Sigurd Bergmann, Irmgard Blindow,
Konrad Ott (Eds.)

Aesth/Ethics in Environmental Change

Studies in Religion and the Environment
Studien zur Religion und Umwelt

published on behalf of the
European Forum for the Study
of Religion and the Environment
by

Sigurd Bergmann

Volume 7

LIT

Aesth/Ethics
in Environmental Change

Hiking through the arts, ecology, religion
and ethics of the environment

edited by

Sigurd Bergmann,
Irmgard Blindow,
Konrad Ott

LIT

Gedruckt auf alterungsbeständigem Werkdruckpapier entsprechend
ANSI Z3948 DIN ISO 9706

Bibliographic information published by the Deutsche Nationalbibliothek
The Deutsche Nationalbibliothek lists this publication in the Deutsche Nationalbibliografie; detailed bibliographic data are available in the Internet at http://dnb.d-nb.de.

ISBN 978-3-643-90292-4

A catalogue record for this book is available from the British Library

©LIT VERLAG GmbH & Co. KG Wien,
Zweigniederlassung Zürich 2013
Klosbachstr. 107
CH-8032 Zürich
Tel. +41 (0) 44-251 75 05
Fax +41 (0) 44-251 75 06
E-Mail: zuerich@lit-verlag.ch
http://www.lit-verlag.ch

LIT VERLAG Dr. W. Hopf
Berlin 2013
Fresnostr. 2
D-48159 Münster
Tel. +49 (0) 2 51-62 03 20
Fax +49 (0) 2 51-23 19 72
E-Mail: lit@lit-verlag.de
http://www.lit-verlag.de

Distribution:
In Germany: LIT Verlag Fresnostr. 2, D-48159 Münster
Tel. +49 (0) 2 51-620 32 22, Fax +49 (0) 2 51-922 60 99, E-mail: vertrieb@lit-verlag.de

In Austria: Medienlogistik Pichler-ÖBZ, e-mail: mlo@medien-logistik.at
In Switzerland: B + M Buch- und Medienvertrieb, e-mail: order@buch-medien.ch
In the UK: Global Book Marketing, e-mail: mo@centralbooks.com
In North America: International Specialized Book Services, e-mail: orders@isbs.com

Contents

THE SACRED IN AND OF EARTH 1
Introductory Remarks on the Challenge of Integrating Aesthetics and
Ethics for the Sake of Our Common Environment
Sigurd Bergmann, Irmgard Blindow and Konrad Ott

LANDSCAPE, RECREATION AND NATURE CONSERVATION – A
CONFLICT SITUATION OR NOT? 13
Case study Hiddensee Island
Irmgard Blindow

ESSENTIAL LANDSCAPE 23
George Steinmann

BEYOND BEAUTY 27
Konrad Ott

"... THE SPACE WHERE I AM" 39
Decolonising, Re-sacralising and Transfiguring Landscapes through the
Aesth/ethic Lens
Sigurd Bergmann

THE GOOD, THE BAD AND THE UGLY 71
Wonder, Awe and Paying Attention to Nature
Celia Deane-Drummond

WORKING WITHIN THE FRAME, BREAKING OUTSIDE THE BORDERS 85
Intersections in the Theological Experience of Art and Place
Forrest Clingerman

FORCES OF NATURE 109
Aesthetics and Ethics
Heather Eaton

WATERWASH AND THE ZEN ART OF PRAGMATISM 127
Lillian Ball

CALL AND RESPONSE 131
Deep Aesthetics and the Heart of the World
Beth Carruthers

LANDMARKS OF THE SACRED IN TIMES OF CLIMATE CHANGE 143
Climate Justice, Icons, and Policy
Thomas Heyd

REPRESENTATIONS OF REALITY, CONSTRUCTIONS OF MEANING 159
Netherlandish Winter Landscapes during the Little Ice Age and Olafur
Eliasson's Glacier Series
Philipp Meurer

BEING ON THE BEACH 177
Exploring Sensomotoric Awareness in a Landscape
Grete Refsum and Ingunn Rimestad

CONTRIBUTORS 205

The Sacred in and of Earth

Introductory Remarks on the Challenge of Integrating Aesthetics and Ethics for the Sake of Our Common Environment

Sigurd Bergmann, Irmgard Blindow and Konrad Ott

How is our perception of the environment connected to our practice with and within nature? Can aesthetics and ethics be integrated for the good of habitats, places and spaces?

How can arts widen our perception of nature and deepen environmental ethics? Where should we seek the Sacred in nature?

Could aesthetics, ethics, religion and ecology transcend contemporary political modes of environmental protection? Could such a multifaceted view, catalyse a truly transdisciplinary environmental science?

Questions like these were formulated in the invitation to the transdisciplinary workshop, which provided the original context for the following chapters. The event took place 24-28 May in 2010 at the island of Hiddensee in the Baltic Sea and gathered together thirty artists and scholars from nine countries. By bringing together ethics, the arts, religion and science, the conference sought to reach a deeper and more complex insight into nature, landscape and its changes, and to widen our practical, artistic and intellectual tools to increase our awareness about the human entanglement with nature.

There are several important reasons to advance an exchange between different disciplines that so far has occurred only loosely in the environmental sphere. First, unbalanced development in environmental science has led to an asymmetry of disciplines in which the natural sciences are placed at the forefront while the environmental humanities and arts are resigned to the margins. An increasingly technocratic ideology is creeping into environmental science; promises of quick technical fixes are gaining priority and investments over long-term complex processes of knowledge seeking. In spite of the fact that environmental problems are human-made, a deeper exploration of the human and cultural dimensions of human interaction with and within nature is constantly marginalized. Although the authors of this book represent the arts, environmental ethics, ecology, religious studies, theology, art history and philosophy, they cannot provide a complete or consistent synthesis of various perspectives in the environmental humanities and the arts. Nevertheless, it is our hope that the reader can see the gainfulness of such a patchwork and be inspired by its exchanges. The last several years have brought a much larger number of perspectives and publications from the environmental humanities to the public; in addition, the field of environmental arts has increased in a surprisingly dynamic way. Despite these advances, we still lack a sustained exploration of transdisciplinary perspectives on human ecology and on questions pertaining to sustainability, climate mitigation and adaptation, and the common future of all living beings and lands.

In order to summarize the task for the new millennium, Wassily Kandinsky wrote in 1927 a pithy, though not very well known, essay entitled "und" (and).[1] In it he claims that now is time for **and** instead of **either-or**. It is for artists to lead in the process of creating culture and together they should put an end to the "either-or" thinking of the 19th century with all its contradictions and conflicts. The either-or structure of thought along with increasing specialization brought about a kind of splintering and separation, such as in the sphere of machines and employment markets. Kandinsky characterized his, and probably also our own, time as a "chaos" in which the quick choices between one thing and another thing are enforcing a tragic and fatal shallowness. For him, an alternative attitude can emerge through synthesis; thus, the artist is encouraged to explore the relations, soundings, and interplays between different expressions of culture and life. Already in 1927, Kandinsky was anticipating, and contributing to the emergence of a social movement focused on the environment, ecology and sustainability. Even though Kandinsky's plea still can motivate us to take care of the **and** (how the one relates to the other), the question arises if this should be taken one step further, expanding the **and** to the **in**. The challenge would then not only be about exploring how the *one* and the *other* relate to each other, but also how the one is situated *in* the other. The intention of this book is to take Kandinsky's demand seriously as well as further and suggest that only a truly multifaceted and transdisciplinary mode of producing knowledge can contribute to the wisdom necessary to clear an alternative path to our common future on and with our common earth.

The second reason for having this transdisciplinary exchange is to address the unsatisfactory relationship between ethics and aesthetics, which is primarily caused by the territorialisation of thematic fields in the history of modern philosophy and the fatal reduction of aesthetics to a reflection on beauty rather than on perception and awareness. The following texts provide different approaches to the challenge of finding new paths towards an integrated "aesth/ethics" in which bodily perceptions of ethical problems in the environment take priority, and in which ethical reflections are embedded in bodily practices that interact with modes of thinking, remembering and acting. In such an account, perceiving the environment is prior to reflecting on and acting within it, even if all three dimensions are interconnected in a circular movement and are driven by the complexities of remembrances, conventions and traditions. Therefore, images and words will stand side by side in the following pages and the reader is invited to move back and forth between the visual and rhetorical sections of the book, letting his/her own imagination (or, in Kant's words, *produktive Einbildungskraft*) be inspired and enlightened. The integration of aesthetics and ethics cannot be achieved by philosophical reasoning alone; rather, it should be an adventure of all the (interacting) senses. To describe this vision, Joseph Beuys coined the phrase *the social sculpture*. Art is, according to Beuys, a social activity that transforms society and the environment. In our estimation, such a social sculpture should also include an alliance between committed artists and scholars. Therefore, this book seeks to contribute to a wider consciousness of the need for such a socio-ecological sculpture, in which modes of perceiving, thinking and acting join together in an experimental communication.

Such an approach resists the reduction of environmental aesthetics to a "handmaiden of environmental ethics" whose sole purview is to correct errors, "such as the sentimental valuing of big eyed mammals over ecologically more important but visually dull organisms, or to realign public taste with ecologically sound landscapes rather than those managed to reflect a cultural ideal."[2] Instead, this approach affirms environmental aesthetics as a foundational activity for the environmental humanities and environmental science in general; this is because our bodily awareness and perception of the environment, the "problems" in it and ourselves within it, necessarily comes first. The aesthetic experience of nature is more than simply another "use-value" to be calculated; it is a deep dimension that is located and at work within other values. An environmental aesthetics enlightened by philosophy, ecology and religious studies/theology not only increases our aesthetic "literacy" regarding (some kind of "reading" of) nature, but it develops our bodily, emotional and rational tools of awareness in a broader synaesthetic sense. Negotiation over what really counts as an environmental problem cannot simply be left to ecologists, economists or activists but must take place in a broad practical discourse where all the concerned parts, including nature, are represented. Without an awareness of the synergies between humans and other bodies and without beliefs regarding what is Sacred, one cannot expect to achieve deep sustainable solutions. The "pragmatic turn" in environmental ethics, therefore should be followed by an aesthetic and spiritual turn.

Finally, a third purpose of the workshop was neither to offer a generalized reflection on the environment nor to simply provide different contextual attempts, but to keep these together through the theme of *landscape*. A focus on "landscape" emphasizes the spatiality of environmental ethics, philosophy and spirituality. The term itself unites "land" and "scape", the physical and the cultural. It also invites an awareness of the spiritual driving forces, since landscapes are never simply coming and going but are emerging and fading as the fruit of the encounter between the Sacred and the Natural, between what people regard as sacred and ultimate and what is given. Landscape also makes it possible to highlight the significance of given and constructed spatialities as a central category of environmental aesth/ethics. Space is a central object in aesthetic experience[3] and in religion,[4] and the experience of landscape offers a vivid and complex revelation of space.[5]

1   *The island of Hiddensee, view from the North Eastern Part, "Dornbusch", towards the "Bodden" (brackish water bodies) and the island of Rügen, photo: © Irmgard Blindow*

Furthermore, "landscape" connects conservation strategies with their foundations in science (mostly ecology) and with environmental politics; in addition, it explores these with regard to the perspectives and values of a landscape's inhabitants and visitors. Should the political meaning of a landscape be defined solely in terms of its economic and ecological values? Or, could aesthetic values be integrated according to conventional norms and/or to subjective emotions and spiritual experiences? How might one integrate the past of a landscape, its nature and culture, into an agreed upon production of its present meaning? And should one include images and experiences of "the Sacred" in the landscape? And how might this be done?

The following chapters approach landscapes in different ways but they might also be transparent for the impact of the landscape of the island itself. One does not need to believe in magic, animism or the divine creation to accept the possibility that a place may participate in the human mode of thinking. Bodily being is deeply rooted in spatial surroundings and flows of movement around and through the body and mind. The impact of places, such as the unique island of Hiddensee, is depicted in literature and the arts in the modern age and further validated by the continued interest of the many short and long term visitors who experience its inspiring power in their bodies and souls.

The island (of Hiddensee) does not calm but rather tempts and stimulates you, the famous dramatist Gerhard Hauptmann once stated. One can only wonder about the island's influence on the perspectives in this book – readers will have to visit the island themselves to discover this. Hiddensee offers rich possibilities for reflection on the strengths and weaknesses of German conservation policies, the meaning of aesthetics in the ecological, spiritual and ethical sense for future policies. The high diversity of ecosystems, species and land/beach constellations on the island invites

2 The lighthouse Dornbusch on Hiddensee, photo: © Irmgard Blindow.

further to a relaxed well being. Due to its intense sand flows in the Southern Baltic Sea, the geological dynamics of the island are always visible, provoking humility before the powers of nature. It is located in the borderlands and margins of medieval and modern empires and its position at the crossroads of Nordic, Central and Eastern European sea routes offers a rich source for experimenting with a complex set of analytic perspectives.

The following chapters approach the theme from different angles. Ecologist *Irmgard Blindow* examines the relation between nature conservation and the aesthetic experience of a landscape. Is there a necessary conflict between the protection of a landscape and touristic recreation within it? Should nature conservation be restricted to the protection of landscapes that are "untouched" or not affected by humankind, or should they include "cultural" landscapes that for long spans of time have been formed and altered by humans? Can protecting nature from humans really conserve nature, given that it always unfolds in a process of change and evolution? The chapter offers a differentiated discussion of the tools of nature conservation, its weaknesses and strengths, and calls for a model that develops the potential of an integration of the interests of humans and ecosystems.

In *George Steinmann*'s chapter entitled "Essential Landscape", the artist invites the reader to meander through a rich diversity of places, to explore different perspectives and to approach the environment from multiple angles. Taking one's time to let the eye move slowly back and forth over the pictures widens our gaze and deepens our insight into what places do to us and what we do to them. Natural and built envi-

3 Stormbeaten hawthorn on the Northern cliff coast of Hiddensee, photo: © Irmgard Blindow

ronments communicate with each other. The chapter's vision of a deep integration of human and non-human living beings in one common complex space – the location of the *in* within the *and* beyond the *either-or* – offers a glimpse of a sustainable future in the here and now of landscapes of co-habitation, which carry and nurture us and invite us to co-operate.

Philosopher *Konrad Ott* examines in depth the challenge of integrating environmental ethics and aesthetics "beyond beauty"; his chapter operates on the cutting edge of aesthetical arguments in the tradition of the aesthetic appreciation of nature. The author explores the significance of such an approach in contemporary models of environmental ethics focussing on what he describes as "transaesthetic experience", that is, the fusion of beauty with something more, such as the Sacred, the Divine, or Existence. Even if the author, mostly at home in discourse ethics, is aware of the moral ambiguity of aesthetic arguments, he clearly shows how transaesthetic experiences with deontic significance should encourage us to further debate the problem of inherent moral values in nature.

The following chapter emphasizes the spatiality of aesth/ethic perceptions, re-

4   Hiddensee, view from the North to the South, photo: © Irmgard Blindow

flections and actions in and within the landscape. *Sigurd Bergmann*, a theologian and scholar of religion, explores the entanglement of external and internal space in "the space where I am". His contribution experiments with three notions, which have emerged in other discourses and so far, have not been used with respect to landscape. He explores the notions of decolonising, resacralising and transfiguring landscapes in order to redirect our imagination towards an alternative common future and world home (Heimat). In the conclusion he offers a brief proposal for an integrated aesth/ethics: landscape acts as both the subject and object of aesth/ethics as it endows us with life, embraces us spatially, evolves in time and contextualises our ethics in a common encounter. To summarize, he states, "I am the landscape where I am" – ontologically, bodily and morally.

The following three theological chapters shift the focus from ethics to belief. Biologist and eco-theologian *Celia Deane-Drummond* focuses on the ability to experience wonder and awe in response to the natural world. "What", she asks, "is the relationship, if any, between the human capacity for wonder and good acts?" Drawing on the work of Simone Weil, the chapter explores how paying attention, understood in religious terms and mediated through beauty, might serve to deepen commitment to environmental responsibility. In asking searching questions about how we come to give value to the natural world in which humanity is grounded, theological dimensions of aesthetics confront not just the bad, but also what is perceived as the ugly.

In his chapter, theologian *Forrest Clingerman* considers the loss of a deep sense of

5   Aerial photo of the North Eastern "Windwatt" of Hiddensee, photo: © Thomas Kepp

6   Aerial photo of Hiddensee (including the Southern "Windwatt", sometimes covered by water depending on the water level), photo: © Frank Martitz

being in our "overhumanized" world in which the poetic and the natural are obscured by a globalization dominated by technical, calculative thinking and where existence has become increasingly alienated from both the natural and the artistic. Exploring the potential of an interconnection between art and place, he asks if a deeper integration of both might serve as an "antidote" for our alienation from nature. Interpreting a project by George Steinmann, the author examines nature spirituality and prepares the ground for an environmental theology of culture.

Ecofeminist theologian *Heather Eaton* dives into the "forces of nature", a term that often refers to the power and presence of thunderstorms, rushing water, unrelenting winds and uncontainable fire. According to her, the forces of nature, as such, are often feared and humans are depicted as other than nature. In contrast, the author presents a new understanding of the forces of nature. She considers various forces within the natural world, such as ingenuity, creativity, interrelatedness and beauty, and explores how immersion in the dynamics and forces of the natural world can become a source of a new ecological vision, a blend of aesthetics and ethics, and of science and spirituality.

"How can an appreciation of place engender public involvement?" asks environmental artist *Lillian Ball*. Her chapter presents the "Waterwash" project, which is located on Long Island's rural North Fork, New York, in a region where the need for restoration and revitalization of areas challenged by storm water issues is widespread. The idea for the project arose out of a discussion with ecological planners and storm water experts and aims to transform a neglected area into a contemplative public outreach space that can inspire community commitment to solving non-point source pollution problems. Ball's project realizes aspects of the vision to integrate site conservation and human experience that is articulated in the foregoing chapters. The coastal landscape, which is carefully designed by the artist and scientist, produces new inspirations for the community to restore and preserve natural (re)sources.

The philosopher and artist *Beth Carruthers* in her chapter explores the approach of Deep Aesthetics, resonating with Deep Ecology, and asks "whether aesthetic engagement might help us arrive at a deep and necessary shift in our understanding of human, culture, and world." In a profound discussion with art theoreticians, environmental philosophers, geographers and psychologists, such as Jeremy Gilbert-Rolfe, Holmes Rolston III, Val Plumwood, and James Hillman, her text challenges and re-envisions our understanding and perception of beauty, of the "face of the Divine" and of the aesthetical in the "Kosmos".

In the same way as the island of Hiddensee evolves in a constant process of change, so too does global climate and local weather. Philosopher *Thomas Heyd* discusses the degradation and loss of significant cultural markers, due to anthropogenic changes in climate, and highlights the importance of the sacred in the landscape. He argues that the disruption of sacred landmarks, resulting from global warming, should lead to a reflection on its implications for climate justice. Furthermore, he considers the role of iconic images, the significance of aesthetic salience, and the relevance of art in the context of global warming, concluding that the sacred in the landscape should be a focal point of concern and interest for policies of climate justice and responsibility.

The winter landscapes of the Netherlands in the 16th and 17th centuries are usually regarded as expressions and evidence of a culture in a time of climatic change, commonly referred to as the Little Ice Age. Art historian *Philipp Meurer*'s careful study of the paintings, however, provides insight into another possibility that may have driven the artists' visualizations of their environment. He compares the Netherlandish painters with the glacier series painted by contemporary artist Olafur Eliasson; in so doing, he suggests that what lies behind the depictions of the Dutch environment was a loss of faith in an immutable and divinely ordered nature represented by coldness, ice and snow. As in the 16th and 17th centuries, the arts can still nurture an awareness of the fragile balance between nature and humankind, as well as a particular "aesthesia" with the ability to challenge our considerations on climate change with the millennia-old quest for the human condition.

The concluding two chapters offer practical glimpses from the conference. Sculptor *Grete Refsum* and choreographer *Ingunn Rimestad* took the group of participants out on the beach near the conference location in order to explore the "sensomotoric" awareness of bodily being in, with and through a landscape. Although such an experience can scarcely be expressed in the genre of the academic essay, nevertheless, it can serve to inspire us to include the senses and modes of movement in our future considerations of the theme.

One of the intentions of the workshop also was to give the island itself an active role regarding the participants' perception and thinking. Therefore, the programme contained two excursions and a craft session where all could produce their own pales by carving and painting heavy planks of oak.

The artists Thomas Jaspert and Tim Adams, both well-known in Germany for a number of different installations in and with the landscape, instructed scholars who usually are not trained in crafts. For the most part, scholars in the humanities express themselves through the written word, through speaking and on their keyboards; and although the hard wood was difficult to work with, they obviously enjoyed using their hands. After experiencing the resistance and the cooperativeness of the wood and the magic of decorating the pale with (eco-friendly) painted ornaments, signs and whatever came into their minds and hands, the participants carried the pales to the garden of the biological research station. Here they were planted into the soil and everyone explained the "meaning" of his/her pale (cf. the images below) where we convenors were especially surprised at the relaxed body language of the attendants. Most of the pales can still be seen today in the garden where they slowly melt down into the vegetation and lend an inspiring atmosphere of the Sacred in the Earth.

Two excursions – one around the hilly north, the other to the coastal dune heath in the middle – likewise connected the participants to the landscape of the island. During the heath excursion, the participants even cleared parts of this area from shrubs in order to conserve the older cultural landscape. One can only wonder to what degree these bodily experiences might have impacted on the explorative wanderings in the chapters in this book.

Neither the workshop nor the book would have been possible without many valued assistants. We, therefore, cordially acknowledge Marie Ulbers, the event's "secretary bird" with many tasks and talents; Fanny Mundt and Katja Vinzelberg, who interrupted their studies to cook and bake for the well-being of the participants; Lothar Spengler and Wolfgang Zenke for technical support; Gerlinde Zenke for administrative support; Rebecca Artinian-Kaiser, University of Chester/University of Notre Dame, who has gracefully turned many of the chapters of non-native speakers into more enjoyable English; Claudia Rettich for stylistic improvements in Konrad Ott's chapter and Eileen Kücükkaraca in Philipp Meurer's chapter; and Ingela Bergmann, Lund, who has assisted professionally with the book's graphical and cover design.

The faculty of arts at the Norwegian University of Science and Technology in Trondheim has provided a generous subsidy for the publication of this book and we are obliged and thankful to "Religionsvitenskapelig Fond" in Trondheim and Greifswald University for their financial contributions to the event.

7   Participants at the craft session present their pales, photo: © Irmgard Blindow

NOTES

[1] Wassily Kandinsky, "und", in: *Essays über Kunst und Künstler*, ed. by Max Bill, Bern: Benteli 3. ed. 1973, (1955), 9-108.

[2] Isis Brook, "Editorial: Ronald Hepburn and the humanising of Environmental Aesthetics", *Environmental Values* 19, 3/2010, 265-271.

[3] Ronald W. Hepburn, "The Aesthetics of Sky and Space", *Environmental Values* 19, 3/2010, 273-288.

[4] S. Bergmann, "Theology in its Spatial Turn: Space, Place and Built Environments Challenging and Changing the Images of God", *Religion Compass* 2, 2007, 353-379.

[5] Cf. further the contributions to the workshop "Wo steht die Umweltethik? Argumentationsmuster im Wandel", arranged by the Rachel Carson Center for Environment and Society, Munich, and the Center for Advanced Studies at Munich University, 23-25 May 2012; and especially its section on "the significance of the category of space", with contributions from Angelika Krebs, Martin Schneider and Sigurd Bergmann. (Forthcoming, ed. by Markus Vogt and Felix Ekardt, in the series *Beiträge zur sozialwissenschaftlichen Nachhaltigkeitsforschung*, Marburg: Metropolis-Verlag 2013).

Landscape, Recreation and Nature Conservation – a Conflict Situation or Not?

Case study Hiddensee Island

Irmgard Blindow

Introduction

The landscape and its flora and fauna have undergone substantial changes both before and after humans started to affect and change it. Beginning with a global or European overview of pre-historical and historical changes, I will "zoom in" on the small the island of Hiddensee, where the workshop "Aesth/Ethics in Environmental Change" took place in May of 2010, in order to explore what it would look like for the landscape to fulfil the demands both of nature conservation and human recreation. What are the aims of nature conservation? Do these aims, necessarily, conflict with recreation?

Animal-landscape interactions in pre-historic and historic time

The Pleistocene landscape was dominated by conspicuous, mainly mammalian, giants commonly referred to as megafauna. The species composition of these large animals varied across continents. Woolly mammoth (*Mammuthus primigenius*), woolly rhinoceros (*Coelodonta antiquitatis*), Irish elk (*Megaloceros giganteus*), scimitar cat (*Homotherium* sp.), cave lion (*Panthera leo spelaea*), cave bear (*Ursus spelaeus*), cave hyena (*Crocuta crocuta spelaea*) and steppe wisent (*Bison priscus*) were among the most important large mammals on the Eurasian continent. As on other continents, some of these large animals were megaherbivores with a body weight exceeding 1,000 kg. Such large herbivores can defend themselves efficiently and are, therefore, rarely threatened by predation, as is the case with contemporary megaherbivores like elephants (Owen-Smith & Mills 2008). This lack of predation pressure results in high densities of herbivore populations that can destroy vegetation (Langendijk et al. 2011) and creates a park-like mosaic landscape of grasslands, woods, shrub land and solitary trees, inhabited by large herds of herbivores (Vera 2000).

Waves of extinctions occurred during the last 100,000 years among the megafauna. Various hypotheses have been put forward to solve this "extinction riddle" (Haynes 2007). The two most popular theories are the climate change hypothesis, suggesting that extinctions were caused by rapid climate shifts, and the overkill hypothesis.

While it has been stated that such extinctions rarely can be attributed to a single cause (Wroe et al. 2004), the overkill hypothesis is supported by the fact that on different continents megafaunal extinctions occurred during different time periods, though relatively soon after the arrival of humans to this continent (Lyons et al. 2004, Burney & Flannery 2005, Martin 2005, Haynes 2007). As Wolverton (2010) argues, understanding the exact timing of extinctions and its connection to human arrival requires further study.

In contrast to these former extinctions, there is no doubt that the disappearances of megaherbivores in historic times were caused by humankind. In Europe, aurochs (*Bos primigenius*) and wisent (*Bison bonasus*) were rendered completely, or nearly, extinct by hunting and competition with domestic cattle, respectively. The interactions between the landscape and these two animals, however, are far from understood. Recently, Hall (2008) has questioned the theory that aurochs are a typical forest species (van Vuure 2005), and instead, has asserted that this large herbivore was primarily a floodplain specialist important for maintaining the openness of floodplain vegetation. Both aurochs and wisent may have played a key role in regulating forest growth and in creating a park-like mosaic landscape (Vera 2000). In Białowieża Forest, Poland, however, wisents prefer forested areas throughout the year (Krazińska et al. 1987, Rouys 2003).

In most of Europe, it is not only the wild megaherbivores that are extinct today; it is also the larger natural predators like brown bear (*Ursus arctos*) and wolf (*Canis lupus*). These extinctions have released smaller herbivores ("mesoherbivores"), such as the red deer (*Cervus elaphus*) and the European roe deer (*Capreolus capreolus*), from predation pressure. If not regulated by hunting, these herbivores often cause severe damage to younger trees and shrubs.

The aims of nature conservation

On first glance, it might seem easy to define the aims of nature conservation – i.e., to preserve or protect nature. But what is nature? And is it possible to create "natural" ecosystems starting from landscapes that have been affected by humans for thousands of years?

Often nature ("wilderness") is regarded as a landscape "untouched" by humankind. Concerning the debate over whether to attribute former megafaunal extinctions to climate change or overkill, we cannot be sure which former changes in landscape and species composition were caused by humans and which were not. If we accept the overkill hypothesis, any attempt to go back to an "original" nature is doomed to fail: it is simply not possible to re-create animals that are extinct. Most drastic is probably the North American conservation agenda to re-wild North America with the closest living relatives of extinct Pleistocean mammals, the pros and cons of which are the subject of an intense "re-wildering debate" (Donlan et al. 2005, Rubenstein et al. 2006, Caro 2007, Oliveira-Santos & Fernandez 2010, Wolverton 2010). The ethical charge of this conservation agenda is that because humans caused the extinctions, they have an obligation to restore North American ecosystems to approximately the state of the late Pleistocene.

EUROPARC, the federation of European national parks and nature parks, recommends a different strategy. In national parks, natural biocoenoses, as well as ongoing dynamic processes in natural ecosystems, should be released from human interference. "Prozeßschutz" ("process protection"), heavily influenced by forest ecologist Knut Sturm, is the basic conservation strategy of national parks in Germany (Jedicke 1998). Within this strategy, there are two different approaches. The first, "segregativer Prozeßschutz", does not interfere with natural processes but, instead, aims at "developing wilderness", whereby a cultural landscape is often the starting point. The second, "integrativer Prozeßschutz", evaluates which natural processes favour the defined aims of landscape development before deciding which of these processes should be admitted and which should be prohibited (Sturm 1993). This approach also aims at conserving land use processes that favour the dynamics of cultural landscapes and have a positive impact on species or habitat protection without applying directional management measures (Jedicke 1998).

"Integrativer Prozeßschutz" is a different approach to nature conservation. It aims to protect the richness and diversity of habitats, flora and fauna and not merely those of "nature", but also habitats affected by humans. This form of nature conservation acknowledges that human interference not only caused "disasters" like species extinction, but, by employing different land use techniques, also created a diverse landscape with a multitude of habitats, each with a specific composition of typical plants and animals. Especially since the beginning of the 20th century, when traditional agriculture was increasingly intensified with the application of fertilizer and herbicides, many species-rich cultural landscapes were replaced by species-poor habitats, which had lost much of its structural heterogeneity and much of its diverse fauna and flora. Nature conservation tries to protect habitat and species richness through directional management practices.

The EU FFH (fauna/flora/habitat) directive obliges EU member states to protect threatened habitats, plant and animal species that are listed in single appendices. The majority of these habitats are traditional cultural landscapes, such as grasslands and heathlands, and are categorized as "seminatural" habitats (EU 2006).

As in the case of defining "wilderness" or "untouched nature", the definition of the "right" state of cultural habitats, essential for a development of management aims and approaches, is a point of debate. Nilsson (1997), who investigated the development of plant species richness in the South Swedish cultural landscape during the last 1,000 years, argued that nature conservation often aims to restore the landscape to the middle of the 19th century, a period when the landscape already had lost much of its former biodiversity. He suggests that the reference condition for restoration should be the period before 1700 A.D. when natural disturbances such as fire, wind-throw, large herbivore grazing and damming by beavers still occurred regularly.

Case study Hiddensee

The island of Hiddensee is situated in the southern Baltic Sea off the island of Rügen. Tourism is by far the most important source of income – during the summer months, the island's 3,000 to 4,000 guest beds are almost entirely occupied. Additionally, several thousand "day visitors" arrive with one of the ferries in the morning and leave again in the afternoon. Considering the island's size of just 19 km^2 and a population of around 1,000, these are high numbers.

Several nature reserves (Naturschutzgebiete) were established during the 1960s, the largest of these representing the biggest coastal dune heath area in the German Baltic coast region. In 1990 the national park "Vorpommersche Boddenlandschaft" was established. Hiddensee is situated within this national park and most of its area, almost 13 km^2, is under the national park's protection, except for some landscape protection areas, three nature reserves and four villages. Most of the island's valuable habitats are cultural landscapes such as coastal dunes, coastal heathlands, dry grasslands, or coastal meadows. To protect these habitats, including their specific fauna and flora, directional management action is necessary. Although this contradicts the basic policy of German national parks, it is part of the national park's management plan (Nationalpark Vorpommersche Boddenlandschaft 2002). These habitats are among the valuable habitats listed in the EU FFH directive (EU 2006) and are home to a number of threatened species also included in this directive.

Nature conservation thus faces two contradictory aims and obligations, which impossibly can be applied simultaneously in the same area. Of those areas under national park protection, 2.5 km^2 are core zones where all human interference is prohibited, and thus, where "hard-core" "Prozeßschutz" is applied. The remaining 10.2 km^2 belong to the so-called "Pflege- und Entwicklungszone" (management and development zone). Within this zone, the dry meadows and the coastal dune heathlands are to be preserved by means of extensive land-use, e.g., grazing (Nationalpark Vorpommersche Boddenlandschaft 2002). To prevent or solve conflict situations, it has to be decided exactly which parts of this zone will be protected from all kinds of human interference and which parts will be dedicated to directional management. In addition, the financial means to support extensive land-use are far from sufficient. Grazing intensity is, therefore, far too low in both dry grasslands and coastal meadows. In these habitats, shrub encroachment and reed expansion, respectively, lead to a decrease in many threatened species (Fig. 1).

Landscape, Recreation and Nature Conservation

1 *Development of shrub encroachment at the viewpoint "Großer Inselblick" on the island of Hiddensee.*

Upper row: In the early 1990s, the landscape below the viewpoint was open with hardly any shrubs (left). Some shrubs began growing during the late 1990s. Photo (right) by D. Engelmann, 1998.

Middle rows: The photo, taken during a course with students in 2007, records the current situation of heavy shrub encroachment below the viewpoint. The further development of shrub and tree expansion is simulated for 2012, 2017 and 2027. Photo and simulation by Christine Börtitz.

Bottom row: As a nature conservation measure, shrubs were removed during 2009, creating an open landscape again below the viewpoint. Photos by Irmgard Blindow.

The core zones include areas with active coastal processes of land formation and land abrasion. Nature conservation here gives space for highly dynamic, natural processes. One of the two core zones, the Neubessin area in the northeastern part of the island, is a young peninsula built up by sand abraded from the exposed northwestern coast of Hiddensee. During the last few decades, this peninsula has been growing by about 30 m per year! An offshore sandbank provides habitat for many breeding pairs of a number of gull, wader and tern species, and, in particular, features the largest breeding colony of little tern (*Sterna albifrons*) in Mecklenburg-Vorpommern, a species given special protection under the FFH directive (EU 2006). Debate among nature conservationists, concerning the possible need for interference within the core zones, is explained by the fact that these zones were subject to human interference before and after their protection by the national park in 1990 and remain exposed to such interference. In the Neubessin area, numbers of little tern breeding pairs have declined continuously mainly caused by predation from the red fox (*Vulpes vulpes*). Due to successful anti-rabies inoculations, this predator occurs on Hiddensee in an unnaturally high population density and causes annual losses of little tern eggs at about 50% on average (Siefke 1989, Dierschke & Helbig 2008).

The other core zone is situated on the southernmost part of Hiddensee, the Gellen area. Here also active coastal formation results in constant and dynamic change and growth of this area and maintains young succession stages that host a number of threatened plant and animal species. In former times, the major part of this core zone was a coastal dune heathland with a dominance of heather (*Calluna vulgaris*); today, however, it is covered by a thick and almost monospecific grass sward built up by sand sedge (*Carex arenaria*) (Remke & Blindow 2011). Cessation of land use combined with elevated atmospheric nitrogen deposition is the most probable reason for this shift in plant dominance. The open landscape of this core zone is increasingly colonized by various shrubs and trees, mainly black cherry (*Prunus serotina*), a neophyte species planted in the coastal protection forest in the immediate neighbourhood of this core zone (Subklew 2007, Remke & Blindow 2011).

LANDSCAPE AND HUMAN RECREATION

National parks and other protected areas not only serve as refuges for valuable habitats and threatened species; they also serve as important places for recreation. Nature is one of the main tourist attractions on Hiddensee Island. In a survey of 400 guests, the nature and landscape was cited as the main reason to visit the island before recreation and beach life (Korp 2008). The community, therefore, sees the protection of nature, guaranteed by the national park status, as an important advantage. The increasing shrub encroachment and forest expansion, a consequence of the national park's policy that threatens the maintenance of open cultural landscapes, however, is regarded as one of the island's primary weaknesses (Gemeinde Seebad Hiddensee 2007).

The survey (Korp 2008) confirms the importance of open landscape and open views for tourism on Hiddensee. 94% of the visitors characterized the open landscape of the dry grasslands in the hilly northern part of the island as "essential" or "important". Forest development would turn this area into an "unattractive" or "fairly attractive" landscape according to 82% of the respondents. A vast majority (around 80%) supports efforts to maintain this open, cultural landscape.

CONCLUSION

Interestingly, most people tend to refer to a forested landscape when asked to describe "wilderness" or "untouched nature". We do not know, however, how much of the landscape really was covered by forests during former times when large herbivores still were present, nor do we know how much was open grasslands or park-like habitats. Today, forest develops in most places when human interference is excluded, while open landscapes are mainly represented as traditional cultural landscapes. For recreation, both forests and open landscapes have high value. Both, natural and cultural landscapes, host a wide variety of habitats and a high number of specialized plant and animal species. Nature conservation should aim at maintaining this richness and diversity of habitats and species: It should be "Prozeßschutz" **and** directional habitat management, not **either** the one **or** the other!

REFERENCES

Burney, David A. and Flannery, Timothy F. (2005), "Fifty millennia of catastrophic extinctions after human contact", *Trends in Ecology and Evolution* 20, 395-401.

Caro, Tim (2007), "The Pleistocene re-wilding gambit", *Trends in Ecology and Evolution* 22, 281-283.

Dierschke, Volker and Helbig, Andreas J. (2008), "Avifauna von Hiddensee", *Meer und Museum* 21, 67-202.

Donlan, Josh, Greene, Harry W., Berger, Joel, Bock, Carl E., Bock, Jane H., Burney, David A., Estes, James A., Foreman, Dave, Martin, Paul S., Roemer, Gary W., Smith, Felisa A. and Soulé, Michael E. (2005), "Re-wilding North America", *Nature* 436, 913-914.

EU (2006), "Council Directive 2006/105/EC of 20 November 2006 adapting Directives 73/239/EEC, 74/557/EEC and 2002/83/EC in the field of environment, by reason of the accession of Bulgaria and Romania", *Official Journal of the European Union*, 20.12.2006, 368-406.

Gemeinde Seebad Hiddensee (2007), *Insel-Entwicklungskonzept*, bearbeitet durch Uhlich Raith Hertelt Fuß, Partnerschaft für Stadt-, Landschafts- und Regionalplanung, Stralsund.

Hall, Stephen J. G. (2008), "A comparative analysis of the habitat of the extinct aurochs and other prehistoric mammals in Britain", *Ecography* 31, 187-190.

Haynes, Gary (2007), "A review of some attacks on the overkill hypothesis, with special attention to misrepresentations and doubletalk", *Quaternary International* 169/170, 84-94.

Jedicke, Eckhard (1998), "Raum-Zeit-Dynamik in Ökosystemen und Landschaften", *Naturschutz und Landschaftsplanung* 30, 229-233.

Korp, Christin (2008), "*Vegetationsdynamik und Naturschutzkonflikte im Nationalpark 'Vorpommersche Boddenlandschaft' am Beispiel des Dornbusch*", Diploma Thesis, Institute of Botany and Landscape Ecology, University of Greifswald, Germany.

Krazińska, Malgorzata, Cabón-Raczyńska, K. and Graziński, Zbigniew A. (1987), "Strategy of habitat utilisation by European bison in the Białowieża Forest", *Acta Theriol.* 32, 147-202.

Lagendijk, D.D. Georgette, Mackey, Robin L., Page, Bruce R. and Slotow, Rob (2011), "The effects of herbivory by a mega- and mesoherbivore on tree recruitment in Sand Forest, South Africa", *PLoS ONE*, Article Number: e17983. DOI: 10.1371/journal.pone.0017983.

Lyons, S. Kathleen, Smith, Felisa A. and Brown, James H. (2004), "Of mice, mastodons and men: human-mediated extinctions on four continents", *Evolutionary Ecology Research* 6, 339-358.

Martin, Paul S. (2005), *Twilight of the Mammoths: Ice Age Extinctions and the Rewilding of America*, Berkeley: University of California Press.

Nationalpark Vorpommersche Boddenlandschaft (2002), "Nationalparkplan: Leitbild und Ziele", Schwerin, <www.nationalpark-vorpommersche.boddenlandschaft.de>.

Nilsson, Sven G. (1997), "Biologisk mångfald under tusen år i det sydsvenska kulturlandskapet", [Biodiversity over the last one thousand years in the cultured landscape of southernmost Sweden], *Svensk Botanisk Tidskrift* 91, 85-101.

Oliveira-Santos, Luiz G. R. and Fernandez, Fernando A. S. (2010), "Pleistocene rewilding, Frankenstein ecosystems, and an alternative conservation agenda", *Conservation Biology* 24, 4-5.

Owen-Smith, Norman and Mills, M. Gus L. (2008), "Predator-prey size relationships in an African large-mammal food web", *Journal of Animal Ecology* 77, 173-183.

Remke, Eva Stefanie and Blindow, Irmgard (2011), "Site specific factors have an overriding impact on Baltic dune vegetation change under low to moderate N-deposition – A case study from Hiddensee island", *Journal of Coastal Conservation* 15, 87-97.

Rouys, Sophie (2003), "Winter movements of European bison in the Białowieża Forest, Poland", *Mammalian Biology* 68, 122-125.

Rubenstein, Dustin R., Rubenstein, Daniel I., Sherman, Paul W. and Gavin, Thomas A. (2006), "Pleistocene Park: does re-wilding North America represent sound conservation for the 21st century?" *Biological Conservation* 132, 232-238.

Siefke, Axel (1989), "Zur Rolle von Prädatoren in den Küstenvogelreservaten der DDR", *Beiträge zur Vogelkunde* 35, 36-51.

Sturm, Knut (1993), "Prozeßschutz – ein Konzept für naturgerechte Waldwirtschaft", *Zeitschrift für Ökologie und Naturschutz* 2, 181-192.

Subklew, Henriette (2007), *"Küstenschutzwald auf der Insel Hiddensee: Einfluss auf die Neophyten Campylopus introflexus und Prunus serotina und rechtliche Grundlagen für einen Rückbau"*, Diploma Thesis, Institute of Botany and Landscape Ecology, University of Greifswald, Germany.

Van Vuure, Cis (2005), *Retracing the aurochs: History, morphology and ecology of an extinct wild ox*, Sofia and Moscow: Pensoft.

Vera, F.W.M. (2000), *Grazing ecology and forest history*, Oxford: CABI Publishing.

Wolverton, Steve (2010), "The North American Pleistocene overkill hypothesis and the rewilding debate", *Diversity and Distributions* 16, 874-876.

Wroe, Stephen, Field, Judith, Fullagar, Richard and Jermin, Lars S. (2004), "Megafaunal extinction in the late quaternary and the global overkill hypothesis", *Alcheringa* 28, 291-331.

ESSENTIAL LANDSCAPE

George Steinmann

Essential Landscape 25

1-7   George Steinmann: From Essential Landscape, © *George Steinmann / BONO, Oslo 2012*

BEYOND BEAUTY

Konrad Ott

INTRODUCTION

The realm of environmental discourse consists of many patterns of arguments;[1] the so-called eudaimonistic arguments form one highly important cluster. These arguments support the conservation, preservation, and even restoration of nature with respect to a rich, joyful, and meaningful human life. According to Martha Nussbaum, the overall capabilities to live a genuine human life include a capacity to live "with concern for and in relation to animals, plants, and the world of nature".[2] This capacity requires access to nature, it must be exercised throughout the course of life, and it can be enhanced by experiences with nature that include aesthetic, biophilic, transformative, cultural-symbolic, and probably even deontic and spiritual experiences. In a recent publication, Nussbaum concedes that these vital issues have not been "exhaustively pursued".[3] Here, I see a close connection between the general capability argument and the more substantial and specific eudaimonistic arguments in environmental ethics. The dimension of eudaimonistic value is not the realm of pure practical reason; instead, it is clearly "a posteriori". Therefore, in this dimension, humans are present with all their senses and with their bodies. Sigurd Bergmann has coined the term "Aesth/Ethics" to describe this dimension.[4]

In the standard account of environmental discourse these eudaimonistic arguments are presented as isolated building blocks. Presenting them this way as building blocks is helpful for students because they can learn how such arguments are intrinsically structured according to philosophical premises and practical consequences. In the real performance of experiences, however, this building-block-approach does not hold. Experiences often are *concrete* in the literal sense of the word ("concrescere") since they draw on aspects from different patterns of arguments. If, for instance, one returns from a journey to the arid regions of Central Asia and experiences late summer in Germany, aesthetic appreciation fuses with the feeling of re-turning and coming home. Transformative experiences often even have deontic elements revealing a vulnerable nature, which can be harmed and, perhaps, even victimized. At the borderlines and edges of specific arguments there seems to be a clearance into different but neighbouring arguments.

This paper explores such visions at the edge of aesthetic arguments. Aesthetic appreciation of nature is pervasive throughout human cultures and throughout human history. It is highly likely that being human entails a richly textured sensual perception of natural environments that is never devoid of aesthetic components. Such aesthetic appreciation might be paradigmatic of a biophilic disposition in humans.[5] Regretfully, mainstream Western philosophy has been highly biased regarding aesthetic perception of nature. Philosophers, even some decades ago, still claimed that a genuine aesthetic appreciation of nature could emerge only under modern Western societal conditions.[6] According to Joachim Ritter, aesthetic appreciation of nature as landscape supposes a societal domination of nature. Ritter argues that the distinction between working hours and leisure time should be seen as a necessary precondition for genuine aesthetic perception of landscapes outside of the sphere of industrial production. Such aesthetic appreciation is a remanent of metaphysical ideas about nature, which modern science defeated and made outdated. Nevertheless, this highly Eurocentric approach has been proven false by many studies in cultural anthropology. Thus, we should assume that there is a genuine human sense for beauty in nature.

Beyond these general anthropological layers, specific cultural and aesthetic traditions are clearly visible. The aesthetic appreciation of nature has played an important role in Germany since the days of Johann Wolfgang Goethe, Friedrich Hölderlin, Alexander von Humboldt, and the Romantic Movement.[7] Goetheans and the Romantics were particularly critical of the modernization of land-use systems in Germany throughout the 19th century.[8] A confluence between the aesthetic appreciation of nature and the wish to preserve at least some parts of unspoiled nature and pre-modern landscapes due to their aesthetic appeal arose from theses traditions. Nature conservation has a long tradition of drawing on aesthetic arguments.[9]

Poets, philosophers and conservationists, influenced by the Romantic Movement, began paying attention to the fusion of aesthetic and spiritual attitudes toward nature; this emphatic fusion is found in Friedrich Hölderlin's poetry, which had a considerable impact on Martin Heidegger (Mögel 1994). As Hölderlin wrote in his *Empedokles*: "… und hebt, wie Neugeborne/Die Augen auf zur göttlichen Natur" ("and lift, as newborns do, the eyes to holy nature").[10] Ernst Rudorff one of the founding fathers of German nature conservation, argued that aesthetic appreciation of unspoiled nature sometimes comes close to a peculiar kind of spiritual revelation.[11] In aesthetic appreciation, one can immerse oneself in the infinite poetry of Godly revelations. In moments of aesthetic appreciation, as Rudorff notes, nature may seem to reveal itself as being something "more" than just a beautiful place or scenery. For Rudorff, the poetry of poets, such as Eichendorff, portrayed this kind of experience.

Although "transaesthetic experiences", as I label them, also occur within modern societies, they have not gained a foothold within a modern framework of thought. The fusion between beauty and something else (sacredness, holiness, revelation) has often been associated with pre-modern societies, which at that point were unable to draw clear distinctions between something being beautiful and something being sacred (holy). For Habermas,[12] it belongs to the modern predicament to uphold the boundaries between science, ethics, art, and religion. I believe that we should at least address these boundary zones, especially since we rely on experiences that touch on these zones.

In this chapter, I wish to focus on the borderlines between aesthetic appreciation of nature and a more "spiritual" encounter with nature. My hypothesis is that this kind of encounter and attitude has remained alive in non-Western cultures. Revitalization from within the Western tradition could and should stimulate intercultural environmental dialogue.

Aesthetic Arguments in Environmental Ethics

In contemporary environmental ethics, it is widely accepted that something beautiful should not be destroyed without sufficient reason. Nevertheless, compared with economic interests, aesthetic arguments have proven inadequate in environmental conflicts given that beauty tends to be seen as highly "relative" and "subjective". Clearly, aesthetic arguments are anthropocentric: beauty is in the eye of the beholder and aesthetic judgments, as Immanuel Kant argued, are based on the faculty of "taste".

As I suggested in the introduction, aesthetic arguments belong to the category of so-called eudaimonistic arguments in environmental ethics.[13] Such arguments emphasize the role nature can (and should) play in an overall rich and flourishing human life. In his book *Eine Ästhetik der Natur* (1991), philosopher Martin Seel provides contemporary environmentalists with a sound argument: the protection and conservation of natural landscapes and beautiful sites belongs to a modern concept of ethics. According to this argument, society should protect nature out of respect for those people whose conception of the good life includes an appreciation of beautiful nature. Seel restricts his argument to the beauty of nature, warning his readers against the metaphysical pitfalls that loom on the borders of aesthetic experience. The beauty of nature is nothing but beauty, period. There is nothing "behind" or "beyond" beauty. There is that much joy in the beauty of nature that no "beyond" is needed.

Seel's warnings are clearly in line with Kant's warnings against embarking on the vast and foggy ocean of deception (Kant: "Ozean des Scheins"). For Kant, a small island of reason is surrounded by an ocean of intellectual deception, confusion, vain speculation, pseudo-philosophy, and the like. Such warnings against metaphysical speculation intrinsically belong to modern philosophy. It is fair to say that Western philosophical discourse since Kant is full of arguments against metaphysical thought. In the Vienna Circle, this attitude was radicalized in order to purify philosophy from speculative pseudo-problems ("Scheinprobleme"). It was argued that prudent philosophers should avoid these time-consuming pseudo-problems and, instead, focus on "real" philosophical problems in epistemology, logic, analytical semantics, metaethics, the theory of rational choice, and mind-brain-relations.

Such a suspicion of metaphysics, however, comes at a price: it may discourage us from seriously considering some kinds of (presumably deeper) experiences that do not fit well into our modern conceptual frameworks. Although a suspicion of metaphysics seeks to purify philosophy, it might end up in the sophisticated boredom of analytical philosophy. Environmental ethics should be more courageous. Thus, I do not adopt Seel's argument against stronger readings of aesthetic experiences. If there is a dilemma, it is between two risks: the risk of being cut off from one's own experiences and the risk of becoming meta-physical, I grasp the second lemma. (Luther: "Peccate fortiter!") Even if this lemma becomes too thorny, the second lemma remains.

In a previous article on the beauty of nature, I coined the term "trans-aesthetic experience".[14] Hepburn in his fine article argued that the experience of beauty in nature sometimes eclipses metaphysical, spiritual, or religious imagination.[15] Hepburn rightly argues that modern Western philosophy lacks in clear language for such imagination. However, it could, perhaps, find a way to describe this imagination through an exploration of language. The experience that underlies the concept of transaesthetic experience could be described in these preliminary terms:

Experiencing beauty in nature (sometimes) gives birth to the intuition that nature "is" both beautiful **and** *"more" than just beautiful.*

The "more" in the above statement is unspecified and unspecified words do not count in modern philosophy. If this is the case, we must add meaning to it or delete such empty words. The experience is not derived from reflection but is immediately given as a phenomenon by and within the experience itself. Since judgments of taste are not immediate transaesthetic experiences, these experiences are not experienced as judgments of taste. If a person has never had this experience or intuition, she will have no problem interpreting it and may find the following exploration pointless and misleading from the start.

I do not claim that all aesthetic experiences are of the transaesthetic kind; they are a (probably small) subset of aesthetic experiences. Transaesthetic experiences neither are freely chosen nor are they brought about by an intention or decision to have them. They simply happen or occur to individuals ("Widerfahrnisse"). I do not address the empirical question here whether such experiences are exceptional, rare or more common than one may believe. At the Hiddensee conference on ethics, aesthetics and religion, many Western scholars and artists confessed that they are quite familiar with trans-aesthetic experiences. I would assume that many indigenous people would also be familiar with these kinds of experiences in which nature at once appears beautiful *and* presents itself as some "thing" more (or some "thing" else).

EIGHT READINGS OF TRANSAESTHETIC EXPERIENCE

If one (even once in a lifetime) has such experience and intuition, certain questions arise: how to communicate it to others and how to cope with it philosophically. Human language, in general, is rich, and thus, it is possible for us to exchange stories in many different natural languages and tell of such experiences to one another beyond cultural borders. I do not wish to relate personal stories here (of Philippine coral reefs, Nepalese mountains, the endlake of the Heihe river, or Siberian sunsets); instead, I want to address the question whether and, if so, how such experiences might deserve philosophical attention and credit. In this section, I offer eight lines of reasoning and, in the next section, criteria for assessing these lines of reasoning. The first two are strategies to explain away transaesthetic experiences.

1. The first reading is *critical*. The experienced intuition is mistaken. The "more" is nothing but a high degree of *intensity* in the aesthetic experience. Intensely felt aesthetic experiences of nature are quite often experiences of the sublime. Experiencing the sublime might provoke other emotions and attitudes, such as feeling small against the "majesty" of nature, or facing "Mother Nature" or the "living forces of the land", but such stimulation should be analysed in a sober manner.
The problem of the high intensity of emotions and perceptions has been debated in poetic traditions since the 18th century.[16] Intensity comes in degrees and high degrees of intensity regarding the perceived beauty of nature may be overwhelming in a way that could suggest something "more" is at stake. High intensity can be deceptive and erroneously confused with some strange and metaphysical "more/else". Avoiding this mistake is coherent with a pattern of reasoning that such an intense aesthetic experience of nature should count as a sound rationale for protecting beautiful nature. As in utilitarianism, high intensity can be taken seriously and respected, as such, without any metaphysical pitfalls. Since Bentham, the intensity of pleasure and joy has to be accounted for in a utilitarian calculus. Even Martin Seel, who is not a utilitarian ethicist, would find this reading appealing. According to this reading, we should emphasize intensity but avoid metaphysics. This critical reading is a first variant of a "nothing-but-ism" argument. A person upon reflection becomes aware that there is nothing more than the simple intensity of one's own feelings.

2. The experienced intuition might be the result of a subconscious interplay between specific neuronal brain structures, early experiences in childhood and peculiar human predisposition for *peak experiences,* which probably have a neuronal basis or might be induced by "psychedelic" drugs (LSD, "magic mushrooms", mescal, and the like). Such a mental state could be projected into nature from a first-person-perspective but should be better explained by neuronal science. Recently, in the field of psychology of religion, religious and other ecstatic experiences have been viewed as something that occurs within the brain. Scientists can provide sound clinical explanations for why such experiences occur and why they are peculiar to human adaptation. Spiritual experiences, it is supposed, provide humans with the strength to cope with life. As some neuronal scientists argue in the mind-brain debate, the human brain may deceive humans for the sake of human adaptation. This is a second variant of the "nothing-but-ism" argument since the "more" does not refer to nature (or something behind nature), but only refers to the proceedings of the brain or, ultimately, firing neurons.

3. The experienced intuition may or may not be mistaken or deluded but it is better to be silent on such points. Becoming silent is the proper attitude; we should

simply smile but not speak. Wittgenstein would sanction such an "*ineffabile*" solution, arguing as he does in the *Tractatus* that all propositions must refer to some state of affairs which is the case. For Wittgenstein, the "that" of being a world remains mystical. If this is the case, the "more" cannot be clarified by propositional language. The "more" being experienced is and should remain ineffable at least in philosophical language, which must be conceptual and discursive.[17]

Some philosophers claim that humans should generally shy away from attempts to specify the "more" by means of language because such attempts destroy the immediacy of experience. It is better to keep and store the "more/else" in the immediacy of experience with gratitude rather than to try to articulate it by means of language. This solution has always been unsatisfactory to me because, in effect, it comes close to the more positivistic strategy to purify philosophical thought; moreover, it shifts such experiences into the domain of privacy. However, for Habermasians, these experiences should be present in the public space of reasoning.

If some x cannot be captured adequately by propositional language, it does not follow that x cannot be expressed at all. A phenomenology of nature[18] might be helpful since phenomenology enables us to describe such experiences as they are given to our minds. The language of phenomenology entails "thick" descriptions full of sensations, experiences, values, metaphors and analogies; often, such language verges on the literary. Phenomenological descriptions are often "hybrids" of philosophy and art (i.e. descriptions of atmosphere in nature, or simply how the odour of different ripe fruits mix to create a "fruit-smell" in late summer). But how should we deal with such hybrids? Habermas proposed a strict division of labour: philosophers ought to leave these fields to poets and other artists (musicians, painters, landscape artists) for unconstrained expression.[19] The peculiar hybrid nature of phenomenology is better resolved by art and, thus, the "more/else" should be expressed in works of art that enrich our perceptions of nature and our attitudes toward nature. The maxim, then, would be: "Leave it to the artists!" However, this solution may only shift the problem to the genre of art criticism. Art critics, then, are seen as experts who decipher meanings in works of art. The direct route of a phenomenology of nature and the more indirect route of a philosophical interpretation of works of art are not mutually exclusive.

4. The experienced intuition should be taken as an indication that everything in nature can be perceived as beautiful. Both Allen Carlson and Theodor W. Adorno (in his *Ästhetische Theorie* 1970) make this assertion. Carlson argued that his claim ("positive aesthetics of nature") could be substantiated by scientific ecology. Carlson's approach failed because scientific ecology is silent on such matters. For Adorno, all parts of nature can become beautiful; it is as if it glows from the inside out.[20] Adorno did not argue for this glowing but he took it as a promise that there would be no final triumph of destruction, barbarism, and domination of nature. As I have argued elsewhere,[21] this claim can be substantiated on aesthetic grounds. The experienced "more/else" is properly represented by the logical

quantifier "∀". Although sometimes the beauty of nature seems to point to some "more/else" beyond beauty, there might be good reasons to hold that nothing in nature is ugly. Having experienced such "more/else", one may feel entitled to speak in a paradox or riddle: "Everything in nature is beautiful regardless of whether it appears beautiful or ugly (to me)." This argument comes close to the approach of Chuang-tzu, as quoted in Krebs:[22] "'Where is it, that which we call the Way?' 'There is nowhere it is not' (...) 'It is in shit and piss.'"

5. This experienced intuition "more than just beautiful" goes beyond the dichotomy of an experiencing individual as subject (I, self) and the objects being experienced as beautiful by the subject. The experience instantly refuses the subject-object distinction on which aesthetic experiences seem to rest. In such an experience, we find ourselves being thrown out there in the world. The "more/else" does not refer to nature itself but to some basic existential structure of human "Dasein" (M. Heidegger) which "is" *with/in* nature before it becomes a knowing subject, a moral person, and a culturally shaped individual. This primary "being human with/in nature" is like a child opening his eyes. From within a more complex aesthetic experience, which presupposes an individual person with some preferences and with culturally shaped tastes, a "flashback" takes place to a more elementary and brute experience in transaesthetic experiences. The experienced "more/else" becomes a "less than" within the humans. In such experience the human reaches a level of being human in which she "is" less than a subject, less than a person, and less than an individual. Less is more and more is less. In particular, such experiences sometimes have a greater quality of a with*in* (being in natural environments) and sometimes a greater quality of *with*in (being together with natural beings). This *with*in can even have deontic meaning (see 7.).

6. Another reading not identical to 3.5 stems from contemporary philosophies of nature. Aesthetic beauty, in its usual sense, can be seen as "first-level" beauty. On the second level, however, the natural world itself is full of beauties given that natural evolution creates heterogeneity, complexity, novelties, emergent projects (as species), autotelic structured organisms, symbioses, and the like. First-level beauty relies on a series of preconditions that are themselves products of evolutionary processes, by which a richly structured world of living nature comes into being and can be experienced by highly complex organisms which have eyes, ears, tongues, skins, noses, and the like. Such a reading can be labelled as "Whiteheadian". First-level beauty is a catalyst into the more epistemic (ecological, evolutionary, "physio-logical") study of biospherical or biophysical nature, which is full of beautiful achievements of many different kinds.[23] First-level beauty strongly indicates that biospheric nature is full of wonders.[24] Transaesthetic experiences may well stimulate new approaches in the philosophy of nature that go beyond an epistemology of science. One might wish to claim that there are achievements of higher complexity and sensual awareness as a result of a prolific and projective

nature; such a claim, of course, must be substantiated philosophically but this is beyond the scope of this article.

7. Transaesthetic experiences are to be regarded as *deontic* (moral) experiences. In such deontic experiences[25] natural beings present themselves as intrinsically valuable and untouchable, and thus, revealing their inherent moral value. Interestingly, philosopher Jürgen Habermas has argued in this vein in his book *Erläuterungen zur Diskursethik*.[26] For Habermas, in specific transaesthetic experiences natural beings seem to reveal their inherent moral significance. In such experiences we strongly feel the intuition to preserve them for their own sake and not just because they give pleasure, joy, or excitement to us. Habermas describes this aesthetic-deontic experience as if natural beings instantly could retreat within themselves *and*, by doing so, reveal their moral significance. Ultimately, Habermas leaves it open whether such revealing is rather a kind of illusion or whether such moral imaginations can enrich our moral theories.

Similar deontic experiences are well known in the history of environmental ethics. Albert Schweitzer, for instance, described the experience of sitting on a boat moving slowly and carefully along a sandy river in the glow of an African sunset, with a herd of rhinos close by and partly in the river. As Schweitzer recounts, suddenly there was the phrase "reverence for life" in his mind's eye, providing him with the supreme ethical principle for which he had been searching a long time. Other deontic experiences are to be found in the writings of Aldo Leopold, Arne Naess, and David Abram. (As I myself observed a beautiful horse closely and patiently, I suddenly seemed to be face to face *with* the horse in a morally significant way).

If the "more/else" refers to moral significance within nature, physiocentric solutions of the demarcation problem deserve ethical credit. Ultimately, I am not convinced that such transaesthetic experiences are clear-cut and univocal deontic experiences by which the demarcation problem can be resolved. As I argued elsewhere, deontic experiences, as such, may be contested, and other tools are available for a reasonable resolution to the problem (Ott 2008). Nevertheless, transaesthetic experiences that have deontic significance should encourage us to debate further the problem of inherent moral values in nature. This reading suggests the need to take the demarcation problem seriously even if environmental ethics may turn to more pressing practical problems, such as water provision, climate change, or agriculture.

8. The final reading does not shy away from religion: the beauty of nature points to a great mystery behind or within nature. The "more/else" really refers to some "thing" as holy (sacred) and which might be conceived using various onto-theological concepts, such as "Deus sive Natura" (Spinoza), "natura naturans" (Schelling), "Creation", "Creator vivificans", "deep incarnation", and the like. Many Western and non-Western theologians have proposed ideas of how to articulate this line of thought. This line of reasoning needs to be analysed by theologians who can free themselves from the clumsy web of metaphysical concepts,

which have originated from late-Roman and medieval scholastic systems. Within the Jewish-Christian tradition, there are good reasons to offer new readings of Genesis 1 which replace the old concept of dominion over nature ("*dominium terrae*") by the idea that humans being blessed by God shall take the very good earth under their feet in order to represent God at any place.[27]

CRITERIA, READINGS, AND CLAIMS

These eight lines of reasoning are not mutually exclusive but can be combined in various ways. None of them is completely unreasonable; however, as philosophers, we would not simply accept them as equally promising. We would not want to say "anything goes", though we would certainly want to judge these lines of reasoning according to some criteria. Such criteria should be able to discriminate between approaches for interpreting transaesthetic experiences. Epistemic criteria as ontological parsimony clearly speak in favour of the first two lines, but philosophers need to carefully evaluate the criteria of parsimony since it may reduce the world of nature to physical entities and laws. Ultimately and regretfully, all criteria, however, may evade the issues at stake. This could be true especially for criteria such as "rationality" which strongly depend on definitions; it could also be true for a criterion such as "depth", since the rhetoric of "deep ecology", "deep incarnation", "deep democracy", and "deep aesthetics" has become pervasive in recent years. It is possible that there may be mere presumptions of depth that cannot be substantiated. Therefore, criteria are not very helpful in judging our lines of reasoning.

This experienced intuition that there is "more/else" than just beauty in nature can be interpreted with the distinction between *ontological* and *existential* categories.[28] This distinction should be acceptable even under a parsimony-criterion and it is compatible with the concept of science. If one favours an *existential interpretation* of this "more/else" experience, reading no. 5 above should receive some philosophical credit. The claims of positive aesthetics, of second-order beauty in nature, and of deontic experiences with non-humans should not simply be put aside, but rather deserve close philosophical attention. If one favours a concept of religion (the "holy"), which reduces ontological commitments ("God") as far as possible, even reading no. 8 remains within the scope of reason. All things considered, reasonable humans are not restricted to no. 1, no. 2, and no. 3:[29] this is the one and only point I wish to make.

FINAL REMARKS

The stimulating effects of transaesthetic experiences cannot be denied. As a result, an open intercultural dialogue of human experiences with and within nature needs to be on the philosophical agenda. In addition, contributions to such a dialogue should not be restricted to Western cultures. The many difficulties inherent in expressing the "more/else" in propositional, conceptual, and discursive language strongly indicate that a gap will always remain between nature and language. By means of language, however, humans can and should try to bridge this gap. Scientific references to natural objects and causal relations are only one way to bridge this gap – there are many other ways to describe encounters with nature. Although any human language carries a specific worldview, we can exchange our experiences and perspectives in living dialogues, as W. von Humboldt has argued.[30] The same can be true for trans-aesthetic experiences, too. The lines of reasoning described in no. 1-8 may prove interesting to non-Western people, while Westerners should not be biased against no. 8 by dogmatic naturalism. It would be a subtle bias against non-Western cultures if we were to restrict their experiences and claims to no. 8.

Transaesthetic experiences have been expressed in many spiritualized ways in non-Western languages. Perhaps Western people should look for wisdom in the stories, songs, prayers and rituals of indigenous people, that is, if they want to know more about such experiences. In this way, indigenous people could be seen as the keepers of the knowledge that has been lost in the West in the project of scientific enlightenment. In some Shaman traditions, the "more/else" will be expressed by saying how clean and sacred the high mountains are where ordinary humans should not go. In First Nation approaches, the "more/else" is perceived as a pervasive and prolific force of the land that is both spiritual and vital.[31] If, as I firmly believe, there is much for us Westerners to re-learn about nature, we can learn from indigenous people without discarding the achievements of the Enlightenment.

The adventure of human experience within nature and the adventure of searching for modes of language to express these experiences has been distorted and silenced by narrow concepts of rationality (as personal utility maximization or the efficient use of the scarce means of production). Therefore, environmental philosophy is faced with several tasks. The first task is to encourage people to express the many ways in which nature can be meaningful to humans. The second task is to provide a postcolonial platform which enables undistorted communication.[32] The third task is to guard such unrestricted communication by some (modest) rules and standards of discourse, logic, and reason. The overall task is an ambivalent one: to make room for fresh and vital expressions and to guard them by standards of reason.

Notes

[1] Krebs, Ott (2010), Muraca (2011).
[2] Nussbaum (2007), 77.
[3] Nussbaum (2011), 163.
[4] This capacity to live with concern for the world of nature can be enhanced by works of art, which can deepen our aesthetic imagination with respect to nature. Therefore, there is an intrinsic relationship between the beauty to be found in art and in nature (Seel).
[5] Wilson, passim.
[6] Ritter, 162.
[7] While Goethe and Humboldt conceived the relationship between natural sciences and

aesthetics as a mutual enrichment and enhancement, the Romantics conceived it as a contrast. For the Romantics, the poets have deeper insights into nature than scientists do.
8   See overview in Blackbourn, passim.
9   Conservationists argued throughout the 19th century that beautiful scenery should be protected by the state for the common good. Even protests against damming the Rhine River relied on aesthetic arguments.
10 Hölderlin, Empedokles I, 1540 f quoted in Mögel 163.
11 Rudorff, 50.
12 Habermas (1985), chapter VII.
13 Ott (2010), chapter 4.
14 Ott (1997), 234-235.
15 Hepburn, passim.
16 Kleinschmidt, passim.
17 Adorno also came close to this solution given that his dialectical philosophy pointed to something that always escapes discursive language (the "Nicht-Identische", see Adorno 1966, passim).
18 Böhme.
19 Habermas (1985), chapter VII.
20 Adorno (1970), 110: "von innen her leuchtend".
21 Ott (2010), 90.
22 Krebs, 61.
23 Muraca (2010), especially chapter II on Whitehead's ontology.
24 Rolston, especially chapter VI on "pro-jective nature".
25 Birch, 322-325.
26 Habermas (1991), 226.
27 Ott (2010), chapter 6.
28 Heidegger.
29 Even if the "ineffabile" solution in no. 3 is rejected, we can keep a silent smile on our face.
30 Lingual worldviews and dialogical reasoning are no logical contradictions but two essential aspects of language. See Humboldt, passim.
31 Armstrong, passim.
32 As the *lingua franca* of our times, English may serve as a preliminary lingual media and turning-table for such an exchange. However, every environmental philosopher probably should learn at least one non-Western language.

REFERENCES

Adorno, Theodor W. (1966), *Negative Dialektik*, Frankfurt am Main: Suhrkamp.
— (1970), *Ästhetische Theorie*, Frankfurt am Main: Suhrkamp.
Armstrong, Jeanette (2009), *Constructing Indigeneity: Syilx Okanagan Oraliture and tmix[w]-centrism*, Inauguraldissertation, Greifswald.
Birch, Thomas (1993), "Moral Considerability and Universal Consideration", *Environmental Ethics* 15, 4, 313-332.
Blackbourn, David (2007), *Die Eroberung der Natur*, München: Beck.

Böhme, Gernot (1997), "Phänomenologie der Natur – ein Projekt", in: Böhme and Schiemann, 11-43.
Böhme, Gernot and Schiemann, Georg (eds.) (1997), *Phänomenologie der Natur*, Frankfurt am Main: Suhrkamp.
Carlson, Allen (1984), "Nature and Positive Aesthetics", *Environmental Ethics* 6, 1, 5-34.
Habermas, Jürgen (1985), *Der philosophische Diskurs der Moderne*, Frankfurt am Main: Suhrkamp.
— (1991), *Erläuterungen zur Diskursethik*, Frankfurt am Main: Suhrkamp.
Heidegger, Martin (1927), *Sein und Zeit*, Tübingen: Niemayer.
Hepburn, Ronald W. (1996), "Landscape and the Metaphysical Imagination", *Environmental Values* 5, 191-204.
Humboldt, Wilhelm von (1829), "Über die Verschiedenheit des menschlichen Sprachbaues", in: Humboldt, Wilhelm von, *Schriften zur Sprachphilosophie, Werke* (ed. Flitner/Giel), Vol. III, Darmstadt 1979, 144-367.
Kleinschmidt, Erich (2004), *Die Entdeckung der Intensität: Geschichte einer Denkfigur im 18. Jahrhundert*, Göttingen: Wallstein.
Krebs, Angelika (1999), *Ethics of Nature: A Map*, Berlin and New York: DeGruyter.
Mögel, Ernst (1994), *Natur als Revolution*, Stuttgart: Metzler.
Muraca, Barbara (2010), *Denken im Grenzgebiet*, Freiburg: Alber.
— (2011), "The Map of Moral Significance: A New Axiological Matrix for Environmental Ethics", *Environmental Values* 20, 3, 375-396.
Nussbaum, Martha (2007), *Frontiers of Justice*, Cambridge, London: Belknap.
— (2011), *Creating Capabilities*, Cambridge, London: Belknap.
Ott, Konrad (1997), "Naturästhetik, Umweltethik, Ökologie und Landschaftsbewertung", in: Theobald, 221-246.
— (2008): "A Modest Proposal about How to Proceed in Order to Solve the Problem of Inherent Moral Value in Nature", in: Westra, Bosselmann and Westra, 39-60.
— (2010), *Umweltethik zur Einführung*, Hamburg: Junius.
Ritter, Joachim (1963), "Landschaft", in: *Subjektivität*, Frankfurt am Main: Suhrkamp 1971, 141-163.
Rolston III, Holmes (1988), *Environmental Ethics*, Philadelphia: Temple Press.
Rudorff, Ernst (1897), *Heimatschutz*, St. Goar: Leuchter (new ed. 1994).
Seel, Martin (1991), *Eine Ästhetik der Natur*, Frankfurt am Main: Suhrkamp.
Theobald, Werner (ed.) (1997), *Integrative Umweltbewertung*, Berlin and Heidelberg: Springer.
Westra, Laura, Bosselmann, Klaus and Westra, Richard (eds.) (2008), *Reconciling Human Existence With Ecological Integrity*, London: Earthscan.
Wilson, Edward O. (1984), *Biophilia*, Oxford: Oxford University Press.

"... THE SPACE WHERE I AM"

DECOLONISING, RE-SACRALISING AND TRANSFIGURING LANDSCAPES THROUGH THE AESTH/ETHIC LENS

Sigurd Bergmann

ALL-EMBRACING SPACE

"I am the space where I am," confesses French poet Noel Arnaud in an often-quoted phrase in architectural theory.[1] In such a view, external space and internal space interact closely, where our surrounding world and our inner world represent a common continuum. This insight is also true for landscapes. The inner world of remembrance, imagination and experience grows together with the landscape that holds us biologically, culturally and historically. "I am the space..." opposes a view of human hubris where one lives under the illusion of a totally invented and managed self. "... the space where I am", and especially the "where", embeds the living in a wider and deeper reality which grounds, anchors and embraces the living.

The reality of dramatically increasing environmental change, which climate science clearly diagnoses as "dangerous" and which is irreducible and scarcely manageable change,[2] sharpens the contours of Arnaud's insight. If I am the space where I am, and if this space at its largest scale is "Earth, our home",[3] how can we make-ourselves-at-home (*beheimaten*) in a world that we are at the same time ruining in autocratic hubris?[4] If "the space where I am" changes in a way that forces a rapidly increasing number of world citizens to either adapt to or escape from inherited lands and if landscapes have to be protected by humans from humans who have lost their ability to live with and through them rather than simply to live in them, then common capitalist modes of socioeconomic and technical (so-called) management will seem to have failed altogether.

Insights like this have been formulated since the early 1970s and have led to a multifaceted environmentalism which has greened many spheres of public life and has given rise to a couple of achievements, even if the basic code of "modern man" ruling over nature, rather than living in and with nature, seems to persist and dominate still. The *either-or* – human or nature – is far from being replaced by the *and* – man, woman and nature – and even lesser by the *in* – humanity in nature and nature in humanity.[5] The contemporary adaption of climate science in politics and economics clearly proves, for example, that technocratic and socioeconomic reactions can only produce short term, unsustainable and cosmetic responses; at the same time, the convergence of worldviews, values, lifestyles and designs of alternative life-worlds, demanded for over forty years, still dwells on the late-modern margins. These margins, nevertheless, offer fertile soil for a surprisingly broad and creative flourishing of alternatives, as seen, for example, in the World Social Forum.

This is why the focus of this book moves towards arts and religion and their cooperation with committed life sciences and environmental humanities. Such a move goes beyond the former conflicts of anthropocentrism versus ecocentrism, and aesthetics versus ethics, since it regards the human skill to perceive, imagine, design and rebuild environments as crucial in the necessary social transformation ahead of us. It focuses on "landscape" not in opposition to urban space or as an idealised (sometimes idolised) idyllic refuge, but as an all-embracing space that through its complex ecologic interplays carries and cares for life on all scales, including human ecology.[6] Our aim is to highlight the perception, imagination and expression of the all-embracing and intrinsic power of "the space where I am" as a source for re-envisioning images of ourselves in nature, modes of thinking and practises within nature.

In what follows, I will experiment with three ideas that have emerged in other discourses and, so far, have not been used in regard to landscape. A rough sketch of decolonising, re-sacralising and transfiguring landscapes may help redirect our imagination towards an alternative common future and a world home. To conclude, the chapter will offer suggestions for creating an integrated aesth/ethics.

Decolonisation

The notion of "decolonisation" is developed in postcolonial discourse where indigenous people, and those in solidarity with them, reflect on their identity – culturally as well as in regard to environmental connections – amid a long history of colonisation, in order to devise potential ways out of this oppressed state of being. Conscious that there can be no "authentic" identity[7] after a long history of cultural exchange and impacts, the reconstruction of traditional and local practises and spiritualities takes place in a desire to be nurtured by ancestral roots as well as by traditional lands. In spite of all its brokenness and ambiguity, decolonisation represents a strong and significant driving force towards an alternative, deliberative and ecologically just handling of nature.

Sami poet Nils Aslak Valkeapää suggests that "belonging to the land" is an essential element of the interplay between people and the landscape that can be applied to other indigenous contexts; he writes:

> To know,
> this is our land,
> we are this land's,
> hosting.[8]

In such a view, the land itself is the active subject to which humans belong. Can the arts and religion help recover this closeness again?

1 Fiona Foley, Winged Harvest, 2001, Australian National University's Humanities Research Centre in Canberra, close to "Old Canberra House", photo: © S. Bergmann, 2003

2 Memorial park at Flinders university, Adelaide, photo: © S. Bergmann, 2003

The first step towards decolonisation is to accept colonial history, which, incidentally, also radically affected colonisers, though in a different mode, and to ask how this can be turned in another direction. Artists play an important role in redirecting decolonisation and in the experimental recovery of traditional spiritual practices.[9]

Contemporary Australian aboriginal art, for example, and its portrayal in cultural studies, show clearly how art and religion develop in synergy with traditional as well as colonised landscapes. Anthropologist Debora Bird Rose in her "Ethics of De-colonisation"[10] clarifies the significance of place and land for the identity and religion of aboriginals.[11] As colonisation has altered large areas of the continent's geography, and thereby violated the sacred sites of the indigenous inhabitants, the future process of reconciliation between settlers, their heirs and the aboriginal population, should in some way transform the spiritual geography, such as through a restoration of sacred places. Colonisation must be turned into de-colonisation; the principle of conquering replaced by justice.[12] De-colonisation offers, in Rose's sense of the term, a "counter modernity" in which the distribution of colonial violence is replaced by the "flourishing" of individuals and their relations in, and within, environments.

Artists have an important role to play in this process of decolonisation, which also implies a religious dimension. Such a process needs to engage the history of de-sacralisation and de-spiritualisation that has characterised the violation of the spiri-

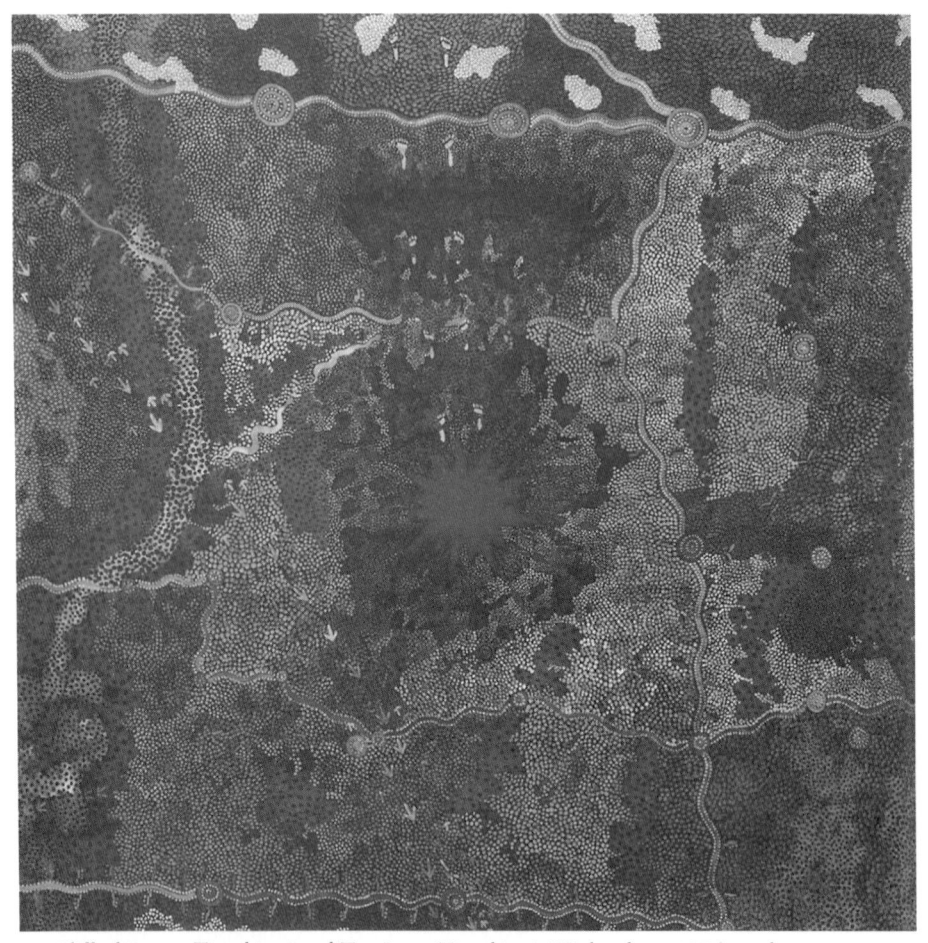

3   Clifford Possum Tjapaltjarri and Tim Leura Tjapaltjarri, Warlugulong, 1976, acryl on canvas, 168,5 x 170,5 cm, Art Gallery of New South Wales, Sydney

tual heritage of the aboriginals.[13] Consequently, the global cultural mobilisation of indigenous populations is at present characterised by a complex entanglement of religious, aesthetic, political and cultural dimensions. This quality of complexity and integration is in itself an important element of decolonisation.

The production of landscape painting and land arts performs a crucial function in this process. The production of landscape paintings represents an important part of the struggle for the aesthetics of a landscape that affects its perception and use.[14] The use of land and the imagining and artistic rendering of it are both elementary in the negotiation of what a landscape is.

As the large field of research on aboriginal arts has shown, the land plays a central and active role in the de-colonisation effort. The land has been created by the mythical animals in the dreamtime and shaped by the walking ancestors. Visual arts, thus, offer a space where one continuously can hand over, reconstruct and transcontextualise the spiritual continuum. Many pictures offer a kind of spiritual map referring to existing places, sites and regions while expressing and manifesting mythical stories about the totemic animals and the ancestors' history then and now. Dreamtime takes place in the image. The production of art is in itself a personal religious experience and, at the same time, it is also a public practice.

Anthropologist Howard Morphy summarises the spiritual content of such an image:

The key difference, however, is that Aboriginal art contains a fourth dimension – the 'inside'. Aboriginal art is as conceptual as it is perceptual. It is concerned with ideas and processes more than with appearances, and the perspective that it illuminates is that from the inside.[15]

Morphy's attempt to clarify the spiritual content of art with the metaphor of "the inside" works in a Western language system, but I am not sure whether the dialectics of inside-outside really can express the specifics of aboriginal arts. It could be argued that the outside is the inside, and the inside expresses the outside. The space where I am generates me, and therefore I am the space where I am. The physical landscape reveals its inner essence by art shaping form and colour in the picture. The pictorial depiction creates a space where, using a classical Christian expression, the Spirit gives life to the "everywhen and now" of the dreamtime. Aboriginal arts express in the picture a spiritual interpretation of life and a concrete perception of it; it is "as conceptual as it is perceptual". Dreamtime must be understood "as an everywhen".[16] In aboriginal consciousness, knowledge of the past carries knowledge of the present. The future lies in the tightest possible consolidation of the old and the new, the past and what emerges in the present. Aboriginal art is characterised by images that can contain memories of the land, but it is also able to move places, landscapes, and insights throughout the images:

Art is a means of transporting place and knowledge of place.[17]

The capacity of art to transport memories and insights about place gives special significance to those pictures created by aboriginals settling in new, urban regions. Moreover, this capacity is important not only in aboriginal contexts, but also in global communication systems in general where images of landscapes are no longer dependent on locally or regionally limited experiences and representations, but rather on productions of locality which emerge from processes of transfer, transculturation and translocal exchange.

This brief exploration opens a new window to a different way of culturally envisioning the deep connection between humans and the all-embracing space of the landscapes that inspire us. Such an insight does not simply represent an exotic inspiration from "the strange"; rather, it can teach us a crucial lesson in the struggle to find paths to future sustainable (zukunftsfähige) practices of landscape handling. If we transfer the dialectic of colonisation and decolonisation to the discourse on

4   George Steinmann's project Komi: A Growing Sculpture, 1997-2006 offers a contrast to such hypertranslocalisation, carefully partaking in, depicting and modelling the Russian cultural forest landscape. Photo: © G. Steinmann, in: George Steinmann, Komi: A Growing Sculpture, 1997-2006, Bern: Stämpfli 2007, 7.

landscape preservation ethics, we could develop a deeper self-critical consciousness. As aboriginal lands have been de-spiritualised, we could interpret the history of European landscape painting as a "distancing of nature" (Die Entfernung der Natur)[18] in light of the process of colonisation. Humans have in this history distanced themselves from nature, even if nature itself never can be set apart from embodied human beings; cities have been turned into polluting monsters and landscapes have been homogenised, cut apart, and overexploited by monoculture cultivation and industrialised territorialisation. Even "toxic landscapes" have emerged in this part of human history, poisoning large portions of nations, ecosystems, human minds and communities.[19]

The antidote of environmentalism, however, should be analysed critically within such a horizon. Is it enough to protect some landscapes from human exploitation, turning them into small refuges for scientists and, at best, eco-enlightened tourists? According to what criteria are some species, ecosystems and landscapes protected while others are left to their destiny in the struggle for the survival of the (financially) fittest? Obviously, biology, in the tradition of empirical rationalism, cannot offer a well underpinned base for decision-making but can only inform it; in addition, as Emily Brady has shown, the local, social and primarily the aesthetical dimensions of landscape handling are constantly underexposed in these decisions.[20] In such a context, what does de-colonisation mean with regard to aggressive, anthropocentric money accumulation and profit-driven exploitation and to a narrow ecocentric rationalistic ideology of clear and unclear preferences for either exclusively defined charismatic species or idealised ecosystems? Beauty in itself, as an aesthetic echo of the early enlightenment times, can scarcely save us either, as many before me stated at our event "beyond beauty" (K. Ott). How can decolonised lands turn into "sentient landscapes"?[21]

5   Max Schulze-Sölde, Zeit der Technik, 1925, oil on canvas, 123 x 94 cm,

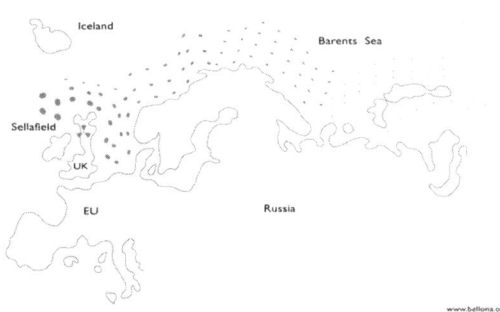

6   Sources of present Arctic contamination, (dumping of radioactive waste and spent nuclear fuel), in: Nils Bøhmer, Aleksandr Nikitin, Igor Kudrik, Thomas Nilsen, Andrey Zolotkov and Michael H. McGovern, The Arctic Nuclear Challenge, (Report 3:2001), The Bellona Foundation 2001, p. 58, <http://www.bellona.org/reports/The_Arctic-_Nuclear_Challenge>

From these reflections on de-colonisation in a postcolonial, and especially Australian aboriginal, context one can formulate five claims:

a) Rather than excluding culture, decolonised landscapes as landscapes of counter-modernity should deepen the ecological and cultural exchange of the inner and outer surrounding: not only "I am the space where I am" but also "we are the space/landscape where we are".

b) In order to avoid the relation of land and people as a bonanza, that is a simple territory for different kinds of technocratic profit-driven exploitation, such as agribusiness, genetic engineering or mass tourism, the entanglement of land and people should be nurtured from a depth of cultural, historical, ecological aesthetical and spiritual dimensions, which govern economic interests instead of being dominated by them.

c) A deep spirituality of belonging to the land, which carries us and cares for us, might be at the core of such an alternative common space and future. Administrations and politics that do not mirror the entanglement of bodies, minds and souls embedded in lands and embraced by life-giving space, can only achieve short-term insufficient responses to violations. This spiritual claim must not be interpreted as an apologetics for views such as "only a God can save us", or "if all become believers all will change, either through ecoreligon, traditional monotheism or new esoteric". A deep spirituality of land means nothing more than what cultures and religions for a long time have preserved as central wisdom, summarised by Valkeapää's humble "this is our land, we are the land's".

d) The connection of the arts, religion and science, and their reciprocal interweavement in new transdisciplinary modes, has an important role to play in catalysing de-colonisation.

e) The production of earthworks and landscape paintings represents an important part of the struggle for the aesthetics of a landscape that affects its perception and use. The sculptural and pictorial expression of how we imagine a landscape is in itself a crucial part of the negotiation about the meaning of that landscape, the values of the environment, and the identity of humans in it. Inner and outer spaces flow into each other in the process of imaging the environment. Religion can hinder as well as nurture and fuel such creative landscape production. Images of landscapes can be stored, remembered and transported through places; in this way they can contribute to a new arena of exchange between different places and regions. Art can indeed transport place.

Aboriginal Australian artist Albert Namatjira (1902-1959) produced all his life a series of landscapes expressing the indigenous understanding of land in a way that allows also the settler and his/her heirs to approach it, to learn from it and to let it enrich and change their mode of seeing. A large exhibition "Seeing the Centre", arranged by the Australian National Gallery in 2002, re-evaluated his work as an outstanding contribution of high national significance to the reconciliation of landscape aesthetics in a colonial context.[22]

RE-SACRALISATION

Secularisation has for some time been regarded as one of the central characteristics of modernity. The diminished influence of religious institutions, traditions, worldviews, values and practices in the public sphere has been interpreted as a kind of natural law in the social sciences, in which increasing enlightenment, rationalisation and "Verwissenschaftlichung" (scientification) has been assumed necessarily to lead to the decline of religion. Today, one can claim without a doubt that this general thesis is no longer valid. Empirically focussed scholars in the social sciences have for too long operated with a far too narrow concept of religion; they have not perceived the upsurge of religion in private and small scale social spheres, nor have they noticed and analysed the multifaceted transformation of religion in the ages of modernisation and globalisation. Consequently, in the last decade, many voices have begun again to acknowledge the significance of religion in late modernity; as a result, discourse about religion in politics, and religion and ecology, in the public sphere has increased. Furthermore, the falsely claimed "clash of civilisations" rooted in different religions (S. Huntington), has been dismantled as an ideologically driven, one-sided distortion of the concepts of culture and religion.[23] Instead, the impacts of globalisation on

7 Albert Namatjira, Ghost gum, (Eucalyptus papuana), ca 1945-53, water colour on pencil drawing on paper, 32,2 x 42 cm, private collection

religious traditions in various geographical and cultural world regions tend to develop in similar, rather than in conflicting, ways, provoking a flourishing of new forms of faith in a globalised late modernity.

For some, this new, and often scholarly, perception of the contextualised and diverse significance of religion in practices, worldviews, values and imaginations of the past, present and future, has been interpreted as a "return of religion".[24] But faith, although it has changed, has never really disappeared, so how can it return? The phrase signals, rather, the return of religion as a phenomenon in scholarly spheres and in the, mainly, European media, where religion has not been on the radar but is now again appearing visibly.

Throughout the entire history of modernity, implicit religious codes have provided a kind of skeleton for modern society's body, for example, through codes suggesting that nature is given to man to steward. Or, that goodness and justice are core values that are somehow hidden in reality and can be perceived, understood and applied by humans. Or, the idea that all human beings are equal, which is rooted in the Jewish Christian view of man and woman made in God's image. All these elements, and many others, form crucial parts of our historical self-understanding that affect our understanding of life and nature. Even the theory of evolution, which is metaphorically anchored in images of the holy scripture as enrolled (as a book role) in the Jewish synagogue liturgy where the signs and letters in the holy book are interpreted, is analogous to the biologist who interprets the on-going story of life as an evolving process in one common book of life. The "evolvere" of the scripture is, as Hans Blumenberg has shown,[25] at its metaphorical depth grounded in the image of reading the holy book of the Creator. Incidentally, in late antiquity, Augustine had already formulated such ideas in his doctrine of the two books, the book of nature and the book of the bible, which were both regarded as equal sources for an experience of God's revelation.[26]

Rather than simply talking about the return of religion in late modernity, however, I want to argue for the use of ideas, such as de-secularisation and re-sacralisation, as some scholars in the sociology of religion have suggested, in these discussions.[27] Even if the "re-" causes similar problems as the "re-turn", as I have noted, the term "sacralisation" might fit better with old as well as new belief systems; furthermore, it fits better with the early history of sociology as well as the rapidly developing field of the study of religion, nature and the environment.

My hypothesis here is that the process of re-sacralisation deeply affects the perception, imagining and usage of landscapes. Sacralisation of the landscape would then mean regarding it not as an empty space where life emerges only according to the laws of biology, geography and other sciences, often learnt in school, but as a complex environment of ecological and cultural processes, historically bound on the one hand and developing as an open system towards the unknown future on the other. Landscape would then not just be a Newtonian space but rather a "third space" (E. Soja), where imagined space and physical space together create a plastic lived space.[28] Landscapes would then represent not simply a realm of life but a world where knots of lines between places interact.[29]

To put it in Jakob von Uexküll's terms, landscape would be a space, where "Wirkwelten" (worlds of action) and "Merkwelten" (worlds of remembrance and orientation) of different organisms and life systems cross each other in a manifold community of paths and places.[30] As far as humans are concerned, "Merkwelten" also implies the images of the Sacred and "Wirkwelten" include sociocultural practices with regard to the Sacred. Subjective, sociocultural and physical dimensions are then, as the model of the so-called human ecological triangle suggests, interconnected and part of a complex interplay of exchanges.

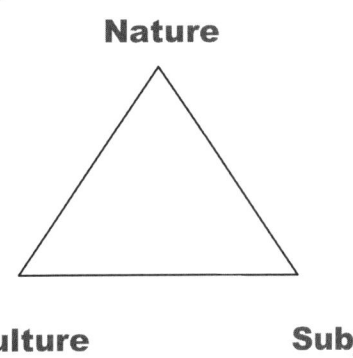

Nature

Society/Culture   **Subject**

8   *The human ecological triangle*[31]

Modern biological ecology, as we know from the history of modern environmentalism, can fuel and catalyse an integrated view of landscape in both its biological and spiritual dimensions. From its modern beginnings, biology, as well as geography, has been driven, I would suggest, by a desire to grasp the Spirit of life and earth. While the aesthetical approach in the early days still played a central role in perceiving, depicting and measuring landscape and life forms (i.e., in biomorphological illustration or in Humboldt's physiognomic cosmos), today it is reduced to a mere illustration that aids the dominate, abstract, mostly computer-based, simulation of diverse taxonomies. In addition, historical dimensions in the entanglement of culture and landscape, in spite of how much these still impact on present relations, move more and more into the shadows of the politics of landscape planning. Historical, cultural, spiritual and ecological values and intrinsic values have to give room to financially defined economic values which emerge on how to use, not just see and live with, landscapes. As in the Renaissance when the term "landscape" was invented, landscape on this account still functions as the body of politics.[32] In a similar way as also the understanding of human welfare has been dominated by accumulation economy and just recently strives for a deeper understanding also landscapes are affected. We would then need to develop something that we could call "landscape welfare economies" in a future still to come.[33] In a pioneering text, landscape architect Ian McHarg was already pointing in this direction in 1969 when he argued for the need to approach landscapes through the framework of "processes as values" and to regard any place as "the sum of historical, physical and biological processes" which dynamically constitute social values.[34]

If regarded from the more open-minded elements of the sociology of religion, or from a phenomenologically inspired theology, without a doubt one can interpret landscape as an arena for religious imagination. This is evident in the overwhelming number of tourists who, for example, pilgrim to places such as Hiddensee Island, seem to be driven by a desire to escape the world. "The world" here is understood in the Apostle Paul's biblical meaning, that is, not the good cosmos and creation but the empire with all its mixtures of enslavement and disempowering, or, as Habermas once phrased it, the life worlds colonised by the system.

In such a context, an open landscape can serve as a refuge and a liberating contrast. On islands such as Hiddensee, the landscape offers open and wide spaces instead of limited ones, green and blue instead of grey surfaces, a wide range of forms, colours and sounds instead of predesigned built surroundings and technically-produced soundscapes and surroundings. It offers a space where a walk along a path can create a special place, and where many visitors return in order to build up an individual, place-based memory of well-being. Such protected spaces, which shelter species, ecosystems as well as human drop-outs, can increase and enrich the visitors' sensitivity: bodily senses and perceiving skills are aesthetically enriched to a high degree, especially if compared to the ordinary life of employment, business or education. Such heightened sensitivity often provokes further experiences with the Sacred, which may not necessarily point to a traditional God, even if s/he also incarnates, resurrects and inhabits landscapes like this where the inner and outer space again open up and flow into each other.

When using a term like re-sacralisation to describe such an aesthetically variant approach to liberating landscape experiences, in contrast to imperial enslaving experiences, it is important to be clear about what is meant by "the Sacred". According to sociologist Bron Szerzsynski, the Sacred is beyond that of Durkheim's and Weber's limited concepts of it. Although he follows Kay Milton's definition of the Sacred as "what matters most to people", Szerzsynski also moves beyond her positive appreciation of the Sacred in nature by also exploring the alienation from, and fear of, nature.[35] For him, sacralisation involves "practices that have religious or quasi-religious aspects", and so, secular treatments of nature can also be understood in religious terms.[36] He makes clear how through the ages monotheistic institutions have influenced and shaped our images of the Sacred; in addition he shows how, what he calls, the postmodern and global Sacred are both dependent on this history and try to establish new practices and images of the Sacred.

Images of landscapes seem to me to play a more prominent role in shaping a global Sacred and in processes of "Beheimatung".[37] From Szerszynski one can learn that images of the Sacred are at work in the cultural process and in different "cultural techniques", and that secularisation has not limited these techniques but rather accelerated their production.[38] Globalisation appears to fuel the construction of religious identities and renewed traditions, both in strict fundamentalism and in creatively open contexts; in a similar manner, the imaging of nature in landscape (and also urban space) also seems to be part of a complex re-sacralisation process.

An inspiring example of what I have in mind is found in German land artist Herman Prigann's (1942-2008) earthworks. In his artworks the physical, historical, sociocultural and spiritual dimensions (including explicit religion) become visible not merely as a sculpture but as a space that becomes a place, a *Raum* one can move in and out of, move around in, and, furthermore, can transport its meanings to other places, as in the aboriginal artefacts mentioned earlier. Rather than working against or merely with the help of a given landscape, Prigann includes the complexities of a landscape's sociocultural and physical histories. The landscape shapes the artist while he works with "her".

According to Prigann and his "ecological aesthetic", "destroyed landscapes are activity fields available for creative remodelling."[39] Prigann belongs to a growing group of creative perceivers, thinkers and actors who experiments with places, artefacts and paths that might lead humanity and the planet Earth through the sufferings of anthropogenic environmental change. In a couple of highly provocative, widely acknowledged projects, the artist has reconstructed urban and industrial landscapes transfiguring them into exciting places of remembrance, contemplation and ritualization.

9 Herman Prigann, Himmelstreppe (stairs to heaven), on top of the dump site of the colliery area Rheinelbe, the Skulpturenwald Rhein-Elbe, 1999, photo: © Thomas Robbin

In his long-term project "Terra Nova", Prigann designed and built his "Himmelstreppe" (Stairs to Heaven) on the site of a dump at an abandoned coal mine near the German Ruhrgebiet. Fragments and debris from built environments are interwoven with new and organic materials. In this manner, the archaeological past does not fade away but receives a new meaning and function. The lonesome artefacts point backwards and forwards in time and as they remain in place, the historical wounds on the landscape begin to heal. Aesthetically, Prigann's work alludes to Mesoamerican ritualistic places as known from, for example, Mayan sacred geography.[40] The religious transfer from one context to another invites us to ritualise the former coal mine anew. What kinds of social actions could and should take place here and now? What kind of awareness might emerge regarding the human skills of destruction and construction? Furthermore, the restoration, or better, the transfiguration of the mine into a new open eco-spiritual place, is embedded in a larger master plan for a landscape park, where large areas of former industrial sites will be turned into a landscape whose future appearance is far from clear and predictable.[41] Land Art thus offers a specific quality of change and uncertainty that might teach us something about the tremble and tremor of social and natural disasters catalysed by dangerous environmental change. One of the challenges in this context is to differentiate between those uncertainties that potentially threaten life and those that can encourage us to increase our dignity for life.

Prigann completes his stairs to heaven with the "Der große Stuhl" (Great Chair), which references an archaic throne but is built from fragments of granite and stone from the old mining company's central building. The "Spiralberg" establishes with its Stairs to Heaven a mythical landmark that embeds the visitor and provides him/her with an orientation in the larger surrounding, inviting him/her to reshape the significance of the place by physically moving around and mentally creating new inner images. The "sins" of the past, represented here by the former mine whose products contributed to the CO_2 emissions driving global climate change, are in this way slowly transformed into landscapes where change can take place in a peaceful, reconciled, non-threatening way.

Furthermore, Prigann's art reminds us that anthropogenic environmental change not only encompasses climate change but also changes in global and regional land use (that is, the widespread conversion of natural ecosystems to arable land, pastures, settlements, etc.), disturbances to terrestrial and aquatic ecosystems that threaten faunal and floral biodiversity, soil and water contamination, and many others. In this vein, we might also consider his restoration of an abandoned water works in which the natural flow of the river has become visible and tactile again. The hill thus "carries" the ruin and the landscape embraces our common past and opens onto our common future. This may remind the passer-by that without intact aquatic and terrestrial ecosystems and without a fair and sustainable use of freshwater, relations between human societies may become increasingly insecure, violent, conflict-laden and painful. A global water ethos is, as Dieter Gerten shows,[42] as essential for establishing patterns of creative adaptation to climate and environmental change, as it is to turn former CO_2-intensive coalmines into flourishing gardens of redemption.

Another crucial challenge, visualised in the artist's transformed site, is to make oneself at home again in a world that is permanently being destroyed by humans themselves. What in general does "home" (German *Heimat*) mean, and how will processes of "earthing and making-oneself-at-home" develop in the context of ac-

10   Herman Prigann, Waterlevel, transformation of a former water-pumping station (near Marl, Germany) into a landscape artwork, 2001, photo: © Herman Prigann

celerating and expanding environmental change, including the related changes in lifestyles, belief patterns and modes of surviving? How can religion itself contribute to the earthing and "Beheimatung" in this world?[43] Or, to put it in Anne Primavesi's terms, what does it mean to be alive with Gaia in a relational world?[44]

The conclusions from this section on resacralised lands can be summarised in the following statements:

a) Landscape is more than simply an empty container where life in a strict biological sense or sociality in a strict geographical or socioeconomic sense takes place; it is a complex space with interwoven physical, sociocultural, historical and spiritual dimensions. In particular, destroyed landscapes are in need of a creative "re-modelling" in order to restore their traces.

b) The sacralisation of a landscape, which can take many routes that scholars of religion and landscape should investigate in a common research field,[45] contributes to this re-modelling. Regarding a place as Sacred has a significant impact on the formation of images, values and norms for the usage of a landscape. The driving forces behind sacralisation can include the accumulation of financial capital as well as a need to shelter endangered species; they can include the desire for alternative, rather than colonised, life worlds as well as the therapeutic need to approach a landscape where outer space can embrace a broken inner space. Religious studies and cultural studies have developed reflections on the Sacred (about what really matters most) and offer a broad range of approaches to keep the diverse entanglement of man/woman and landscape open.

c) The explicit and visible interchange of images, expressions and practices of the Sacred and the landscape creates, not just an etheric spiritual mood or beautiful decoration but atmospheres of a wonder-working power. To build on my arguments about de-colonised landscapes, the re-sacralised landscape can contribute, in this sense, to a liberation from narrow, rationalist, economic and anthropocentric images and can catalyse, if not necessarily in itself create, a sacred geography that again one can approach, experience, interpret and walk through with the assistance of many different religious traditions.

d) In such a horizon of re-sacralisation, the cooperation of the arts, religion and science does not serve to re-conquer a Christian-European identity and territory.[46] Neither should it uncritically support the nationalist and regional restorations of power constellations through landscape management or restoration of landscape symbolics; instead, it should visualise for all the senses the visible and hidden forces and intrinsic values of landscapes which open themselves for a spiritual exchange with humans. To put it into Alexander von Humboldt's language, the face of the landscape invites the faces and bodies of humans to interact with the other. Formulated in Emmanuel Levinas' terms, landscape becomes the other whom I must see, respect and encounter; the strange landscape then can embrace and embody man and women. Put in religious terms, landscape embraces and interacts with its inhabitants before God's face.

TRANSFIGURED LANDSCAPES

The dialectics of transcendence and immanence, so common in Western philosophical and religious ontologies for about 700 years, has caused much harm to human modes of perceiving, thinking about and acting with nature; it should be overcome. The split between transcendence and immanence mirrors what art historians call "the distancing of nature"; it can be clearly traced in the history of European landscape painting in the late medieval, enlightenment and modern periods and it mirrors the well-known Cartesian split of mind, body and surrounding life.

If man is separated from nature, then God, the Creator, is separated from the world. Since its beginning in the early 1970s, ecotheology has critically analysed this one-sided thinking and has offered several alternative models of God being in and with nature.[47] Even before late nominalist scholasticism, classical theology and, in particular, Eastern Orthodox theology has always imagined the Divine in, with and through nature. At its roots, Christianity developed a unique, radical and, in the context of antiquity, a revolutionary revaluation of the body, especially the poor and suffering body as a locus of encounter between the created and uncreated, the divine and living beings. In late antiquity systematic theological models emerged, such as

Augustine's account of the two books of nature and the holy scripture as two equal sources of God's revelation and liberating work, along with his account of the image of the Holy Spirit as a liberating Life-giver who acts in synergy with humans and other life forms to realize a new world and a new era beyond contemporary suffering. Such ideas have inspired ideologies of European empire building as well as those of solidarity, emancipation and love of neighbour. Transcendence and immanence are not classical Christian images of God.[48] What is at stake, in classical as in contemporary Christianity, is what we might call the *transparency* of created life towards the Divine and God's visibility in the material world. In such a view, life worlds and ecosystems, to phrase it in modern terms, are perceived, interpreted and experienced as open, given spaces where places of different kinds serve as arenas for encounters with the Triune on earth, with earth and for the sake of creation.

The incarnation of God as a human being, and the dwelling of the Spirit in human bodies and on earth, forms the centre of Christian faith. Such a rich view of the close interplay of created beings of all kinds with the experience of the God who acts and the Spirit who liberates life, is expressed in Paul's letter to the Romans, where he confesses

... that the creation itself will be liberated from its bondage to decay and brought into the glorious freedom of the children of God. We know that the whole creation has been groaning as in the pains of childbirth right up to the present time. (Romans 8:21-22)

For the Christian tradition and its reconstruction, such a theology is crucial as it expands upon the notion of the unity of human and other creatures and imagines this as a community of suffering, hope and liberation.[49] Landscapes, thus, are necessarily included among those awaiting liberation from the bondage to decay. Landscapes co-act with the Triune in the synergy of liberation.[50] For our context, I would like to offer the idea of *transfiguration* as a point of departure for this experimental alternative.

In Christian theology, "transfiguration" is defined narrowly as the transfiguration of Jesus upon a mountain (later identified as Mount Tabor) (Matthew 17:1-9, Mark 9:2-8, Luke 9:28-36), where he became radiant, spoke with Moses and Elijah and was called "Son" by God. The transfiguration is celebrated commonly in the Eastern churches, while Western Catholic churches only memorialise it locally. For some early theologians, transfiguration points to a personal transformation where the senses are enabled to perceive Christ. This event has offered widespread inspiration for artists and composers.[51]

Transfiguration can also serve as an aesthetic category (in German *Verklärung*), whereby it sometimes is used to characterise the least attractive of religious artefacts, for example, souvenirs, that aim to transfer the observer and user of the artefact into a specific transfigured state – in other words, to draw him/her, analogous to the ascending Christ, out of this world and into a purely spiritual and holy one. In this sense, transfigured objects mirror the recently criticised dichotomies of nature and

11/12   Raphael's The Transfiguration of Christ (1518-1520), oil on woods, 405 x 278 cm, Pinacoteca Vatican) includes trees, rock and sky in the mystical event and distributes the divine light to the whole surrounding landscape and figures. While Raphael elevates the Son of God, the Greek Icon with the same title (ca 1600, 76,5 x 51 cm, Ikonen-Museum Recklinghausen) anchors Christ at the mountain and depicts the landscape scenery, in all its elements, as transparent to the divine light. While Western believers are drawn up to heaven, the Eastern believers experience Christ coming down to earth. Bellini, in contrast, ascribes to the landscape, including its built and rural environments, an intrinsic value by virtue of its participation with the event; it shares, carries, and adopts a smoothly greening light from Christ as well as from the embracing heavens.

spirit, man and life, God and world. They draw you out of this world into another one; they do not transfigure creation in the classical sense but leave this world to its own devices and in its bondage to decay.

Transfiguration is also developed, primarily in Eastern Orthodox liturgies and theologies, as an inspiring and broad notion for comprehending how on-going change in creation takes place in synergy with a Creator, which Jewish mystics have called the Lover of life. Transfiguration then points to the on-going transformation and metamorphosis of creation as a whole and in its various parts. To visualize what this might mean in evolutionary terms, we could suggest that, while evolution biologically describes both the mysterious and intelligible dynamics of on-going change in life systems, transfiguration describes the spiritual dimension within, not above or beyond, evolution. However, one should not equate evolution and transfiguration ontologically. The two processes cannot and should not be forced to converge; science and religion ought not to be dissolved into one another but should interact

13   Giovanni Bellini, Transfiguration, ca 1490-1495, tempera on panel, 115 x 151,5 cm, Capodimonte National Gallery, Naples, Italy

on various levels. As this discussion is explored in other discourses on science and theology/religion,[52] I will focus instead on transfiguration in the religious sense and examine how it operates as a quality of change within, not beyond, natural life and its evolution.

In classical Trinitarian terms, the incarnation of the Son is followed by the indwelling of the Spirit; extending this image to the transfiguration of landscapes would require us to revise our theology and, especially, to emphasise its spatial ecology. The notion of transfiguration plays a central role in Eastern Orthodox theology: in various contexts, it serves as an interpretive lens for God's encounter with creation. Furthermore, the ascension story circumscribes Christ's bodily return with the bloody marks of his bodily suffering to the Father; it also describes the Trinitarian mystery of the Son, "the wisdom of the Cross",[53] and the Spirit who continues God's salvation history on and with the earth. For eastern believers, all creation takes part in this transformation; and thus, the transfiguration of the cosmos is a key doctrine that connects the doctrines of creation and redemption. As God created the world, God also sustains the world and leads it to its end; in the words of patristic theologian Gregory of Nazianzus: What God has begun he also fulfils.[54]

In such a view, all life is given and in the process of becoming. The transfiguration of the cosmos draws created life closer to God; this includes what the Orthodox faith calls the "deification" of man and woman, the maturation of the human person closer to God so that he or she can become a true icon of God. This process of spiritual change embraces all material life and non-human life forms. Creation is, to put it simply, on its way to God with God, or, to put it in Trinitarian terms, on its way through and in the Spirit with the Son to the Father (or, if you prefer, Mother) of Life. As part of the ecumenical process for "justice, peace and the integrity of creation" (JPIC), the Orthodox Church issued this official ecumenical statement in 1987:

> The value of the creation is seen not only in the fact that it is intrinsically good, but also in the fact that it is appointed by God to be the home for living beings. ... Ultimately, however, the whole of the creation is destined to become a transfigured world, since the salvation of humankind necessarily involves the salvation of its natural home, the cosmos.[55]

14   Basilica of St. Apollinare in Classe, Apse mosaic, Ravenna, ca 549

The apse in the Basilica in Ravenna dates to the same era as the emergence of patristic theologies of transfiguration and offers us a glimpse of the integrated entanglement of humans and landscapes in the process of becoming closer to the triune God.

Giovanni Bellini's marvellous landscape compresses the whole Christian story – Genesis, incarnation and spiritual vivification – in a dense landscape comprised of places from Christian salvation history. More than simple scenery, his landscape performs in synergy with the acting God and his creatures. Soaked in warm, soothing

15 Giovanni Bellini, *The Holy Allegory*, ca 1490, oil on wood, 73 x 119 cm, Galleria degli Uffizi, Florence

colours, it embraces natural and built environments, figures and places. The artistically construed atmosphere of such a landscape provides a visual of the Creator's revelatory and liberating work with creation.

I am well aware that such foundational theological declarations have their limits, both inside and outside of Christian and public spheres; however, for me it is important to show that a classical theological view can fully support a complex view of landscape that includes a spiritual dimension. Such a view of landscape can enable us to overcome reductionist, mechanistic or empiricist approaches combined with applied utilitarian ethics, and instead regard them as animated sociocultural and historical arenas of evolutionary life.

It does not matter to me whether one follows, as Heather Eaton does,[56] the path of Teilhard de Chardin, or whether one takes a more detached stance on systematic change. As one among several possible approaches, a synthesis of the belief systems of classical late antiquity and early enlightenment patterns of thinking, which both can inspire a spiritually deepened human ecology, would be perfectly acceptable.

In opposition to the dogmatism of mechanistic science developed by Goethe, Humboldt, Herder and many others in the early 17th century, *enlightened vitalism* ontologically operated with the central intention of understanding *life forces*. For the enlightened vitalists, as the prominent historian Hannes Reill calls them,[57] these hidden forces were implicit in various life forms, interacting and creating a field of energies that could be identified by scientists in medicine, biology, chemistry and geography. Science at that time was not territorialised but able to observe on both macro and micro levels, crisscross. The morphological approach, as biologists are well aware, was more deeply integrated in an aestheticological understanding of the connection between our own body's perception and the study of life, its change and continuity. The Romantics, much acclaimed in environmentalism, seem to have destroyed this genuine acknowledgement of manifold in science production and casted it again in one mould but that is another story.

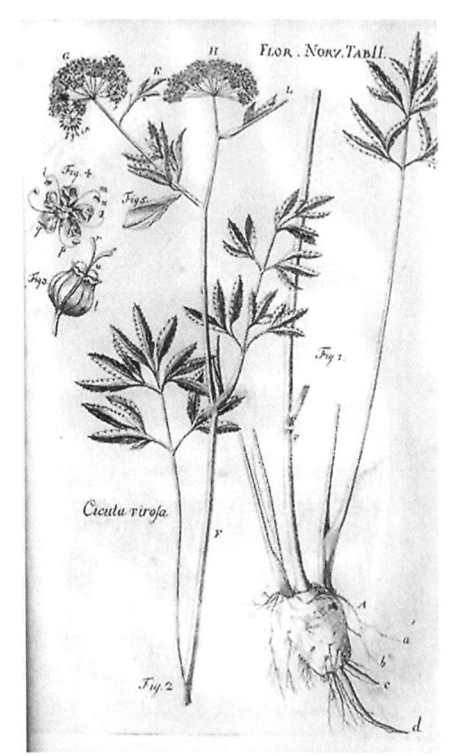

16   Cicuta virosa, in: *Johann Ernst Gunnerus, Jo. Ern. Gunneri Flora Norvegica: observationibus praesertim oeconomicis, panosque norvegici locupletata, Nidrosiae: Typis Vindingianis, 2 b, 1766-1772,* <http://www.ub.uib.no/avdeling/spes/godbit97/-august.htm>

17   Corals, in: *Johann Ernst Gunnerus, Om nogle Norske Coraller, in: Det Kongelige Norske Videnskabers Selskabs Skrifter, Vol. IV., Trondheim 1768, 38-73.*

Merging the concept of transfiguration as a common divine process on the micro and macro scales of nature, society and culture, with the early enlightenment concept of life forces, might throw new light on the unfolding sacred geography of landscapes. Scientists would then need to be transparent and open concerning how their methodology works with what we can know and especially with what we *cannot* know and grasp. Believers, then, would no longer need to regard scientists as threats to their dogmatically formulated traditions of creation as a simple *theatrum mundi*, an empty arena for God's performance; instead, like scientists, they would need to operate carefully with the unknown in *the strange* of nature and *the strange* in God.[58] Theology would then need to recover its older apophatic method[59] in which one can never fully know God's essence but can learn about God through bodily and spiritual experiences in places where the Spirit acts. Science could learn to apply the same epistemology in regard to nature – that is, to operate with an unknown "within life" that changes attitudes while they continue to research. Artists could then begin to operate between both camps, without prostituting themselves too much to science or without copying religious practices, and develop carefully designed artefacts in the field between religion, nature and culture.

Aesth/ethics

So far in my appeal for decolonised, re-sacralised and transfigured landscapes I have drawn experimental sketches and presented alternative understandings of landscape other than those that reign in contemporary discourses in politics and science. Some might argue that what is missing in this is an environmental/ethical dimension and they might overlook the implicit challenge here concerning how to practically manage and design landscapes of and for a sustainable future. While such criticism may seem relevant, my intention simply has been to meander through the worlds of words, memories and images to find new and inspiring constructive tools to break through the contemporary, ill-fated and limited modes of thinking about landscape. In conclusion, I want to explore a more theoretical tool, developed earlier mainly in architecture and environmental ethics: an integrated concept of aesthetics and ethics, where both stand not simply as equals side by side, but where aesthetics generates the space in which ethics can work and moralities can flourish.

The concept of "aesth/ethics" brings aesthetics to the forefront of ethics.[60] "Aesthetics" is here understood not as a theory of beauty in the narrow philosophical sense, but as a discursive and artistic production and reflection of practices and discourses on synaesthetic perception, creation and reception. Following German philosopher Gernot Böhme, an ecological aesthetics is a self-aware human reflection on one's living-in-particular-surroundings.[61] The slash between aesthetics and ethics suggests two things. First, it signals the intention not to leave moral philosophy and ethics to themselves but to embed them continuously in bodily perceptions. If ethics is defined as a discursive reflection on moral problems, it becomes difficult to exclude people's mental capacities and to separate aesthetic competence from moral competence. Ethics, therefore, must be embraced by aesthetics. The perception of moral problems must precede their reflection and solution. It requires a sharp mind and the capacity of the senses to see our neighbour's misery and to answer Cain's question: "Lord, am I my brother's keeper?"

Second, prioritizing aesthetics over ethics shall prevent us from regarding ethics as a superior, dominant, and neo-colonial "modern ethics" (in the sense of Zygmunt

Bauman).[62] The embodied and sensitive perception of oneself and others in a common environment[63] will not only precede moral agency and reflection, it will also continuously regulate it. The experience of space not merely as a physically perceived space or an ideationally conceived space, but as a truly plastic lived space is at the core of such a trialectic "aisthesis" embedding "ethos".[64] This means that an *aesth/ethics of landscapes*, and especially of landscapes experiencing dangerous environmental change, emphasises bodily perception of a landscape that is deeply integrated with rational reflection about the history, use and management of the landscape. In such an account, Landscape is more than a territory, area or scenery, it is complex human-ecologic space that emerges by "doing the landscape",[65] that is, by human practises in and with the landscape rather than simply observing and seeing it ("practises" here broadly refers to perceptions, actions and emotional conditions). The geometry of a living environment depends on the mental state of the person who moves in it.[66]

An utilitarian concept of ethics violates such integration because it immediately departs from a negotiation about an alleged highest value and its maximisation (defined in accordance with modern economic thinking), which determines the whole further ascription of values to landscapes and development of human moral agency. A deontological concept of ethics, even in its best form of discourse ethics, cares most about keeping intact the intrinsic value of nature and its life evolving in landscape; however, at best, it only can translate this into an abstract principle to be either respected or violated. In contrast, aesth/ethics departs from the bodily being of humans and seeks, instead, a foundation of moral perception, imaging, reflection and action in a sustained bodily interconnection with the environment. To re-phrase it in Arnauld's words in my title: landscape acts as both the subject and object of aesth/ethics as it endows us with life, embraces us spatially, evolves in time and contextualises our ethics in a common encounter. Ontologically as well as bodily and morally, *I am the landscape where I am, – and through which I am.*

18   Grieben, Hiddensee, in August, photo: © Ingela Bergmann, 2009

Notes

1 Noel Arnaud, quoted in: Bachelard, 137.
2 On "dangerous climate change", see Schellnhuber, Cramer and Nakicenovic. On "dangerous environmental change" (which broadens the term and research field), see Bergmann and Gerten.
3 <http://www.earthcharter.org/>, 18 September 2006.
4 Geographer Yi-Fu Tuan emphasises in his latest book what is different and what is common in geography and religion, and he regards, 15, religions in general as practices with a central meaning "to make a home for humans." Religion, for him, 70, is "the core idea of which is that humans are most deluded when they believe that they can feel, even in the best of times, at ease and at home on Earth."
5 Cf. Kandinsky declared the end of the age of *either-or* and replaced it with the age of the *and*.
6 Historically regarded, the notion of "landscape" (invented in Dutch and German languages) is not an innocent one; it represents a deeply political and exploitative view of the land as "a place that found itself at the center of Renaissance struggles to represent the nature of the polity." Olwig, 214. Landscape represents both a panorama view with man at its center and a reification of the land for his sake, as well as the body of politics. Olwig identifies two different discourses that are intertwined: in the first sense, land represents the terrain upon which the nation state is constructed; in the second sense, land

is established through the people who inhabit it. My reflection in the following aims at a revaluation of the second discourse.
7   Cf. Shiff about famous Cherokee artist Jimmie Durham and his criticisms of "authenticity".
8   Nils-Aslak Valkeapää, in: *Nu Guhkkin Dat Mii Lahka/Så Fjernt Det Nære*, (without page numbering): "vite,/ dette landet er vårt,/ vi er dette landets,/ vertskap".
9   For a continuous covering see the journal *Third Text*, and for a depiction of Sami arts see Bergmann (2009b) (2008ab).
10 Rose (2004).
11 Rose (2000), 40.
12 Ibid., 48f.
13 Eggington, 5f.
14 Morphy (1998), 266: "The colonial process has been a battle not only between different economies but between different ways of relating people to land, and since aesthetics has been close to the heart of Aboriginal relationships with land, colonialism has also been a struggle over the aesthetics of the Australian landscape."
15 Morphy (2000), 130.
16 Stanner, 29.
17 Morphy (1999), 65.
18 Bätschmann.
19 Cf. Nye.
20 Brady, 246ff.
21 The notion of "sentient landscapes" captures the (indigenous) way of conceiving the whole ensemble of entities, made up of human and non-human beings as well as landscape elements. Cf. Heyd, and Cruikshank.
22 Alison. Cf. Bergmann (2009), 299-302.
23 Scholar of Islam Oliver Roy offers, for example, in his recent book detailed insights into the diversity of interconnections (and disconnections) between religion and culture in the times of globalisation.
24 Cf. Bell, and Scruton. In connection to a postulated "return of religion" one can further speculate about the return of atheism and a new aggressive criticism of religion by some media-noisy elites in rich Western contexts.
25 Blumenberg, 19.
26 Augustinus, *De genesi ad litteram*, PL 32, 219ff. Later, Thomas Aquinas sought to read in nature "the knowledge of God like in a book". On modernity's absolutization of the metaphor of the book of nature, see Blumenberg, 267-299.
27 On *re-sacralisation*, see Beyer, 25, who emphasises that re-sacralisation does not mean a simple renegotiation of the secularisation thesis, but that religion must be studied in a new key in the context of pluralism and globalisation. Already in 1977, Daniel Bell observed the re-sacralisation of society when Protestant fundamentalism became a political force in the United States. On *de-secularisation*, see further Knoblauch.
28 A sensitive question would be to explore how so-called real and un-real space, that is virtual space (which in fact is neither un-real nor simulated), affects religious imagination and our orientation in physical and cultural spaces as well our normative practices with regard to it. For exciting insights on this topic in Japanese and Russian Orthodox philosophies of cultural space, see Botz-Bornstein, 21ff. On the "reversed perspective" in

Russian early modern philosophy of religion, see Bergmann (2009a), 63f. For the impact of virtual spaces on urbanism, see Löw, Steets and Stoetzer, 81. One can only wonder how virtual space impacts on landscape images and practices in the present and in the future. Historically speaking, such a question continues the early enlightenment split in "landscapes of doing" (different usages with regard to goals such as food production, building, energy) and "Kopflandschaften" (head landscapes), as Küster and Küster, 351, call them (such as landscape paintings and parks). Contemporary landscapes seem however to have dissolved completely the earlier distinction of gardens on the one side and wilderness on the other. On "mental maps/Landschaften im Kopf" cf. further Schlögel, 243ff.

29 Ingold.
30 Cf. Uexküll and Kriszat.
31 Cf. Steiner, 47ff.
32 Cf. above note 6.
33 Cf. Diefenbacher.
34 McHarg, 104.
35 Szerszynski, 10.
36 Szerszynski, 11.
37 Cf. Bergmann, "Beheimatung: Making-oneself-at-home with the Spirit – a collage".
38 Cf. also Deane-Drummond (2006), 162f., who agrees with Szerszynski that late modernity offers a fragmentation of organised religion in Western societies that does not form a secular wasteland but a huge diversity of enchantments, "rich profusions of the sacred, bridging the technological and natural worlds".
39 Herman Prigann, <http://www.terranova.ws/tnvision.htm>, 26 October 2009. On Prigann's ecological aesthetic, see Strelow.
40 On Mayan sacred geography cf. Bergmann, "Städte auf dem Strom der Götter: Streifzüge durch die heilige Landschaft der Maya", chapter 4 in Bergmann (2010).
41 The "Emscher Landschaftspark" forms, with the participation of twenty cities, a part of the broader transformation of the central German industrial region "Ruhrgebiet" into a so-called post-industrial cultural landscape. Cf. <http://www.rvr-online.de/landschaft/Emscher_Landschaftspark/emscherlandschaftspark.php>.
42 See Gerten.
43 Cf. Bergmann (2010).
44 Primavesi.
45 In order to accelerate such investigations and strengthen the cooperation of scholars in different fields, the symposium *Conserving nature at sacred sites* was held at the University of Zurich on the 25th October 2011. Among other projects it led to the establishment of the ambitious newsletter *Sacred Sites Research Newsletter (SSIREN)* edited by Emma Shepheard-Walwyn and Fabrizio Frascaroli.
46 Pope Benedikt XVI often talks gladly about "reawakening Europe's Christian roots" and "rechristianisation" of secular societies.
47 For a survey see Deane-Drummond (2008), and Hallman.
48 Bergmann (2005), 347ff.
49 Bergmann (2005), 273, and (2011a).
50 Cf. Moltmann Wendel.
51 Cf. for example Richard Strauss' tone poem about the death of an artist from 1988/89: *Tod und Verklärung*, op. 24.

[52] See, for example, the journal *Theology and Science* edited by the Center for Theology and the Natural Sciences in Berkeley and financed by the Templeton foundation, which supports most of the dialogues in the field.
[53] Deane-Drummond (2006), 117-121.
[54] Sigurd Bergmann (2005), 107.
[55] *Orthodox Perspectives on Creation*, Report of the WCC Inter-Orthodox Consultation, Sofia, Bulgaria, October 1987, § 7, <http://www.goarch.org/ourfaith/ourfaith8050>, 21 April 2010.
[56] Eaton, chapter 4 (on evolution and politics).
[57] Reill.
[58] On the difference between *the other* and *the strange*, between alterity and alienation, see Bergmann (2008a).
[59] On apophatism and the knowledge about nature, see Bergmann (2005), 339-352
[60] Cf. Bergmann (ed.) (2005) and (2006).
[61] Böhme, 8f.
[62] Bauman.
[63] Cf. also Deane-Drummond (2006) who departs from our capacity of wondering as an evolutionary developed skill *to pay attention*, which is interwoven with practical human wisdom as well as other "natural wisdom", and which can be theologically interpreted in the light of Triune Wisdom.
[64] Cf. Bergmann (2010), chapter one.
[65] Olwig (2008).
[66] Cf. Bollnow, 191-202, and his reflections about "hodological" space, the space which emerges by walking along paths, and which also structures landscapes. On the dimension of movement, motion, and mobility in the contexts of urban design and the widening mobility discourse, which cannot, although it should, be mined deeper here, see Bergmann and Sager. Cf. Bergmann (2011b). On the concept of *transient space* in architecture and phenomenology, which could offer rich perspectives on movement in landscapes, see Bergmann (2007). On emotional geography, see Davidson, Bondi and Smith, and Nynäs.

References

Alison, French (2002), *Seeing the Centre: The art of Albert Namatjira 1902-1959*, Canberra: National Gallery of Australia.
Bachelard, Gaston (1969), *The Poetics of Space*, Boston: Beacon Press.
Bätschmann, Oskar (1989), *Entfernung der Natur: Landschaftsmalerei 1750-1920*, Köln: DuMont.
Bauman, Zygmunt (1995), *Postmodern etik*, Göteborg: Daidalos, (*Postmodern Ethics,* 1993).
Bell, Daniel (1977), "The Return of the Sacred? The Argument on the Future of Religion", *The British Journal of Sociology* 28, 4, 419-449.
Bergmann, Sigurd, "Beheimatung: Making-oneself-at-home with the Spirit – a collage", chapter 2 in: *Religion, Space and the Environment*, (forthcoming: Transaction Publishers 2013).
— (2011a), "Aware of the Spirit: In the lens of a Trinitarian aesth/ethics of lived space", in: Bergmann and Eaton, 23-40.

— (2011b), "Religion in the Built Environment: Aesth/Ethics, Ritual and Memory in Lived Urban Space", in: Goméz and Van Herck, 73-95.
— (2010), *Raum und Geist: Zur Erdung und Beheimatung der Religion – eine theologische Ästh/Ethik des Raums*, (Research in Contemporary Religion 7), Göttingen: Vandenhoeck & Ruprecht.
— (2009a), *In the Beginning Is the Icon: A Liberative Theology of Images, Visual Arts and Culture*, London: Equinox.
— (2009b), *Så främmande det lika: Samisk konst i ljuset av religion och globalisering*, [So strange the similar: Sami art in the light of religion and globalization], Trondheim: Tapir.
— (ed.) (2009c), *Theology in Built Environments: Exploring Religion, Architecture, and Design*, New Brunswick NY/London: Transaction.
— (2008a), "The Strange and the Self: Visual Arts and Theology in Aboriginal and Other (Post-)Colonial Spaces", in: Bychkov and Fodor, 201-223.
— (2008b), "'It can't be locked in' – Decolonising Processes in the Arts and Religion of Sápmi and Aboriginal Australia", in: Stålsett, 81-101.
— (2007), "Theology in its Spatial Turn: Space, Place and Built Environments Challenging and Changing the Images of God", *Religion Compass* 1, 3, 353-379.
— (2006), "Atmospheres of Synergy: Towards an Eco-Theological Aesth/Ethics of Space", *ECOTHEOLOGY: The Journal of Religion, Nature and the Environment* 11, 3, 326-356.
— (2005), *Creation Set Free: The Spirit as Liberator of Nature*, (Sacra Doctrina: Christian Theology for a Postmodern Age 4), Grand Rapids, MI: Eerdmans.
— (ed.) (2005), *Architecture, Aesth/Ethics and Religion*, Frankfurt am Main/London: IKO-Verlag für interkulturelle Kommunikation.
Bergmann, Sigurd and Eaton, Heather (eds.) (2011), *Ecological Awareness: Exploring Religion, Ethics and Aesthetics*, (Studies in Religion and the Environment 3), Berlin/Münster /Zürich/Wien/London: LIT.
Bergmann, Sigurd and Gerten, Dieter (2010), "Religion in Climate and Environmental Change: Towards a Symphony of Voices, Memories and Visions in a New Polycentric Field", in: Bergmann and Gerten, 1-12.
Bergmann, Sigurd and Gerten, Dieter (eds.) (2010), *Religion and Dangerous Environmental Change: Transdisciplinary Perspectives on the Ethics of Climate and Sustainability*, (Studies in Religion and the Environment 2), Berlin/Münster /Zürich/Wien/London: LIT.
Bergmann, Sigurd and Sager, Tore (eds.) (2008), *The Ethics of Mobilities: Rethinking Place, Exclusion, Freedom and Environment*, (Series "Transport and Society"), Aldershot: Ashgate.
Bergmann, Sigurd, Scott, Peter, Jansdotter Samuelsson, Maria and Bedford-Strohm, Heinrich (eds.) (2008), *Nature, Space and the Sacred: Transdisciplinary Perspectives*, Aldershot: Ashgate.
Beyer, Peter, "Globalization and Glocalization", <http://learners.in.th/file/asakya/globgloc.pdf>, 20 April 2010.
Blumenberg, Hans (1993), *Die Lesbarkeit der Welt*, 3. ed. Frankfurt am Main: Suhrkamp, (1981).
Böhme, Gernot (1989), *Für eine ökologische Naturästhetik*, Frankfurt am Main: Suhrkamp.
Bollnow, Otto (2004), *Mensch und Raum*, 10th ed. Stuttgart: Kohlhammer, (1963).
Botz-Bornstein, Thorsten (2009), *Aesthetics and Politics of Space in Russia and Japan: A Comparative Philosophical Study*, Plymouth: Lexington.

Brady, Emily (2003), *Aesthetics of the Natural Environment*, Edinburgh: Edinburgh University Press.
Bychkov, Oleg V. and Fodor, James (eds.) (2008), *Theological Aesthetics After Von Balthasar*, Aldershot: Ashgate.
Cruikshank, Julie (2001), "Glaciers and climate change: Perspectives from oral tradition", *Arctic* 54, 4, 377-393.
Davidson, J., Bondi, L. and Smith, M. (2005), *Emotional Geographies*, Aldershot: Ashgate.
Deane-Drummond, Celia (2008),*Eco-theology*, London: Darton, Longman and Todd.
— (2006), *Wonder and Wisdom: Conversations in Science, Spirituality and Theology*, London: Darton, Longman and Todd.
Diefenbacher, Hans (1995), *Der "Index of Sustainable Economic Welfare" – Eine Fallstudie für die Bundesrepublik Deutschland, 1950-1992*, Heidelberg: FEST.
Eaton, Heather (2005), *Introducing Feminist Ecotheologies*, London/New York: T&T Clark International.
Eggington, Robert (1996), *Bulyer Boona Boodja Koora Kooralong Ale Nyoongah Myar,* Perth: Dumbartung Aboriginal Corporation.
Gerten, Dieter (2010), "Adapting to Climatic and Hydrologic Change: Variegated Functions of Religion", in: Bergmann and Gerten, 39-56.
Gómez, Liliana and Van Herck, Walter (eds.) (2011),*The Sacred in the City*, London/New York: Continuum.
Hallman, David G. (1994), *Ecotheology: Voices from South and North,* Geneva/Maryknoll: WCC/Orbis.
Heyd, Thomas (2010), "Sentient Landscapes, Vulnerability to Rapid Natural Change, and Social Responsibility", in: Bergmann and Gerten, 73-86.
Ingold, Tim (2008), "The Wedge and the Knot: Hammering and Stitching the Face of Nature", in: Bergmann, Scott, Jansdotter Samuelsson and Bedford-Strohm, 147-161.
Ingold, Tim and Vergunst, Jo Lee (eds.) (2008), *Ways of Walking: Ethnography and Practice on Foot*, Farnham/Burlington: Ashgate.
Kandinsky, Wassily (1955), "und", in: *Essays über Kunst und Künstler*, ed. by Max Bill, 3. ed. Bern: Benteli 1973, 97?108.
Kleinert, Sylvia and Neale, Margo (eds.) (2000), *The Oxford Companion to Aboriginal Art and Culture*, Oxford: Oxford University Press.
Knoblauch, Hubert (2007), "The Sociology of Religion – and the desecularisation of society", *Revista Lusófona De Ciência Das Religiões*, Ano VI, 11, 247-256.
Küster, Hansjörg and Küster, Ulf (eds.) (1997), *Garten und Wildnis: Landschaft im 18. Jahrhundert*, München: Beck.
Löw, Martina, Steets, Silke and Stoetzer, Sergej (2008), *Einführung in die Stadt- und Raumsoziologie*, (UTB 8348), 2. ed. Opladen/Farmington Hills: Verlag Barbara Budrich.
McHarg, Ian L. (1969), *Design with Nature*, New York: The American Museum of Natural History, Doubleday/Natural History Press.
Moltmann Wendel, Elisabeth (1993), "Rückkehr zur Erde", *Evangelische Theologie* 53, 5, 406-420.
Morphy, Howard (2000), "Inner landscapes: The fourth dimension", in: Kleinert and Neale, 129-136.
— (1999), "Manggalili Art and the Promised Land", in: Taylor, 53-74.
— (1998), *Aboriginal Art,* London: Phaidon.
Nye, David E. (2009), "Anti-Landscapes: Superfund Sites, Toxic Narratives", keynote at the

International Research Symposium *Counter Nature(s): Revising Nature in an Era of Environmental Crisis*, Uppsala University, 20-22 November 2009.

Nynäs, Peter (2009), "Spatiality, Practice and Meaning: The existential ambiguity of urban chapels", in: Bergmann (2009c), 131-150.

Olwig, Kenneth Robert (2002), *Landscape, Nature, and the Body Politic: From Britain's Renaissance to America's New World*, Madison: The University of Wisconsin Press.

— (2008), "Performing on the Landscape versus Doing Landscape: Perambulatory Practice, Sight and the Sense of Belonging", in: Ingold and Vergunst, 81-91.

Primavesi, Anne (2010) "What's in a name? Gaia and the reality of being alive in a relational world", in: Bergmann and Gerten, 87-102.

Reill, Peter Hanns (2005), *Vitalizing Nature in the Enlightenment*, Berkeley/Los Angeles/London: University of California Press.

Rose, Deborah Bird (2004), *Reports from a Wild Country: Ethics for Decolonisation*, Sydney: University of New South Wales Press.

— (2000), "The power of place", in: Kleinert and Neale, 40-49.

Roy, Oliver (2010), *Holy Ignorance: When Religion and Culture Diverge*, New York: Columbia University Press, (*La Sainte Ignorance,* Le Seuil, 2008).

Schellnhuber, Hans Joachim, Cramer, Wolfgang and Nakicenovic, Nebojsa (2006), *Avoiding Dangerous Climate Change*, Cambridge: Cambridge University Press.

Schlögel, Karl (2003), *Im Raume lesen wir die Zeit: Über Zivilisationsgeschichte und Geopolitik*, München/Wien: Hanser.

Scruton, Roger (2008), "The Return of Religion", Axess Magazine 1/2008.

Shiff, Richard (1992), "The Necessity of Jimmie Durham's Jokes", *Art Journal* 51, 3, (Recent Native American Art), 74-80.

Stanner, W. E. H. (1979), "The Dreaming (1953)", in: *White Men Got No Dreaming*, Canberra: Australian National University Press 1979, 23-40.

Steiner, Dieter (1993), "Human Ecology as Transdisciplinary Science", in: Steiner and Nauser, 47-76.

Steiner, Dieter and Nauser, Markus (eds.) (1993), *Human Ecology: Fragments of antifragmentary views of the world*, London/New York: Routledge.

Strelow, Heike (2004), *Ökologische Ästhetik: Theorie und Praxis künstlerischer Umweltgestaltung*, Basel: Birkhäuser.

Stålsett, Sturla J. (ed.) (2008), *Religion in a Globalised Age: Transfers and Transformations, Integration and Resistance*, Oslo: Novus.

Szerszynski, Bron (2005), *Nature, Technology and the Sacred*, Malden/Oxford/Carlton: Blackwell.

Taylor, Luke (ed.) (1999), *Painting the Land Story*, Canberra: National Museum of Australia.

Tuan, Yi-Fu (text), and Strawn, Martha A. (photographs and essays) (2009), *Religion: From Place to Placelessness*, Chicago: The Center for American Places at Columbia College Chicago.

Uexküll, Jakob von and Kriszat, Georg (1983), *Streifzüge durch die Umwelten von Tieren und Menschen, Bedeutungslehre*, new ed. Frankfurt am Main: Fischer, (Hamburg 1956).

Valkeapää, Nils-Aslak (1994), *Nu Guhkkin Dat Mii Lahka/Så Fjernt Det Nære*, Kautokeino: DAT.

The Good, the Bad and the Ugly
Wonder, Awe and Paying Attention to Nature

Celia Deane-Drummond

Introduction: Wonder and Environmental Responsibility

One of the great environmentalists and naturalists, Rachel Carson, believed passionately in the protection of nature, and the human capacity to spoil its beauty. She also presupposed that the capacity for humans to experience wonder in relation to the natural world is a prelude to proper treatment of it. I am defining the human capacity for wonder here as that heightened psychological and emotional state engendered by different experiences. Wonder may, however, include undertones of fear or anxiety as well as joy. Wonder is almost always elicited when human beings encounter natural or cultural "wonders", since the noun is defined by the verb. Historically, however, the particular occasions that may have elicited the experience of wonder, or what has been considered wonderful, has varied in different periods of history, as well as the relative academic or scientific respectability of the experience itself.[1] For Carson, however, the experience of wonder is explicitly grounded in contact with the natural world, so that "The more clearly we focus our attention on the wonders and realities of the world about us, the less taste we shall have for destruction" and "A child's world is fresh and new and beautiful, full of wonder and excitement. It is to our misfortune that for most of us that clear-eyed vision, that true instinct for what is beautiful and awe inspiring is dimmed and even lost when we reach adulthood".[2] She is certainly not alone in expressing such a sentiment. Ecologists and biologists from Charles Darwin in the nineteenth century to E. O. Wilson and Richard Dawkins in the twentieth century have testified to the importance of wonder as a means of motivating their passion as scientists.[3] But only some experience this wonder as a specific motivation for environmental protection.

The difference seems to be related to the occasion provided by that wonder. In the case of Richard Dawkins his experience of natural wonder is indirect, as a result of his own perceived insights about the scientific mechanisms involved in the intricate working of the natural world. His own atheism dominates in as much as he compares the kind of wonder he experiences as based on scientific "fact" with that of religious believers that he considers to be based on "fantasy", so for him only the former is credible. But Dawkins' wonder is arguably self-referential, for it is experienced through belief in insights gained through the filter of his scientific analysis. The wonder that he experiences might even be related to the kind of elation that comes not just from a satisfaction of curiosity, but through a form of knowledge that lends greater power to the observer to manipulate or change what is observed.[4] For naturalists like Rachel Carson wonder is experienced in direct contact with living forms and her attitude is one that is associated with gratitude for her encounter with them, rather than desire for control. Yet E. O. Wilson occupies an uneasy space between Dawkins and Carson, since he both affirms the human ability to experience wonder as a naturalist, but then ties this in specifically with biological knowledge. Wilson contends that humans possess an innate tendency to focus on life and life-like processes, such a tendency he calls *biophilia*.[5] He argues that modern biology is a genuinely new way of looking at the world that happens to be in tune with this tendency. Yet it is through such a search that he believes we discover the core of wonder, for our search is still replete with this wondrous capacity due to the rich abundance of life in comparison with our relative ignorance of it. He links such wonder with mystery, implying an almost implicit religious sense of awe in the face of the sheer diversity of life. Accordingly:

Now to the very heart of wonder. Because species diversity was created prior to humanity, and because we evolved within it, we have never fathomed its limits. As a consequence, the living world is the natural domain of the most restless and paradoxical part of the human spirit. Our sense of wonder grows exponentially. The greater the knowledge, the deeper the mystery and the more we seek knowledge to create new mystery.[6]

Wilson wonders at simple biological facts, such as that a handful of soil and litter is home to hundreds of insects, nematode worms and other larger creatures, alongside a million fungi and ten billion bacteria. So much does the experience of wonder begin to impinge on his thinking that for Wilson the mysteries of nature are analogous to a "magic well".[7]

Wonder for Wilson, seems then, to be as much about an experience of a gap in our knowing that is then filled by biological knowledge, as about a direct encounter with living forms in the manner of Carson's reflections. He is certainly not sentimentally inclined towards other creatures. His philosophy remains somewhat mechanistic when he describes an ant colony in these terms: "I never see the colony as anything more than an organic machine".[8] But, at the same time, he has campaigned long and hard for a deeper sense of environmental responsibility. However, he does this on the basis of a staunchly empiricist base for ethics, rather than through what he terms a "transcendental" approach, which, according to him, assumes that there are objective natural laws to be discovered and adhered to, given by God and written into the laws of nature.[9] Wilson argues that if we protect species, then other aspects of the physical environment will automatically be protected, so that the former should come first in setting our priorities. His vision is for a *biologically* grounded, internationally based vision of species protection, along similar lines to the Intergovernmental Panel on Climate Change (IPCC), except now rooted in the science of biodiversity, rather than that of climate science. In an interview for New Scientist in August 2009 he suggested that:

> I am working on a joint proposal with Simon Stuart, head of the Species Survival Commission at the IUCN. I want to set up an effort along the lines of the Intergovernmental Panel on Climate Change to protect species. The panel has had huge success marshalling global science to address climate change, providing models and the evidence to show climate change is happening, and that it is due to human activity. But it is still all about the physical world.[10]

What he craves for is some way or means in order to convince people to support the protection of species. The way the IPCC was set up was through a strictly scientific approach to climate change, even if it acknowledged the possible contribution of social analysis in assessing the resilience of different communities to climate change impacts. What remains debatable, however, is whether Wilson's empiricist method, filtered through current biological knowledge of the widespread loss of different species, can ever be sufficient to motivate widespread environmental responsibility. Further, the isolation of the protection of species from other aspects of environmental concern and climate change may highlight the specific problems of species loss, but the latter will also have to be tackled through a more holistic approach that includes social, political and perhaps religious dimensions of human relationships with other creatures. His argument that wider issues will automatically follow a focus on species loss is not all that convincing.[11]

In *Hell and High Water*, for example, Alastair McIntosh bemoaned the fact that however much we know about the facts of climate change still the human person suffers from an amnesia that remains bent on committing what he calls *ecocide*.[12] Are facts about climate impacts or even species loss or loss of biodiversity *ever* really going to convince people, or is it more likely that a direct encounter with nature in all its wild and raw beauty will provide the motivation for change? Such an encounter borders on what we might call awe, and in order to develop this idea further, I will first touch on the pre-modern Celtic tradition of affiliation to nature that still persists in areas local to my own context,[13] before turning to the religious philosophy of Simone Weil.

CELTIC SAINTS AND THE WISDOM OF THE LIMINAL

The Celtic saints that populated what is now known as Scotland, Wales, Cornwall, Ireland and parts of Brittany and Spain lived in a world that was, by all accounts, very different from our own. The technological inventions of post Enlightenment society had yet to be born, along with the battery of scientific inventions that allowed the manipulation of the natural world through experimental science. The living conditions of these early saints were, by all accounts, simple, yet the location of monastic centres was more often than not at the boundary between two different natural landscapes. Here consciousness of the divine was understood to be particularly present, and the history of repeated pilgrimages to such sites reinforced the experience of awe-intimations of the transcendent at particular places where the boundary between heaven and earth was thought to be "thinner". Ian Bradley who has arguably done much to reawaken interest in Celtic thought in the English-speaking world, cautions that we need to be wary of becoming too romantic in our interpretation of Celtic Christianity.[14]

The early Celtic saints were certainly not "green" in the modern sense of self-conscious protection of the natural world, since for these early peoples the separation of self from the natural world was not self-conscious. Hence it is fair to suggest that, following the Eastern Orthodox tradition that Celtic Christianity seems to have partially echoed, humanity and nature were viewed as an integral whole, with God understood as Lord of all, and the natural world perceived as a blessing and a gift. It also seems highly likely that stories and religious instincts of the Egyptian ascetic desert tradition impinged on the indigenous Druid tradition of the early Celtic saints, providing a motivation for religious pilgrimage, *peregrini*, associated with persistent contact with the landscape and other creaturely kinds.[15] Oliver Davies believes that key elements in Celtic Christianity, such as the central role of poetry, a special emphasis on Trinitarian thinking, a strong sense of community and an unusually positive attitude to the natural world came from pre-Christian religious elements.[16] The attitude of the Celtic saints to other animals as expressed in hagiographic accounts of their lives was one that expressed relative compassion and companionship, in some cases treating the suffering and loss of other creatures as if they were part of the human family.[17]

The experience of wonder arising in this tradition was certainly not self-referential, but mediated through the natural so that it was directed towards God as Creator and Lord of the Universe. In the Welsh poem "Loves of Taliesin", for example, admiration at the "beauty of an eagle on the shore when the tide is full" sits alongside celebration of the covenant.[18] While many of the stories of the close relationship between saints and the natural world are hagiographic rather than factual history, the existence of such stories does point to the intimacy of the relationship between a life lived out in commitment to religious belief, and joyful celebration of the natural world and its creatures. The struggle against nature that these early ascetics spoke about is that of human desire and attachment to material things, rather than a negative attitude towards the natural world as such.[19]

For the early saints a pregnant sense of the world infused with the presence of God inspired a strong sense of wonderment, so, according the Eastern Orthodox scholar Elizabeth Theokritoff, the early saints' "vivid sense of God's hand constantly at work in all his creation fuels their sense of the universe as a great wonder, a continuing miracle".[20] There are likely to be differences between the Eastern tradition and that of the early Celtic writers. Davies contrasts the lives of the Desert Fathers from the Eastern tradition where humanity is considered the crown of creation, and the Welsh lives, where nature herself actively cooperates. He puts this down to the influence of primal religion, though this contrast seems too sharp, since a strong tradition of active cooperation with nature is also present in Eastern Orthodox Christianity.[21] For Theokritoff, the key point of a "miracle" was not so much the thought that something appeared to go against the laws of nature, but the wonder that it inspired.[22] For the saints of the early church a profound sense of the "depth" of created things pervaded their experience, in such a way that the sense of their own limitations come more clearly into view. Knowledge of the natural world is grounded on this profound sense, so that "as our knowledge of the workings of nature increases, this does not explain away the wonder of creation, instead, it deepens our sense of awe at the intricacies of divine wisdom".[23] As the intelligibility of the world becomes clearer, faith is not so much dimmed as celebrated in the light of divine wisdom.[24] The natural world therefore acts like a mirror for the presence of God, but also implies that "our primary task in our dealings with the rest of creation is to 'listen' to it, and respond by praising God".[25] The outworking of a religious experience of wonder leads to praise for the Creator. But what does this "listening" to creation entail, and how is this related to care for the natural world?

SIMONE WEIL ON PAYING ATTENTION

So far the general sense of respect and no doubt awe that early Celtic saints and mystics felt towards the natural world demonstrates an attitude that comes close to that expressed by Rachel Carson in that it implied deep companionship with other creatures and the natural world, rather than manipulation. However, what does this wonder really mean? It is worth asking a little more clearly what wonder involves when it emerges from human contemplation of the natural world in an explicitly religious context. While the emotion of awe has much in common with wonder understood as amazement at something unusual or breaking the boundary of the known, wonder *as such* will not necessarily lead to practical action that favours environmental responsibility or a compassionate attitude to other animals, even if it is in some sense a pre-requisite for it. Wonder is also highly ambiguous when it comes to religious belief; for while the experience of wonder through the miraculous in Mark's Gospel, for example, increased believers' faith, by contrast, in John's Gospel, wonder was more commonly associated with unbelief.[26] The difference between wonder and religious awe becomes clearer in the light of Simone Weil's religious philosophy.

For Weil paying attention is not the kind of concentrated mental effort that is normally conjured up by the term, rather:

Attention consists of suspending our thought, leaving it detached, empty and ready to be penetrated by the object. It means holding in our minds, within reach of this thought, but on a lower level and not in contact with it, the diverse knowledge we have acquired which we are forced to make use of. Our thought should be in relation to all particular and already formulated thoughts, as a man on a mountain who, as he looks forward, sees also below him, without actually looking at them, a great many forests and plains. Above all our thought should be empty, waiting, not seeking anything, but ready to receive in its naked truth the object which is to penetrate it.[27]

Weil was no romantic, but allowed attention to be directed to *truth* and to *suffering*. For her, the human soul had to "pass through its own annihilation to the place where alone it can get the sort of attention which can attend to truth and to affliction ... he name of this intense, pure, disinterested, gratuitous, generous attention is love".[28] Her discussion of beauty is also highly relevant to the present discussion, since for her "Beauty is the supreme mystery of the world", it "attracts the attention and yet does nothing to sustain it". It is like a promise that "feeds only the part of the soul that gazes". But "If one does not seek means to evade the exquisite anguish it inflicts, then desire is gradually transformed into love; and one begins to acquire the faculty of pure and disinterested attention."[29]

This implies that at its best aesthetics has to *face up to anguish*, and in a paradoxical way true beauty confronts suffering, so that the "radiance of beauty illumines affliction with the light of the spirit of justice and love".[30] The thought of true beauty being somehow present even in suffering and in spite of evil or even ugliness is a strong theme in the theological aesthetics of the theologian Hans Urs von Balthasar.[31] His approach is more radical than Weil in that he suggests that the image of the suffering Christ not only confronts the evil of crucifixion, but also overturns the common meaning of beauty. He also envisages beauty in a classic sense as one of the transcendentals, along with goodness and truth. For Balthasar, an encounter with the true beauty of Christ crucified does not just transform suffering, but challenges a transformation of human consciousness as to what beauty is like. Like Weil, Balthasar links the transcendental of beauty with love, but he appeals to Denys in linking God's Beauty with God's passionate love, the revealed love of a Person. Stephen Fields remarks: "Shining forth in the scandal of the cross, this love, grasped in faith, transforms an image assessed as ugly by intramundane norms into an icon of beauty."[32] On this basis we can go on to suggest that Christ the form of Beauty challenges humanity to appreciate not just those forms of creation that seem most appealing to us, but also those creatures that seem to us to be repellent or even repugnant.

There is a paradox here that is worth addressing. On the one hand, in as much as humanity experiences wonder through an encounter with the natural world, such wonder is a possible response to paying attention to nature as it is, including facets that seem to us to be "good", or "bad" or "ugly" according to our own human standards. On the other hand, that does not mean that either the direct or indirect infliction of suffering on other creatures by human actions is acceptable or to be tolerated. We might experience a sense of wonder at the capacity for humanity to inflict cruelty, but this is not a form of wonder that is appropriately disciplined by love or justice. In parallel with Weil's insight into the nature of beauty, wonder that is grasped after for its own sake is unhelpful, but the ability to experience true religious wonder is in alignment with the kind of beauty that Weil articulates. Such wonder is experienced not simply in romantic relationship with other creaturely beings, but instead does not flinch in the face of suffering, for it perceives the hidden beauty within. Further, subsequent human action is guided by a strong sense of love towards the natural world, so that where that suffering is caused by human beings it deliberately seeks for its amelioration. In Christian terms this wonder in the presence of beauty is expressed in the encounter with the figure of Christ who confronts injustice of all kinds, including that inflicted on other creatures.

The studied attention of a biologist might come to much the same conclusion without necessarily appropriating this in explicitly religious terms by pointing out the wonder and fascination of a multitude of different species, even in the midst of apparent ugliness and cruelty of at least a proportion of them. So we might ask ourselves: does contemplating the natural world in explicitly *religious* terms make any difference or not? For Simone Weil paying absolute attention is like a letting go of all pride, and is the same thing as prayer. For her "Extreme attention is what constitutes the creative faculty in man and the only extreme attention is religious".[33] But she also warns against the kind of religious experience that is itself too attached in an excessive devotion. In this sense it is the *transformation of our desires* in heightened experience of explicitly religious wonder disciplined by love and justice that is particularly important to consider. In this way, crucially, she can claim that "The attention turned with love towards God (or in a lesser degree, towards anything that is truly beautiful) makes certain things impossible for us".[34] She implies, then, an *ethical* outcome of such studied attention. Attention in Weil's thought needs therefore to be interpreted as a particular kind of looking that then leads to an openness to an experience of deep wonder and awe, without becoming too attached to the creatures that are contemplated.

ENTANGLED LIFE LINES?

How might such a view cohere with the idea of human entanglement in the world that Tim Ingold, in a fascinating way, argues is necessary in order to inhabit a place properly?[35] Ingold contrasts the detached observation of a biologist influenced by Darwinian thinking that he likens to "a wedge" of human insertion into the natural world, with that of a knot, where human life is completely interlaced in a meshwork with other creatures and the natural world in a way that is essentially and deeply entangled. For Ingold a true ecology of life is one that is deeply immersed in an open world where there are no boundaries of inside or outside, or objects that are "others".[36] The suggestion of entanglement is perhaps closer to the pre-Enlightenment attitude of the early Celtic saints discussed above, who seemed to have less self-conscious distance from other creatures or the natural world as "others" distanced from humankind. While Ingold's suggestion is both fascinating and deeply provocative, I suggest that encouraging a passing over to total entanglement is an over-reaction to the objective detachment arising out of modern experimental science. Total attachment in Ingold's schema replaces total detachment, arguably a mirror image of the curse of modernity.

As an alternative, along the lines that Simone Weil has hinted, I suggest that paying attention in love can still permit us to inhabit the world deeply in the way Ingold suggests without falling into the negative trap of just living on its surface. We also need to ask the question: what kind of environmental ethics might be fostered through such notions of entanglement? It might bring a deeper appreciation of wonder for the microbial entanglement in all life forms. But wonder that is disciplined through love in the manner I have suggested above is not an inevitable outcome of entanglement. John Dupré and Maureen O'Malley, for example, also argue that cooperation rather than competition characterises higher organisms in their mutual relationship with microbes, and that the boundary between life and non-life blurs the definition of life in relation to non-life and viruses.[37] Ironically, perhaps, the deliberate genetic manipulation of plants and animals is viewed as completely compatible with such a position of total entanglement.[38] This seems to be the end point once the integrity of an organism as a particular species is dealt a deathly blow through the complete dismembering of the tree of life in notions of absolute entanglement.

One of the intriguing charms of the idea of entanglement is that it seems to get to the heart of the problematic associated with our misuse of the natural world, namely, that in our disassociation from it we have become consumers of nature as a resource for human benefit. But does a return to what might be called the innocence of the open, where boundaries no longer make any sense, necessarily point the way towards an appropriate ethic of environmental responsibility? It might enhance our experience of wonder, but that wonder is undisciplined, and in the context of a culture dominated by Western science, may even lead to further manipulative attitudes insidiously coming to the surface in a way analogous to the story of Medussa.[39]

Towards Environmental Responsibility

Paying attention, understood according to Simone Weil, demands that our looking is no longer possessive, and such an encounter is also crucially informed by love and justice. It therefore seems to me at least to take into account the criticism that entanglement seeks to address, without the dangers of either passivity or manipulation in the name of a lost identity. Further, reawakening a religious sense of paying attention in a non-possessive way not only challenges the kind of egocentrism that fosters environmental irresponsibility. It also encourages environmental responsibility when that attention is directed towards love of the natural world that is freed from the bondage of possessive desires. This may be one reason why Rachel Carson was intuitively accurate when she suggested we needed to recover something of the innocence of childhood in order to experience wonder that will lead to appropriate action.

The shape of that environmental responsibility could take at least some its cues from the agrarian context of the biblical world, appropriated by some contemporary American environmental writers. Such an agrarian context affirms kinship and solidarity between different life forms, without maintaining a total loss of boundary conditions between different species. Such an agrarian approach of belonging to a specific place finds modern expression in the work of authors such as Wendell Berry. Berry made it his life's ambition to find a way of deeply belonging to a place.[40] In a manner similar to the above account in engagement with Simone Weil, Norman Wirzba, drawing on Berry, argues that the first step in such a process of deep encounter with creation is detachment from the egoism that dominates Western cultures in particular.[41] Wirzba also names beauty as that which unites all things, citing Pseudo-Dionysius as one who speaks of the "intermingling of everything", but, crucially, at the same time, in ways that "do not obliterate identity".[42] Wirzba also presses for patient, attentive and humble regard for creation, but it is to be expressed most explicitly in relation to land and place. Further, in a manner analogous to my earlier argument, reason becomes disciplined and qualified through love so that the intellect is able to resist scientific or economic reductionism. In practice, therefore,

True farmers and gardeners have tamed the ego by making care of another their first priority. They have submitted their plans and designed their economies in such a way as to contribute to processes of fertility and growth. They have brought personal desire into alignment with the needs, potential, and limits of another in its particular place.[43]

But such close encounter with creation shows up a darkness of incomprehension in the face of beauty alongside unspeakable suffering and pain. In this way, humanity is forced to acknowledge its own ignorance, and therefore adopts a modest view of how to approach environmental responsibility. It therefore encourages what might be termed biblical wisdom, understood as one that is schooled through the experience of patient connectivity with the land. As biblical scholar Ellen Davis suggests:

the sages treat agriculture as a primary realm in which God's wisdom is needed and utilized by humanity. Proverbs includes various instructions for farmers (e.g. 24:27; 27:23-27); moreover, the bad farmer is for the sages the epitome of *aslut*, 'sloth', the destructive quality that constitutes the antithesis of wisdom (24:30-34).[44]

Yet while such an agrarian dimension reminds human beings of the importance of local, contextual patterns of responsibility, in the wider interests of social justice that Simone Weil was so acutely aware, there also needs to be ways of moving beyond this localised orientation towards a strong sense of global environmental responsibility. I suggest, therefore, that an agrarian reading of environmental ethics has considerable advantages over other forms of commercial agriculture, but the sheer ignorance of human impacts on the natural world can also come to the surface from consideration of the global issues in relation to climate change and species diversity as well as through local, situated issues concentrating on a given place. The scale through which we consider different ecological events and contemplate in wonder will therefore affect our perception of what is of most ethical importance and what must take priority in contested decision making. The complexities involved in climate change is a stark reminder of the need for global solidarity and the difficulties of working out an adequate politically negotiated settlement at a national as well as an international level.

Some Tentative Conclusions

I have argued in this Chapter that the human experience of wonder is an important first step in contemplating the natural world and energizing our sense of responsibility for it. Wonder may also be positive in freeing up an egoistic attachment to purely rationalistic goals. However, wonder on its own is ambiguous, in that it may arise from different human experiences in relation to the natural world that could be morally good or bad. If we ask ourselves how the early saints contemplated the natural world, then their experience of wonder was most likely to be associated with a prior deep sense of the presence of God in all created things, leading to a strong affinity between humanity and the natural world. While we must guard against a romantic return to associating Celtic saints with ecological harmony, their humble attitude towards other creaturely kinds is self-evident. I have argued here, however, that a rich vein of religious philosophy can be gleaned from the mystical writing of Simone Weil, who was particularly attentive to issues of justice as well as encounters with beauty. For her beauty encountered through careful *paying attention* needs to be disciplined through love and justice and face up to suffering. We can widen this notion to suggest that the experience of explicitly religious wonder in encountering beauty is shaped not so much through intramundane examples of what beauty is like, but in a Christian context is filtered through the mystery of the cross of Christ. This is not so much a glorification of suffering, but an experience of solidarity with those who suffer alongside a protest against that suffering, including that inflicted by humans on other creaturely beings. If we compare this approach with that of anthropologist Tim Ingold, who has argued for an embedded approach to our relationship with the natural world, then there are some lines of continuity as well as discontinuity. His sharp disjunction between what he terms a Darwinian approach and a deeply entangled approach to human life may be somewhat overdrawn. Further, I have my doubts if entanglement is as liberating as he suggests it is when it comes to generating appropriate environmental responsibility. Instead, I am arguing more along the lines of the work of Wendell Berry, who opted for an agrarian approach to the natural world, and emphasised the importance of rootedness in place, without adopting a total blurring of boundaries between different creaturely forms. Yet there are some drawbacks to this position, not least because both Ingold and Berry's views tend to eclipse a wider sense of environmental responsibility towards the global sphere as such. Wonder, as that which is elicited according to different ecological scales, will lead to different priorities of vision. My suggestion, therefore, is that we need a wisdom that comes not just from a localised, nurturing sense of agrarian living, but also from a wider sense of solidarity with different nations, cultures and contexts.

NOTES

1. In post-Enlightenment thought, for example, wonder was often derided as either childish or an expression of ignorance. In earlier centuries, however, wonder was associated with the border between the known and unknown. In religious terms, linking wonder with religious awe was an innovation of writers such as Augustine. The advantage of the experience of wonder in philosophical terms is that it provides a possible opening for alternative ways of thinking about issues compared with pure rationalism that assumes a more contained or controlled psychological state. All these various elements of wonder may come to the surface in contemporary discussion. For a discussion of the history of wonder specifically in relation to scientific knowing, see Deane-Drummond. For a discussion of the specific role of wonder in philosophy, see Miller.
2. Cited in Locker and Bruchac, 32.
3. Dawkins, Darwin, Wilson (1984).
4. Dawkins regrets the fact that scientific work is not used to inspire poets in their writing, but if his experience of wonder begins in an encounter, the scientist then has to press to understand the phenomenon. Dawkins, 17. Further, he presses to understand the evolutionary origin of the human capacity to make metaphors, while, ironically perhaps, at the same time opposing scientific ways of perceiving the universe to religious beliefs about it. So, in speaking of the capacity of human beings to imagine a model of the universe, this permits "A big model, worthy of the reality that regulates, updates and tempers it; a model of stars and great distances, where Einstein's noble spacetime curve upstages the curve of Yahwch's covenantal bow and cuts it down to size; a powerful model, incorporating the past, steering us through the present, capable of running far ahead to offer detailed constructions of alternative futures and allow us to choose", 312.
5. Wilson (1984), 1.
6. Ibid., 10.
7. Ibid., 19.
8. Ibid., 36.
9. As discussed in Wilson (1999), 265-296.
10. Opinion: Highfield.
11. Ulrich Beck has argued that if we focus just on the science of climate change specifically then there is a danger that we will loose sight of the importance of social dimensions that underlie the problem in the first place. See Beck, 254-266. For further discussion of Beck see, Deane-Drummond and Bedford-Strohm, 1-14. In a similar way, if we focus specifically on the science of species loss, and ignore the social factors that lead to those losses, then it is likely that the problems associated with species loss will not be resolved. Both the work of the IPCC and that of any international effort in relation to species loss needs, therefore, to be set in an appropriately modest context of what it might achieve.
12. McIntosh.
13. Chester, where I lived for seventeen years, is situated on the border with Wales, an area of the United Kingdom that is still deeply immersed in its Celtic heritage. This is reinforced by the restoration of the use of the Welsh language, so that Welsh is now a compulsory

subject in all Welsh schools, and the relative independence of Welsh governance from the Houses of Parliament in Westminster, London.

14 Bradley. Bradley's study of the history of interpretation of Celtic Christianity shows how readily it can become incorporated into different standpoints. Certainly the idea of a fixed Celtic Church is inappropriate, and other elements in Celtic thought that are less friendly towards the natural world need to be held in tension with more positive renditions. See, for example, Clancy and Markus (1995). Bradley also raises the possibility that references to the natural world are "symbolic". A similar reading has been suggested in relation to Eastern Orthodox appropriations of the natural world. What is far more likely is that there is a combination of imagery serving human ends, and delight in the natural world for its own sake.

15 Schaefer, 150-151.

16 These pre-Christian indigenous elements were most likely to be Druid. Davies.

17 Hagiographic accounts are certainly not intended to be literal, but the persistent trend to treat other creatures as companions with humans, alongside a desire to preserve the natural environment, influenced later traditions such as that associated with Francis of Assisi in the twelfth century. Schaefer, 151.

18 Davies, 86-88.

19 Elizabeth Theokritoff's survey of Eastern Orthodox approaches to asceticism probably comes close to the type of asceticism adopted in Celtic traditions in the first centuries, even though the existence of a definitive Celtic "church" following common or universalised practices is unlikely. See Theokritoff, 97, and O'Loughlin.

20 Theokritoff, 43.

21 Davies, 86-88.

22 While there is no evidence that the Celtic saints showed an interest in science, early church fathers such as Basil the Great of the fourth century or John of Damascus of the seventh century showed a keen interest in science that was entirely compatible with a strong sense of God in the natural world.

23 Theokritoff, 45.

24 The difference between Stoic philosophy of a world soul and Christian belief is that in the latter the paradox exists: the Word is both in the world, but at the same time is God, and so is uncreated, rather than created.

25 Theokritoff, 48.

26 For further discussion on this topic see Deane-Drummond, 134-136.

27 Weil (1951), 62.

28 Weil (1943), 92.

29 Ibid.

30 Ibid.

31 Balthasar.

32 Fields, 180.

33 Weil (1952), 117.

34 Ibid., 119.

35 A summary of his approach is in Ingold, 147-161.

36 Ibid., 155.

37 Dupré and O'Malley.

38 While perhaps correctly reacting against overblown claims of genetic determinism, the approach to genetic engineering of crops is highly optimistic. See Barnes and Dupré.

[39] The ancient classic story of Medussa recounts how two new heads of the monster grew every time one was cut down.
[40] Berry, 150.
[41] Wirzba, 151.
[42] Ibid.
[43] Ibid., 159.
[44] Davis, 35.

References

Balthasar, Hans Urs von (1982), *Glory of the Lord, Vol. 1: Seeing the Form*, (tr. Erasmo Leivà-Merikakis), Edinburgh: T & T Clark and San Francisco: Ignatius Press.
Barnes, Barry and Dupré, John (2008), *Genomes and What to Make of Them*, Chicago: University of Chicago Press.
Beck, Ulrich (2010), "Climate for Change, or How to Create a Green Modernity", *Theory, Culture and Society* 27, 254-266.
Bergmann, Sigurd, Scott, Peter Manley, Jansdotter Samuelsson, Maria and Bedford-Strohm, Heinrich (eds.) (2009), *Nature, Space and the Sacred: Transdisciplinary Perspectives*, Farnham/Burlington: Ashgate.
Berry, Wendell (1969), "The Long-Legged House", in: *The Long-Legged House*, Washington DC: Shoemaker and Hoard 2004.
Bradley, Ian (1999), *Celtic Christianity: Making Myths and Chasing Dreams*, Edinburgh: Edinburgh University Press.
Clancy, Thomas Owen and Markus, Gilbert (1995), *Iona: The Earliest Poetry of a Celtic Monastery*, Edinburgh: Edinburgh University Press.
Darwin, Charles (1859), *On The Origin of Species*, (ed. by Gillian Beer), New York: Oxford University Press 2008.
Davies, Oliver (1996), *Celtic Christianity in Early Medieval Wales: The Origins of the Welsh Spiritual Tradition*, Cardiff: University of Wales Press.
Davis, Ellen F. (2009), *Scripture, Culture and Agriculture: An Agrarian Reading of the Bible*, Cambridge: Cambridge University Press.
Dawkins, Richard (1998), *Unweaving the Rainbow: Science, Delusion and the Appetite for Wonder*, Allen Lane: The Penguin Press.
Deane-Drummond, Celia (2006), *Wonder and Wisdom: Conversations in Science, Spirituality and Theology*, London: DLT.
Deane-Drummond, Celia and Bedford-Strohm Heinrich (2011), "Introduction", in: Celia Deane-Drummond and Heinrich Bedford-Strohm (eds.), *Religion and Ecology in the Public Sphere*, London: Continuum, 1-14.
Dupré John and O'Malley, Maureen (2009), "Varieties of Living Things: Life At The Intersection of Lineage And Metabolism", *Philosophy and Theory in Biology* 1, <http://quod.lib.umich.edu/cgi/t/text/text-idx?c=ptb;view=text;rgn=main;idno=6959004.0001.003> 8 February 2010.
Fields, Stephen (2007), "The Beauty of the Ugly: Balthasar, the Crucifixion, Analogy and God," *International Journal of Systematic Theology* 9, 2, 172-183.
Highfield, Roger (2009), "E.O. Wilson: We Must Save the Living Environment", *New Scientist*, 2722, 22August, <http://www.newscientist.com/article/mg20327224.600-e-o-wilson-we-must-save-the-living-environment.html> 10 February 2010.

Ingold, Timothy (2009), "The Wedge and the Knot: Hammering and Stitching the Face of Nature", in: Bergmann, Scott, Jansdotter Samuelsson, and Bedford-Strohm, 147-161.
Locker, Thomas and Bruchac, Joseph (2004), *Rachel Carson: Preserving a Sense of Wonder*, Golden: Fulchrum Publishing.
McIntosh, Alastair (2008), *Hell and High Water: Climate Change, Hope and the Human Condition*, Edinburgh: Birlinn.
Miller, Jerome (1992), *In the Throe of Wonder: Intimations of the Sacred in a Post-Modern World*, Albany: State University of New York Press.
O'Loughlin, Thomas (2000), *Celtic Theology: Humanity, World and God in Early Irish Writings*, London: Continuum.
Schaefer, Jame (2009), *Theological Foundations for Environmental Ethics: Reconstructing Patristic and Medieval Concepts*, Washington: Georgetown University Press.
Shuman Joel James and Owens, L. Roger (eds.) (2009), *Wendell Berry and Religion: Heaven's Earthly Life*, Lexington: The University Press of Kentucky.
Theokritoff, Elizabeth (2008), *Living in God's Creation*, Crestwood: St Vladimir's Seminary Press.
Weil, Simone (1943), "The Human Personality", in: Sian Miles (ed.), *Simone Weil: An Anthology*, London: Penguin 2005.
— (1951), "Reflections on the Right Use of School Studies with a View to the Love of God", in: Leslie A. Fiedler (ed.), (tr. Emma Craufurd), *Waiting for God*, New York: Herperperennnial 2009.
— (1952), *Gravity and Grace*, (tr. Emma Crawford and Mario von der Ruhr), London and New York: Routledge 2002.
Wilson, E. O. (1984), *Biophilia: The Human Bond with Other Species*, Cambridge/Mass.: Harvard University Press.
— (1999), *Consilience*, London: Abacus.
Wirzba, Norman (2009), "The Dark Night of the Soul: An Agrarian Approach to Mystical Life", in: Shuman and Owens, 148-169.

Working within the Frame, Breaking Outside the Borders

Intersections in the Theological Experience of Art and Place

Forrest Clingerman

How do we seek, find and express the Sacred in nature and in culture? The present essay asks this question in order to show how theology can bring together environmental concerns and human culture. Such conversations are significant and necessary, for at least two reasons: First, in our "overhumanized"[1] world we have lost a deep sense of being in the world. In a globalized world dominated by technical, calculative thinking, our sense of the poetic and the natural are obscured.[2] Contemporary existence has become increasingly alienated from both the natural and the artistic. The commodification and globalization of the world threatens to render both nature and culture bereft of anything beyond superficial meaning.

However important it is to combat this superficiality, my reflections here concentrate on a second reason for the importance of the present theme: Despite this alienation – or perhaps because of it – there are liberative possibilities that surface through understanding the interconnection of art and place. Therefore, in the present essay I wish to challenge some dimensions of the boundaries between art and nature, aesthetics and ethics. We frame art and nature in a variety of ways, and often narrowly focus on a "surface hermeneutics" to interpret our experience. But a reductive approach is neither liberative nor ultimately satisfying. In contrast, the redemptive possibilities that emerge from the *intersection* of art and place point toward transcendent, imaginative variations of viewing the world. To see this requires understanding how and why we interpret the world as we do. Art and place are important elements that gather together the meaning of our world, and in conjunction with each other they illuminate a sacred depth. The theological task is to investigate the Sacred as it presences itself at the intersection of culture and nature, art and place, aesthetics and ethics. This convergence identifies, in a fragile but important way, what Tillich called the ground and abyss of Being itself.[3]

Thus the intent of this essay is to question the boundaries of categories that we use to name our theological encounters with (on the one hand) cultural works and (on the other hand) natural environments: Are these two quite different classes of things, treated by theology in two entirely different ways? Or are they manifestations of a single thing and part of a unified theological project? My proposal is to expose the limits of these two extremes, by showing that there is a complex and dialectical relationship between works of art and the environment in theological thinking. In other words, I examine a way past a two-dimensional, technical reasoning of both art and place, toward what Tillich called an ecstatic reasoning of the world. If Tillich was correct that faith is the fulfillment of reasoning,[4] then the Sacred is found when our thinking of art is the embodiment of our sense of place, and our thinking of place is fully envisioned in art.

THE BOUNDARIES OF CULTURE AND NATURE

To begin, I argue that environmental theology – theological reflections on nature and environments – should be considered a form of theology of culture. Yet it is a paradoxical form of a theology of culture, for its object (nature) moves outside culture. That is, environmental theology works as a study of boundaries: the boundaries of culture, nature, and the human itself. We encounter such boundaries, however, when we see how these categories are fluid and porous, and in turn, we discover how the sides framed by these boundaries enrich each other. Thus we must break out of an absolute culture/nature divide, which admits no dependencies or interaction; this is a task that many others, including John Rodwell, Thomas Heyd, and Sigurd Bergmann have sought to do philosophically and theologically.

In order to show the confluence of art and place, then, we must first explore how we might bridge two areas of theology that have long been separated. The first area is ecological or environmental theology. In his comprehensive bibliographic survey of the field, Ernst Conradie offers us a succinct definition of this form of theological thinking:

Ecological theology is an attempt to retrieve the ecological wisdom in Christianity as a response to environmental threats and injustices. At the same time, it is an attempt to reinvestigate, rediscover and renew the Christian tradition in light of the challenges posed by the environmental crisis. . . . In other words, ecological theology is not only concerned with how Christianity can respond to environmental concerns; it also offers Christianity an opportunity for renewal and reformation.[5]

Environmental theologies can take several forms. These differences have led to several typologies of Christian environmental thought, including those of Conradie, Peter Scott, and Willis Jenkins.[6]

The second area is the theology of culture. Paul Tillich has given us the most decisive formulation of the meaning of a "theology of culture". As William Schweiker noted, "Tillich believed that theological reflection on culture was both possible and necessary in order to disclose the religious meaning of an increasing secular world and also in order to clarify the relevance of Christian faith to contemporary life."[7] In several essays, beginning with his lecture "On the Idea of a Theology of Culture",[8] Tillich explains how theology can interpret the spiritual substance of a given culture.

For Tillich, a theology of culture begins with a recognition that religion is "being ultimately concerned about that which is and should be our ultimate concern. This means that faith is the state of being grasped by an ultimate concern, and God is the name for the content of such concern."[9] In other words, "Religion is not a special function of man's spiritual life, but it is the dimension of depth in all of its functions."[10] This depth of existence or ultimate concern means that there is not a gap between the religious and the secular. However, the secular tends to separate itself, as does the religious – this is the human predicament.

Theology gathers the secular and the spiritual, insofar as the theological task is to interpret contemporary culture in light of its depth. Cultural manifestations express the substance of a culture's ultimate concern, thereby allowing us to correlate secular culture with theological understanding. Tillich explains the theology of culture as the normative discipline that seeks to interpret the substance or depth of cultural manifestations, in light of the cultural values and expressions. Substance is not content – substance is not simple existence, but is meaning and what gives significance to the form of the work. This means that substance "is grasped by means of a form and given expression in a content."[11] Tillich says content is accidental, substance is essential, and form is mediating. Taken together, "Religion as ultimate concern is the meaning-giving substance of culture, and culture is the totality of forms in which the basic concern of religion expresses itself. In abbreviation: religion is the substance of culture, culture is the form of religion."[12] In essence, the theology of culture defines the task of theological thinking as a form of "cultural hermeneutics",[13] interpreting the meaning of artifacts and human works.

In light of these definitions, I argue that environmental theology is a particular form of theology of culture. At the heart of my claim is the acknowledgement that the object of environmental theology is an object of a theology of culture, and we attend to environments (in both "natural" and non-natural forms) theologically by seeking to interpret its substance or meaning. This is indirectly apparent, because culture is influenced and defined by the natural world, making necessary at least some recognition of environmental influences on cultural objects. But more directly, we can see that nature is not simply an external force *upon* culture, but a participant *within* culture – at least, in an unusual way.

Of course Tillich and others have claimed that nature does not fit into such a cultural hermeneutics. Kevin Vanhoozer asserts a fundamental difference between culture and nature, supported by Dilthey: the way of hermeneutically understanding the human runs parallel to how scientific causality explains nature, meaning that they are fundamentally different.

Whereas the natural sciences seek explanation by law, the human sciences seek understanding. To be sure, we cannot study freedom or mind or spirit directly, but we can do so indirectly. Humans 'objectify' their 'spirits' (e.g., their thoughts, values, beliefs) through concrete objects and works (e.g., poems, buildings, games) that call not for explanation but interpretation.[14]

Vanhoozer further writes, "Culture is the realm of these objectified expressions of human freedom."[15] In contrast, science and explanation examines causality. Tillich also argues against seeing nature through the deliberations in a theology of culture. After asking whether nature is part of a theology of culture, he replies, "The answer is that for us nature can only become an object through the medium of culture, if at all."[16]

Departing from Tillich and Vanhoozer, within environmental thought most philosophers and theologians recognize the interconnection and interpenetration of nature and human culture. In some ways, nature and culture offer two quite different perspectives through which to categorize things. But the boundaries between nature and culture are not clear. Culture overlaps with nature, nature overlaps with culture, and both push outside each other's boundaries. Human beings are embodied, fleshly creatures. Sinew, bone and tissue allow us to stand in the world, to feel the embrace of our surroundings. Our physicality – or to use a term with theological resonance, our incarnation – becomes a frame through which to encounter artifact and human production. From one point of view, *culture is simply a desire to pinpoint and emphasize certain facets and perceived excellences of human life and embodiment – thus participating in our naturalness*. One of the tasks of culture, then, is to account for this "cultural naturalness", since our naturalness is essential to who and what we are. Sometimes this connection to nature is forgotten. H. Paul Santmire has given theological expression to this by critiquing the presumption that human existence is divorced from nature in a motif of ascent from the natural world.[17]

At the same time, any description of the human condition cannot remain focused simply on raw stuff. Individuals and communities emerge from the act of stepping outside and reflecting upon nature, through society, technology, the arts, or other elements of culture. We are not exclusively matter, nor are we solely defined through biology or ecology. Humanity moves beyond what is commonly referred to as "natural" in several ways; abstract thought, imagination, memory and reflection are ways that culture is highlighted as another dimension of human being. As Tillich noted, we use cultural means to understand the natural world, from science and technology to the arts; culture en-frames nature. So while humans use "nature" and "culture" as frames through which to understand the world, perhaps more significantly humans stand at an inevitable fracture: Gordon Kaufmann points out that we are "bio-historical" and Philip Hefner similarly calls human beings "bio-cultural".[18] Philosophers interested in ecosemiotics, ecophenomenology, and environmental hermeneutics have made similar arguments. Humans are paradoxical creatures of nature and culture.

If humans are paradoxical, so too does nature itself have a paradoxical quality. This paradox can be delineated by noting the two ways of referring to "nature": on the one hand, nature is viewed as the opposite of culture, as other, and as separated from the human. The natural serves as the counterpoint to the artificial. On the other hand, nature is the totality of all processes and things (including the human and the artificial). In this sense of nature, the cultural aspects of the human are beholden to her or his genetic and biological constraints; thus, even human culture is contained within the natural, for nature is the constitutive framework that the laws, structures, and processes within which all matter and life functions. Nature can be defined as the opposite of culture, separate from the human world and its artificiality. Discussions of wilderness areas and "pristine" nature show such a distinction.

On the other hand, debates over the meaning and value of wilderness show another side of nature: nature is all-embracing and includes culture as well. As constructivists have argued, nature is intertwined and is defined by the cultural frameworks of human society. Going further, nature also defines culture and places constraints on our interpretation of culture. Philosopher Martin Drenthen has correctly argued for the paradox in wild nature (and thereby in other forms of nature), insofar as wilderness is the cultural manifestation of the otherness of culture.[19] Nature participates in, encompasses, and is involved in the dialectic of cultural definition, including culture.[20] As both other and totality, Heidegger's claim of the en-framing of nature by technology[21] is completed in the ways that nature challenges and en-frames culture. Simultaneously, as Thomas Heyd has argued, humans are always actors in the change and maintenance of our surrounding environments (suggesting the need for a "culture of nature").[22]

Because of the complex overlapping of culture and nature, environmental theologies benefit from being conceptualized as a mediating, reflexive form of knowing, which is part of a broader theology of culture. Environments interact with and challenge human culture, and therefore are valuable objects of theological study. But the inclusion of environments is ambiguous, for *nature exists apart from and eludes culture; yet nature constructs culture; and nature is constructed by culture*. It is for this reason the title of the present essay references frames and boundaries: both nature and culture work within frames, but are fully understood only from beyond their respective borders. In other words, while our investigations approach culture and nature in different ways, environments and humans cause the breaking of any strict nature/culture dichotomy.

To be sure, environmental theology is a strange type of theology of culture, in that the object of study – nature – transcends cultural analysis and fractures the boundaries of our understanding of human cultural meaning. But given these definitions, a theology of culture offers a model through which to understand the task of environmental theology. On the one hand, environmental theologies – theologies concerned with ecological wisdom in a time of crisis – deepen and challenge the concerns and aims of contemporary culture. There are radical changes in global and local ecologies: examples of this are climate change, migration patterns, marine dead zones, and the spread of GMOs. These are not simply questions of nature. In each case such environmental changes (and even the fact that we see them as "problems" rather than mere fluctuations) have cultural import, and must be accounted for. At the same time, the study of culture offers us important resources for environmental theology. *A theology of culture is a hermeneutical enterprise that seeks a depth or substance found within changing forms, styles, and contents.* If seen along these lines, environmental theologies are meant to interpret the human condition, the natural world, and built spaces in light of questions of ultimacy. In the case of environmental theology, the substance of the spirit is found not only within "nature", but within the human interaction with environment – in other words, the divine depth dwells at the intersection of culture and nature itself.

ART AND PLACE

The previous section investigated the commonalities between nature and culture. But we cannot reduce nature to culture, lest we erase the differences between them and assume nature to be a social construction. While we have highlighted the fact that understanding created cultural artifacts and understanding natural environments are similarly hermeneutical tasks, we must also recognize that there are differences between them as well. It is evident that a theology of the arts (as one form of the theology of culture) looks to objects – such as paintings or architecture – and develops a hermeneutical structure that relates art, viewer, and artworld.[23] That is to say, a specific whole, a "work", is identified and its meaning sought. Does environmental theology have a similar but unique structure? It initially might appear less evident that this is so. If environmental theology interprets the meaning of the natural environments as paradoxically cultural, what is actually being interpreted?

In the case of environmental theology, what emerges as comparable to works of art are specific manifestations of environments – that is to say, places or landscapes. Works of art and particular places become objects within the so-called hermeneutical circle: whether or not we agree with Friedrich Schleiermacher that the task of hermeneutics is "to understand the text better than the author", Schleiermacher was correct in saying that interpretation involves understanding the whole through its parts, and each part is understood fully only in light of the meaning of the whole.[24] In fact, artworks and places are unified, meaningful entities, open to interpretation. In contrast, "culture" and "nature" are ambiguous and abstract genres, we might say, making it difficult or even impossible to directly confront either as objects of interpretation for theology.[25] Thus the hermeneutical project of the theology of culture is not oriented exclusively toward "culture", but rather reaches fulfillment through the investigation of specific creations: Theologians approach individual elements of culture and seek to determine what insights such creations provide. As a form of theology of culture, environmental theology can approach specific places and landscapes in order to develop a theological interpretation of the meaning of environments.

To state this more systematically: the theology of culture can be divided into domains of study, such as the visual arts, environments, etc. While every domain is hermeneutically investigated, each domain has certain unique features that differentiates it from others. And while each domain can be differentiated from each other, they are nonetheless somehow connected to each other through a reflexive, hermeneutical theological thinking of culture.

It should be clear that the present essay is interested in two domains. The first domain is the visuals arts. In a theology of art, the theologian not only seeks to determine the theological import of the process of creation in the visual arts but also discusses the spiritual depth of individual works of art as manifestations of particular theological insights. For example, Mark C. Taylor's *Disfiguring* constitutes a form of a theology of culture, in that it seeks to interpret specific manifestations of art and architecture in light of aesthetic-cultural narratives of postmodernity. An example of a more Trinitarian and environmentally-attuned theology of art is found in Sigurd Bergmann's *In the Beginning is the Icon*. Bergmann examines a contextual, liberative art theology not only by investigating the theological definitions of art, icon, and "art theology", but also through a detailed interrogation with specific works of art. Throughout, there is a need to understand the reflexivity of thinking within the visual arts: a work of art encourages us not simply to perceive, but to think about the process of perception – and ultimately to think about how our perception of a particular work of art offers a portrayal of a more transcendent truth or meaning to us.

The second domain is the meaning of place. "Place" provides a useful determination for what is meant by the "whole" to be interpreted by environmental theology. "Place" includes geometric space and chronological time, but it is more than this. Tim Cresswell writes, "This is the most straightforward and common definition of place – a meaningful location."[26] Similarly, Arto Haapala has noted, "Place is, indeed, the horizon that determines our perceptions and preferences."[27] Following Heidegger, we might further say that place is where humans dwell and encounter the other, human and non-human alike.[28] To interpret this sense of place, I have elsewhere argued that knowing "place" is a threefold mediation. First, the interpretation of place includes the thinking of the concept "place," which serves as a categorization. Much like "art" identifies a cultural creation as an artistic work, "place" serves as a guideline for what constitutes an acceptable or truthful interpretation of an environment or landscape. The concept of "place" explains the possibility of space and time as lived particularities. A second quality of understanding place emerges: place is simultaneously the thinking of specific manifestations; places are experiences of unique, individual sites and locales. A particular place, together with its objects, inhabitants, and visitors, can serve as an element of environmental theology. Finally, interpreting place includes an element of reflexive thinking: being situated in place means our thinking includes a mediating correlation between specific manifestation and general concept. Knowledge of place therefore includes thinking about how environments are interpreted as an understanding of how we are emplaced. Humans (as natural and cultural, situated and distanced, inhabitants and observers) find themselves in particular places, and how such embodiment is understood in light of our conceptualizations of place.[29]

Already we can see common traits between these two domains. For instance, in both we encounter specific, concrete objects of reflection. Further, theological reflection seeks in both to find a meaning that is not subjective or exclusively dependent upon the observer or participant. But this does not mean that our interpretation is entirely objective, either. For Emily Brady remarks,

> Interpretation is the activity of discovering meaning. It is "making sense of" something, and involves exploration and putting together various perceptions into a coherent whole, so that we are able to grasp or take in an aesthetic object. In the artworld, one is trying to make sense of a work and the meanings it has. … With environments that are mostly natural, this question would be odd since there is no meaning internal to landscapes. We bring meaning to them or assign meaning through cultural frameworks. There is still an attempt to make sense of something, but not in terms of searching for meaning that already exists.[30]

I agree with Brady, to a point: we bring meaning to nature culturally. But the work of art, too, has no clear and final meaning that exists apart from the interpreter. Interpretation is a relational task that requires not only the world of the work, but also the world of the reader. In this way, art and place are approached intersubjectively, and thus in analogous ways, in the hermeneutical task of theology.

Another common trait is that we find a common ground outside the respective borders that enclose each domain. Stepping back from our particular deliberations on art and place, we see a common theological task: namely, *to investigate the Holy, insofar as we can correlate the Sacred with a numinous quality found in the reflexivity between the conceptual and the lived particular*; or differently stated, thinking about how thought correlates the idea of creation and its manifestation. Theology desires the ground on which the part and the whole are gathered together and exhibited to thought and feeling. Approaching domains such as visual arts or music, theologians might seek to interpret Barnett Newman's *The Stations of the Cross* or Arvo Pärt's *Passio* as manifestations of theological and artistic truth. As Bergmann writes,

> The contextual art theologian does not transpose his or her theology onto the images; rather, s/he seeks to discover and understand the 'theo-iconic,' God's revelation in images, in the making of pictures, in pictures as objects and in their reception. … Simply put, art theology involves discoveries and interpretations of God and images of the divine in art. Art is keeping the image of God alive.[31]

In like manner, the theologian approaches places and landscapes, because places emplace the image of God. For each domain, the spiritual is situated in a point of mediation; the divine depth is the infinite ground of the conceptual frames of thinking and the particular manifestations of experience. The theologian attempts to understand the theological meaning of nature not only in the abstract, but through the depth of particular places – this is truly an "environmental" theology, when we emphasize "environments" as places or locales in which we are situated. In turn, the theological opens a perspective of this ground by a reflexive reflection of thinking about thinking; the theologian seeks the sacred not simply through the mediation of concepts and the content of thought, but also through the reflection on how such thinking instantiates the infinite ground of finite thought.

CONNECTING ART, PLACE, AESTHETICS AND ETHICS

With the foregoing, it is possible to posit a framework for a meaningful theological dialogue between the work of art and natural environments. In fact, a fruitful framework for dialogue emerges in a parallel structure that exists between them: Aesthetics and ethics are the avenues through which we interrogate and entwine both art and place. As noted earlier, the common aim of the theological investigation of art and place is to investigate the Holy, insofar as we can correlate the numinous with a quality found in the reflexivity between the conceptual and the lived particular. In the case of art and place, the interweaving of aesthetics and ethics provide an enactment of theological reflexivity. In other words, there is a connection between the theology of culture and environmental theology, not simply because art and place are understood hermeneutically in similar ways, but also because *art and place are ensconced between the poles of aesthetics and ethics*. In turn, aesthetics and ethics are part of the framework for interpreting art and place, then these four terms – art, place, aesthetics, and ethics – create together a reflexive intersection for a meaningful theological dialogue of culture.

AESTHETICS

Aesthetics bridges art and place in the way it frames our understanding of perception. The discipline of aesthetics is oriented toward perception and the judgment of aesthetic qualities such as beauty. Thus we can differentiate two meanings for aesthetics. As theologian Edward Farley writes,

'Aesthetic' refers to an aspect of human experience evoked by an immediate relation to what is beautiful ... 'Aesthetics' refers to a branch of philosophy or art criticism whose task is to understand the unity and features of works of art and the experience of art.[32]

Of course, increasingly after Hegel, the natural world has been excluded from the concern of philosophical aesthetics, insofar as aesthetic qualities are limited to artifacts and cultural works. Environmental aesthetics has challenged this view, reasserting the older view that nature has aesthetic qualities. This has ushered in a broader view, in which aesthetics seeks to describe how we appreciate and understand certain perceptual experiences.

From the perspective of theology, the interpretation of any manifestation of art or place includes (but is not limited to) aesthetics. Through this connection of art and aesthetics, we see that (1) *Art is an attunement to the flourishing of embodied, perceptual life of individuals and communities*. Artworks are models necessary to train our sense of contemplation of the material world, especially if Heidegger was correct in saying that "Art then is a becoming and happening of truth."[33] Each work of art,

Table 1

	Aesthetics	**Ethics**
Art	Art is an attunement to the flourishing of embodied, perceptual life of individuals and communities. (point 1)	Art envisions liberative possibilities for ethics. (point 4)
Place	Place localized and situates aesthetics, our perception of embodied existence. (point 2)	Place traces the limits of ethics. (point 3)
Theological Convergence	Theological thinking discovers the Sacred when place and art exhibit the placeless creativity that covers and reveals the finite, material creation encountered by our interpretations of perceptual experience.	Theological thinking investigates how the Sacred exists at the ecstatic union of understanding; poetic and platial theological reasoning centers on the intersection of emplaced stability of responsibility, the freeing novelty of liberation, and the Sacred dialectic between them.

as an instance of embodied, creative expression, proclaims a novel way of perception in this broader sense of aesthetics. Even a picture frame takes on new importance, for as Arnold Berleant writes, "The picture frame has come to function not so much as an enclosure but rather as a facilitator for focusing our gaze into the painting, and this internal focusing eludes the very objectification that the traditional aesthetic intended to promote."[34] For example, the contemplation of Ralph Albert Blakelock's *Brook By Moonlight* guides a sense of nighttime and the darkened crags of a tree; Caspar David Friedrich's *The Monk by the Sea* offers a unique lens through which to aesthetically perceive solitude, spirituality, and the vast expanse of the sea. One of the outcomes of the ongoing engagement with the visual arts is the distillation of our ability to perceive. We encounter the material world with a new sense, a new discernment. With that in mind, we can affirm Crispin Sartwell's statement that "Art ... is a form of immersion and connection; art is a way of entering deeply into relationship with non-human materials and with human communities."[35]

The theology of place also has need for aesthetics – especially if we agree with Kim Dovey that beautiful places make us whole.[36] Places are breathed in and encountered perceptually, and aesthetics is one way of framing and thinking in place. On a superficial level, we can immediately accept that places have aesthetic qualities akin to the visual arts. It is even arguable that environments have a greater degree of aesthetic qualities than the visual arts, because environments engage all of the senses. But there also is a deeper connection between aesthetics and place: place forms the site of aesthetic contemplation. That is to say, (2) *place localizes and situates aesthetics, our perception of embodied existence*. Whether we are contemplating a painting in a gallery, creating the work of art, or encountering the natural environment, *it occurs in place*. Our perceptions rest in space and time, in the midst of other denizens and objects. The judgment of beauty, the recognition of aesthetic value, the experience of the sublime – these all occur in space and time. Even determining the applicability of aesthetic judgment is localized and "platial".[37] Place, in this case, can be defined as the locale in which the aesthetic object is emplaced.

But what if we take these two points together? It appears that art allows for an aesthetic openness (within a frame), whereas place provides aesthetic boundaries (albeit permeable ones). Or we might use Arto Haapala's terms, to suggest that art moves toward strangeness and the novel, whereas place revels in familiarity.[38] Interestingly, even change becomes perceived differently in each: art seeks novelty, place seeks stability in its flux. The aesthetic convergence of art and place, then, is found at the tension of the releasement of art and the enfolding of place. We in turn can identify the theological dimension as the grace of the Sacred, which allows for a unity in which the fragile tension exists – *theological thinking discovers the Sacred when place and art exhibit the placeless creativity that covers and reveals the finite, material creation encountered by our interpretations of perceptual experience*. To put this another way, the world of the work and the world of the interpreter – to adapt Ricoeur's language – are inadequate to understand how art and place meet. We must seek another world – a world of the Sacred – that emerges in the aesthetic encounter of place and art. The convergence of a theology of art and a theology of place, then, seeks a depth to aesthetics by proposing a limit question: What brings to being the imperceptible meaning of the perceived creation – the meaning of that materiality that we touch, taste, smell and see as art and environment? This can only be satisfactorily answered in terms of the sacred, transcendent dimension of creativity.

Ethics

Ethics also participates in the theological reflexivity of art and place. Ethics bridges art and place in the way it frames our understanding of moral goodness and action. More generally, we can say that ethics is the reflection on how we are what we are in the world. The traditional view of environmental theology has this kind of direct, explicit ethical dimension. That is to say, a commonly-stated aim of environmental theology has been to explicate an environmental ethics as a response to Christian faith and theological reflection. But then ethics is distanced from, and merely enacted upon, nature. In light of the hermeneutical orientation we have toward place, our thinking – ethics included – is grounded in place. Thus we can make a rather different claim: (3) *place traces the limits of ethics*. We live and act in space and time, through physical bodies and material environments. Our relationships and interactions are bounded by spatial and temporal limitations. Place thereby puts a claim on us, insofar as ethics is always already emplaced – connected to our embodiment in spatial and temporal meaning. Ethics has a spatial dimension, occurring within the confines of bodies and spheres of actions. It also hinges on the temporal aspect of place; elsewhere I have argued that memory is vital for understanding the temporality of an ethics of place. In terms of both space and time, morality occurs *in situ*.

At the same time, art is not absent from or irrelevant to our discussion of ethics. (4) *Art envisions liberative possibilities for ethics*. Art can do this directly – for example, the Quaker painter Edward Hicks' numerous versions of *The Peaceable Kingdom*. It can do this through a confrontation of the injustice and horrors of the world, such as Picasso's *Guernica* and Anselm Kiefer's *Athanor*. Or it can do this indirectly, by allowing us to encounter – perceptually, visually, materially – some of the imaginative variations that constitute our enactment of the world. In this way, a work such as Joseph Beuys' *Show Your Wound* challenge us to rethink or re-envision our ethical relation with what is perceived, and by extension with the world itself. When we confront the work of art, and truly contemplate its meaning, we are seeking to understand not only the work but also ourselves. Play and imagination allow us to "try on" the world of the work, and thereby find new moral possibilities. Paul Ricoeur has argued in this way, and tied it to the Pauline language of the New Being:

Play also opens in subjectivity the possibilities of metamorphosis which is a purely moral vision of subjectivity cannot see. Imaginative variation, play, metamorphosis – all of these expressions seek to discern a fundamental phenomenon, namely, that it is in imagination that the new being is first formed in me.[39]

As with aesthetics, ethics presents a theological correlation between art and place. This is because place provides a structure for ethics, offering the necessary perspectives on how we enact our place in the world. Place grounds our actions, particularizes our world, and offers limits to ethical reflection. At the same time, art provides an openness and novelty to confront different situations through imaginary possibilities. It allows us to live and act in ways that are dis-placed – that is, it presents pictures of a life otherwise lived. Together, art and place confront each other in light of the tensions inherent in the ways that humans enact their world and environments. Therefore the theological dimension here correlates with the grace of the Sacred to allows for a unity in which the fragile tension exists: *Theological thinking investigates how the Sacred exists at the ecstatic union of understanding; poetic and platial theological reasoning centers on the intersection of emplaced stability of responsibility, the freeing novelty of liberation, and the Sacred dialectic between them.*

Place is the site of aesthetics and emplaces the sphere of responsibility in ethics. Art envisions ethics and provides a novel attunement toward aesthetics. For both art and place, the interrelationship between aesthetics and ethics incorporate a sense of reflexivity. For example, an aesthetic appreciation of art can echo and foster a reflection on an ethics of locality that bounds the possibilities of the visual art with temporal change and situatedness. Similarly, an ethical interpretation of place, through its fragile temporality, beckons to be re-placed in an imaginative temporal and spatial possibility that is envisioned by ethics. In turn, this dimension of reflexivity allows us to retrace our steps: aesthetics and ethics bridges the domains of art and place. Art no longer simply lifts us outside of time and present situations, but embeds us more thoroughly in place. Place no longer emplaces us in a temporal and spatial shroud, but elevates us to seek beauty, justice, and goodness in the here-and-now. Art is that which provides an openness to place; place is that which issues the setting of the work of art. Theologically we seek to interpret the intersection, sensing the sacred ground of such permeable boundaries.

GEORGE STEINMANN'S THE SAXETEN WORK

Having suggested ways in which aesthetics and ethics bridge art and place, it is now possible to show more concretely how environmental theologies and theologies of the arts enrich one another. Throughout I have suggested that our sense of place illuminates our perceptions of art, and simultaneously poetic reflections on art sharpen our sense of place. Our interpretations of art and place, I have argued, are theologically, aesthetically and ethically correlated. By focusing on the correlations of art, place, aesthetics and ethics delineated above, we are able to sketch a theological interpretation of individual works of art or particular places. In other words, the foregoing orients us to find the sacred depth of particular manifestations of art and place.

Bernese artist George Steinmann's *The Saxeten Work, a Growing Sculpture* (original German: *Das Werk Saxeten, Eine Wachsende Skulptur*), created 2002-06, shows how these theological correlations aid in how we approach art and place. This work is a poignant example for many reasons. Foremost, it is simultaneously a work of art and a reflection on place; it naturally serves to reflexively mark both culture and nature, creation and environment. Further, Steinmann's work is unusually sensitive to its transdisciplinary boundary-crossing; as an artist he creates works that transcend the gallery, in many ways. Finally, Steinmann is open to the theological resonance of both art and the spirit of place. Thus Steinmann's work confounds any attempt to frame his work simply as art or environment, conceptual or perceptual, aesthetical or ethical, sacred or secular. By reflecting on how *Saxeten* concretizes the discussion above, then, we are able to analyze the theological importance of this work of art.

Saxeten is a work created for the Canton and the University of Bern. While commissioned as part of a renovation of a former hospital into a new building for the University of Bern, the work extends past this site into the village of Saxeten and the Alps. Saxeten is a small, economically poor village in the canton, and thus the work has a significant impact there. Steinmann explains the work in this way:

The work consists of three parts – a bridge for pedestrians, a cabin, and photographs. The bridge has two functions: it is a bridge that restores the hiking trail across the Saxetbach that was interrupted by the floods of summer 2005. It is also a symbolic act of crossing a boundary and a symbol of the dialogue between town and country. Between center and periphery. The second part, the cabin, is accessed by the hiking trail; it's a place where you can rest, think, or meditate and is available to everyone, irrespective of their background or views. This lends the space another, higher significance. It embraces the world symbolically and invites the visitors to the mountain valley of Saxeten. From the cabin there are sweeping views to the north, beyond the valley, to the south into the valley, and towards the Alps. It is a motif from landscape painting, a quote, and yet tangibly real at the same time. The third part is the location of the work in photographs at the University of Bern.[40]

Steinmann's work is centered on bridging art and place through ways of knowing. For Steinmann, it is important to approach this as more than simply an aesthetic object, and instead to see it as part of a transdisciplinary way of knowing. The work, in other words, is grounded on a conviction that everything is related – to recall the hermeneutical circle, the whole and the parts necessarily intertwine in *Saxeten*.

Steinmann's concerns in *Saxeten* illuminate much of the theological discussion above. Foremost, he is interested in a reflection the entwined categories of culture and nature, but recognizes the need to look at these categories through the particular. Thus, in *Saxeten* we see a dismantling of the nature/culture divide, toward a more satisfying mediation of art and place. To be sure, the work contains created objects and visual images. At the same time, it attempts to open up a place for perception and poetic reflection. In other words, Steinmann drinks deeply of a *particular place* through a *particular work of art*, and *vice versa*. Art becomes a lens, a poetic way of knowing. This echoes our concern to move from nature and culture to the hermeneutical investigation between place and art. In fact, many of Steinmann's other artworks share with *Saxeten* a sense of reflection on the meaning of place from a transdisciplinary perspective. His restoration of the Tallinn Art Hall – a work called *The Revival of Space* – is Steinmann's concern for broadening the meaning of art, just as *Komi* seeks to know the place of the northern forests. Thus, Steinmann reaffirms in *Saxeten* and other works the strict separation between culture and nature. It cannot adequately be analyzed as environment, nor is it simply a cultural artifact. It is, rather, a work at the boundaries. In turn, *Saxeten* becomes an object of study for several different forms of theology of culture, insofar as it can be explored as a work of fine art, and as an instantiation of place and environment.

Insofar as Saxeten is both art and environment, it is bridged by aesthetics and ethics. In terms of aesthetics, we noted above (point 1) that the work of art becomes a way of orienting perception in light of individuals and communities. Gerhard Mack suggests, in relation to Steinmann's *Metalog*, "Art has the task of inventing so that we

1-5 George Steinmann, *The Saxeten Work, a Growing Sculpture, 2002-2006,*
photo: © George Steinmann

can have experiences that make us aware of modes of perception, of their possibilities and limits."[41] Art is an opening, a manifestation of how we are embodied and interacting in the world. A place, in this view, becomes a boundary that situates and grounds the perception (point 2). Approaching *Saxeten*, we can see that Steinmann seeks to incorporate both of these aesthetic responses into the work. *Saxeten* is concerned with connecting communities with each other, and opening up new ways of viewing. The cabin within the work, for instance, marks the ways through which we can re-envision the world around it. But at the same time, this is not a disembodied piece that seeks only intellectual reflection. And thus Steinmann has also created a definite space in the world, using local timber and craftsman to create a place through which such perception is gathered and rendered meaningful. Insofar as these two points are applicable to Steinmann's work, so too is the theological correlation noted above: *Saxeten* is finally a reflection on the Sacred, insofar as it is where place and art exhibit the placeless creativity that covers and reveals the finite, material creation encountered by our interpretations of perceptual experience.

Just as our understanding of Saxeten can be understood through aesthetics, it also illustrates the ethical dimensions of art and place. In fact, many of Steinmann's works are concerned with the need for art of advance our sense of responsibility; his art shows a concern for ethics and healing that is evocative of earlier artists such as Beuys. Thus Hildegard Kurt writes of *Komi*,

Conceived as a *growing sculpture*, *Komi* undermines the growth dogma of industrial modernity, i.e. the ideology of faster, higher, further, more. The growth that Steinmann has in mind does not involve more and more of everything – in a bio-physically limited system. It does not mean the macabre programme of material accumulation that is threatening to drive our whole world into a kind of collective suicidality. ... [The] collapse of false wealth is necessary for the long-term well-being of mankind. Only Earth's material, biophysical dimension is limited. The spiritual-cultural dimension of our existence on this Earth wants to grow and do so continuously – the evidence for this lies in *Komi, a Growing Sculpture*.[42]

Certainly this reflection is applicable to *Saxeten*, and shows the ethical groundwork of Steinmann's work overall.

When discussing ethics above, we noted that art is an opening for liberation, while place provides us with a situation or limit from ethical responsibility. This we see in *Saxeten*. Certainly *Saxeten* opens ethical possibilities for us (point 3). By the creation of the work, Steinmann asks us to reimagine place: to see the village of Saxeten – and the Canton of Bern, the Alps, and finally our own sense of being in the world – with new eyes. He has described this as a process, and suggests that the work contains a theme of future viability. The artwork is concerned with perception, to be sure, but it deals with the problems of society, economics, environment, etc. – that is to say, all of the problems in our world that stem from the same problem: our "crisis of perception". In other words, *Saxeten* contains the process for a new way of knowing, which is inherently ethical. In discussing the work, Steinmann said, "If you consider art as an epistemological medium, it does contain an immaterial ethical dimension and, with that, a universal culture of responsibility, which is to say, actions based on an ethos for posterity."[43] But such liberative possibilities must be grounded somewhere, lest they become mere utopian fantasy (point 4). Saxeten drew together specialists and works around a particular site. By concerning himself with the revitalization of a particular space, Steinmann was able to focus us on a particular ground or foundation for ethical reflection. The work sees itself addressing the concrete and particular, highlighting the limits of place – and only thereby its future. This ethical concern points us toward a theological message implicit in Steinmann's work: *Saxeten* is a manifestation of how the Sacred exists at the ecstatic union of understanding; poetic and platial theological reasoning centers on the intersection of emplaced stability of responsibility, the freeing novelty of liberation, and the Sacred dialectic between them.

Conclusion

As seen in the brief description of Steinmann's intervention, art and place provide the possibility of spiritual depth. To conclude, we can see that the foregoing discussion shares much with Bergmann's recommendation of an aesth/ethics of the Spirit, that is, a sense of the spirituality that finds the placeless depths of God precisely in the midst of particular places, within space and time, in light of the revels of sight, smell, hearing and touch. Aesth/ethics – a term Bergmann coined in order to show the "aesthetical dimension of moral acting and ethical reflecting"[44] – sees places and art within "the all-embracing space of creation". To see a connection between aesthetics and ethics in this way seeks to understand both disciplines more fully; in Bergmann's words, "The invented notion of 'aesth/ethics' summarizes the need to integrate ethics into an aesthetics that should not be misunderstood as a theory of beauty but as a concept of bodily perception of the self in the surrounding where ethical demand appears."[45] He elsewhere elaborates:

Aesthetics is here understood not as a theory of beauty in the narrow philosophical sense, but as a discursive and artistic production and reflection of practices and discourses on synaesthetic perception, creation and reception. ... The slash between aesthetics and ethics has been invented to signal the intention not to leave moral philosophy and ethics to themselves but to embed them continuously in perceptions. If ethics is defined as a discursive reflection on moral problems, it becomes difficult to exclude people's mental capacities and to separate aesthetic competence from moral competence. Ethics must necessarily be embraced by aesthetics. The perception of moral problems must be prior to their reflection and solution.[46]

The aesth/ethics of spirit re-places religion, promoting a sense of living spirituality fully dwelling in space and time, involving all of our senses in the thirst for justice and peace. It points to an "environmental aesthetics and a theory of justice".[47] In this desire, both art and place have an essential religious role in aesth/ethics that, as Bergmann says, "seeks for a self-critical and ethically significant awareness of inherent dazzlements and for justice through sensitization for what is unknown and different."[48] Using domains such as art and place, a hermeneutically oriented environmental theology become fully reflexive through the interplay of aesth/ethics.

Foremost, this reflexive interconnection of art and place, aesthetics and ethics is an ingredient to human well-being more broadly. As theories of ecojustice point out, human well-being is obviously tied to place. This is not only the case in situations of local environmental degradation and pollution, but also in the case of global environmental changes. But perhaps not as obvious, art also is fundamental for human well-being, insofar as it presents us with imaginative and beautiful ways of perceiving the world. Birgit Cold, discussing Gadamer's aesthetics, correlates human well-being in environments with the artistic portrayal of beauty. Gadamer argues how artists "discovered" natural beauty. Artists use a "common cultural and aesthetic perception and hence develop knowledge of the beautiful."[49] "The norms of beauty, if we accept Gadamer's view, are influenced by the abilities of artists as well as architects to be open and curious, perceiving, discovering or imagining and mediating unnoticed or new aesthetic qualities in such a way that both the observer and the creator are *seduced.*"[50] Aesthetics and ethics are essential for human well-being; place and art provide the dialogue of changeability and stability for this human well-being.[51]

An environmental theology of culture is local, occasional, fleeting. It engages the never-ending hermeneutical task of encountering the world. Situated in place, recognizant of change, concerned with the material and spatial qualities of the good, perceiving of the beauty of justice – it is a theology outside the frame that transcends the boundaries. Thus we might end with the questions that emerge from this aesth/ethical, environmental theology of culture. There are basic questions: What is the morally good way to approach landscapes and places? How does one judge the beauty of a work of art? But the aesth/ethical theology moves to questions that cross the boundaries: What is the meaning of beauty in the places of lived experience? How do we interpret and enact the meaning of natural beauty in an overhumanized world? What justice is embodied in a work of art? Does the meaning of art provide us with imaginative possibilities of renewal in the world? How might our ethical and aesthetic deliberations on the visual arts redefine our dwelling, and how might we create in the act of dwelling? And, most importantly, what are the spatial and temporal qualities of spirituality, such that these qualities guide us to create in place and dwell in art?

Acknowledgements

I have benefited greatly from comments by Dan Boscaljon, Verna Ehret, and Mark H. Dixon. My heartfelt thanks go to George Steinmann and Sigurd Bergmann, both for conversations on Hiddensee and for comments on this essay. Their suggestions greatly advanced my reflections on art and place.

Notes

1. Klemm and Schweiker, 13ff.
2. Heidegger (1966), 45ff., Tillich (1951), 71ff.
3. Tillich, (1951), 110-118, 155-157, Tillich (1952), 155-190.
4. Tillich (1952), 71ff., Tillich (1957), 74-98.
5. Conradie, 3.
6. Conradie, 121-136, Scott, 8-19, Jenkins, especially part I on "strategies of grace".
7. Schweiker, 138.
8. Tillich (1973), 155-181.
9. Tillich (1959), 40.
10. Tillich (1959), 6.
11. Tillich (1973), 165.
12. Tillich (1959), 42.
13. "Cultural hermeneutics" is a term for the theology of culture used by Kevin Vanhoozer. See Vanhoozer, 15-60.

14 Vanhoozer, 22.
15 Vanhoozer, 22.
16 Tillich (1973), 174.
17 Santmire, 13-29.
18 Hefner, 48, writes that, "The challenge that poses to human being can be stated thus: Culture is a system of information that humans must construct so as to adequately serve the three tasks of interpreting the world in which humans live, guiding human behavior, and interfacing with the physico-biogenetic cultural systems that constitute the environment in which we live."
19 Drenthen (1999), 163-175, Drenthen (2005), 317-337. For a theological assessment of Drenthen's view of wilderness, see Clingerman (2010), 211-232.
20 There is a wide-ranging literature on this concern. For a helpful discussion through a theological lens, see Wallace, 97-120.
21 Heidegger (1977), 19ff.
22 Heyd, passim.
23 Haapala (1999), 254ff.
24 Schleiermacher, especially 24-27, Palmer, 87ff.
25 I hesitate to exclude culture or nature entirely from the discussion of theology, though this might prove impossible. My argument is slightly more limited: to discuss either nature or culture means first and primarily focusing on the partial manifestations of these two.
26 Cresswell, 7.
27 Haapala (1999), 260.
28 Heidegger (1993), 343-363. For discussions on whether only humans dwell, see Young, 63-104, and Clingerman (2008).
29 This discussion of place is heavily indebted to previous research. Clingerman (2004) and (2009).
30 Brady, 2.
31 Bergmann (2009b), 98-99.
32 Farley, 117.
33 Heidegger (1993), 196.
34 Berleant, 165
35 Sartwell, 70.
36 Dovey, 93-101.
37 A term coined by philosopher Bruce Janz.
38 Haapala (1998), 108-125.
39 Ricoeur, 33.
40 Fiedler, 163.
41 Mack, 107.
42 Kurt, 18-19.
43 Fiedler, 165.
44 Bergmann, (2005), 96.
45 Bergmann (2007), 364.
46 Bergmann (2009a), 108.
47 Bergmann (2006), 339ff.
48 Bergmann (2009b), 49.

[49] Cold, 20.
[50] Cold, 21.
[51] Here there is a strong connection between Ricoeur's dialogue concerning ipse and idem identity, and the conversation regarding aesthetics, ethics, art and place. Tracing the discussion of this essay, it is arguable that art is important for determining the changes to the self, whereas place is important for determining the stability and continuity of the self. At the same time, art draws upon place, and place upon art, meaning that the continuity and stability of the self is not strictly a dialectic of (1) art and (2) place, but rather a dialectic of (1) art within place and (2) place within art.

REFERENCES

Bergmann, Sigurd (2005), "Space and Spirit: Towards a Theology of Inhabitation", in: Sigurd Bergmann (ed.), *Architecture, Aesth/Ethics and Religion*, Frankfurt am Main: IKO-Verlag für Interkulturelle Kommunikation, 45-103.
— (2006), "Atmospheres of Synergy: Towards an Eco-Theological Aesth/ethics of Space", *Ecotheology* 11, 326-356.
— (2007), "Theology in Its Spatial Turn: Space, Place and Built Environments Challenging and Changing the Images of God", *Religion Compass* 1, 353-79.
— (2009a), "Climate Change Changes Religion", *Studia Theologica* 62, 98-118.
— (2009b), *In the Beginning is the Icon: A Liberative Theology of Images, Visual Arts and Culture*, London: Equinox.
Berleant, Arnold (1992), *The Aesthetics of Environment*, Philadelphia: Temple University Press.
Brady, Emily (2002), "Interpreting Environments", *Essays in Philosophy* Vol. 3, as found at <http://commons.pacificu.edu/eip/vol3/iss1/16>.
Clingerman, Forrest (2004), "Beyond the Flowers and the Stones: 'Emplacement' and the Modeling of Nature", *Philosophy in the Contemporary World* 11, 17-24.
— (2008), "The Intimate Distance of Herons: Theological Travels Through Nature, Place, and Migration", *Ethics, Place & Environment* 11, 313-325.
— (2009), "Reading the Book of Nature: A Hermeneutical Account of Nature for Philosophical Theology", *Worldviews: Global Religions, Culture, and Ecology* 13, 72-91.
— (2010), "Wilderness as the Place between Philosophy and Theology: Questioning Martin Drenthen on the Otherness of Nature", *Environmental Values* 19, 211-232.
Cold, Birgit (2001), "Aesthetics, Well-Being and Health", in: Birgit Cold (ed.), *Aesthetics, Well-Being and Health: Essays Within Architecture and Environmental Aesthetics*, Aldershot: Ashgate, 11-48.
Conradie, Ernst M. (2006), *Christianity and Ecological Theology: Resources for Further Research*, Stellenbosch: SUN Press.
Cresswell, Tim (2004), *Place: A Short Introduction*, Malden, MA: Blackwell.
Drenthen, Martin (1999), "The Paradox of Environmental Ethics: Nietzsche's View of Nature and the Wild", *Environmental Ethics* 21, 163-175.
— (2005), "Wildness as a Critical Border Concept: Nietzsche and the Debate on Wilderness Restoration", *Environmental Values* 14, 317-337.
Dovey, Kim (2001), "The Aesthetics of Place", in: Birgit Cold (ed.), *Aesthetics, Well-Being and Health: Essays Within Architecture and Environmental Aesthetics*, Aldershot: Ashgate, 93-101.

Farley, Edward (2001), *Faith and Beauty: A Theological Aesthetic*, Aldershot: Ashgate.
Fiedler, Andreas (2007), "Art as a Characteristic and Indicator of Change: A Conversation with George Steinmann", in: *George Steinmann: Blue Notes,* Nürnberg: Verlag für Moderne Kunst, 160-171.
Haapala, Arto (1998), "Strangeness and Familiarity in the Urban Environment", in: Arto Haapala (ed.), *The City as Cultural Metaphor*, Jyväskylä: Gummerus Kirppaino Oy, 108-125.
— (1999), "Aesthetics, Ethics, and the Meaning of Place", *Filozofski Vestnik* 20, 253-264.
Heidegger, Martin (1966), *Discourse on Thinking,* New York: Harper & Row.
— (1977), "The Question Concerning Technology", in: Martin Heidegger, *The Question Concerning Technology and Other Essays*, New York: Harper, 1-35.
— (1993), *Basic Writings*, 2nd edition, San Francisco: Harper San Francisco.
Hefner, Philip (1993), *The Human Factor: Evolution, Culture, and Religion,* Minneapolis: Fortress Press.
Heyd, Thomas (2007), *Encountering Nature: Toward an Environmental Culture,* Burlington: Ashgate.
Jenkins, Willis (2008), *Ecologies of Grace: Environmental Ethics and Christian Theology,* New York: Oxford University Press.
Klemm, David E. and Schweiker, William (2008), *Religion and the Human Future,* Malden, MA: Blackwell.
Kurt, Hildegard (2007), "Growing Beyond Accumulation", in: George Steinmann, *Komi: A Growing Sculpture,* Bern: Stämpfli Verlag AG, 11-20.
Mack, Gerhard (2003), "Making the World Appear: George Steinmann's Metalog", in: *Gentle Bridges: Architecture, Art and Science,* Basel: Birkhäuser, 104-119.
Palmer, Richard E. (1969), *Hermeneutics,* Evanston: Northwestern University Press.
Ricoeur, Paul (1975), "Philosophical Hermeneutics and Theological Hermeneutics", *Studies in Religion* 5, 14-33.
Santmire, H. Paul (1985), *The Travail of Nature: The Ambiguous Ecological Promise of Christian Theology,* Minneapolis: Fortress Press.
Sartwell, Crispin (2000), *The End of Story,* Albany, NY: SUNY Press.
Schleiermacher, Friedrich D. E. (1998), *Hermeneutics and Criticism,* Cambridge: Cambridge University Press.
Schweiker, William (2009), "Theology of Culture and Its Future", in: Russell Re Manning (ed.), *The Cambridge Companion to Paul Tillich*, Cambridge: Cambridge University Press, 138-151.
Scott, Peter (1998), "Types of Ecotheology", *Ecotheology* 4, 8-19.
Taylor, Mark C. (1992), *Disfiguring: Art, Architecture, Religion,* Chicago: University of Chicago Press.
Tillich, Paul (1951), *Systematic Theology, Volume I,* Chicago: University of Chicago Press.
— (1952), *The Courage to Be,* New Haven: Yale University Press.
— (1957), *The Dynamics of Faith,* New York: Harper.
— (1959), *Theology of Culture,* New York: Oxford University Press/Galaxy.
— (1973), "On the Idea of a Theology of Culture", in: James Luther Adams (ed.), *What is Religion?* New York: Harper Torchbooks, 155-181.
Vanhoozer, Kevin (2007), "What is Everyday Theology? How and Why Christians Should Read Culture", in: Kevin J. Vanhoozer, Charles A. Anderson and Michael J. Sleasman

(eds.), *Everyday Theology: How to Read Cultural Texts and Interpret Trends,* Grand Rapids: Baker Academic, 15-60.

Wallace, Mark I. (2005), *Finding God in the Singing River,* Minneapolis: Fortress Press.

Young, Julian (2002), *Heidegger's Later Philosophy,* Cambridge: Cambridge University Press.

Forces of Nature

Aesthetics and Ethics

Heather Eaton

From ecological crisis to ecological imaginary: a new bridge between religion and science

As the complexity and enormity of socio-ecological issues encase us, we see causes entangled as much within our cultural ideologies and worldviews as within economic systems and social organization. Yet what is considered to be effective action depends on how we analyze and interpret the socio-ecological crisis, what question we are trying to answer, and from what horizon. For many the ecological crisis is understood as a problem of resources. Good stewardship and resource management are sensible responses. For others questions of justice and the equal distribution of resources are the most significant frameworks. Such ecojustice analyses lead to grappling with systemic inequities and global schemes of privilege and impoverishment based on gender, ethnicity, and financial capital. For still others it is the level of worldview, values, and assumptions about "nature" and human-Earth relations that needs addressing. In each horizon, the socio-ecological crisis can be a religious and moral problem. However the solutions differ accordingly.

For many years I have worked with others to engage religions on ecology issues, within the Christian traditions as well as in multi religious and multi disciplinary contexts. In order to understand the roots of this crisis much has been required: rethinking the confines of modernity and Eurowestern worldviews; addressing environmental justice and ecofeminism; connecting issues of militarism, globalization, poverty creation, and food and water crises. This has involved analyzing, exposing and critiquing anthropo- and androcentric systems of domination enmeshed in myriad bases of socio-ecological stresses and inequities. Such work was indispensable to gain a basic understanding of the depth and breadth of the many dimensions of this socio-ecological crisis. As we move to greater awareness, apocalyptic scenarios are filling the human imagination, as seen in an small selection of popular books: *The End of Nature* or *Enough* (McKibben, 1989, 2004), *The Heat is On* (Gelbspan), *Toxic Turmoil* (Havenaar et al.), *Field Notes from a Catastrophe: Man Nature and Climate Change* (Kolbert), *Bring On the Apocalypse* (Monbiot,) or *The World Without Us* (Weisman).

There is no shortage of disaster data, and we cannot evade the magnitude of the issues. However, perhaps there is less need for assessing causes and calamity and more need for something upon which to base hope (Hawken, Goudzwaard). Thus, with others, I have changed orientation in a quest of an ecological imaginary, and specifically one germane to religion. Success as an ecological society will depend, at least in part, on the generation of a powerful ecological imaginary to challenge the governing utilitarian and exploitative social imaginary, or dominant worldview.[1] The claim, as some suggest, is that decisive moments in social transformation require the development of a counter-imaginary. The counter imaginary for our moment is an ecological imaginary

In order to move in this direction, we need a bridge between religion and science. We require a particular bridge between the best of the Earth or natural sciences and a fresh approach to what *religious imagination* means. The assumption is that such a bridge may contribute to a nascent ecological counter-imaginary. There are both scientific and religious companions on this quest. Many are exploring new images and novel approaches to science as is evident in a sample of publication titles: *Reinventing the Sacred: A New View of Science, Reason and Religion* (Kauffman), *Earth's Imagination* (Swimme), *Dazzle Gradually: Reflections on the Nature of Nature* (Margulis and Sagan), *Animate Earth: Science, Intuition and Gaia* (Harding), *Biomimicry* (Benyus), *The Sacred Depths of Nature* (Goodenough), *Earthdance: Living Systems in Evolution* (Sahtouris), *The Symbiotic Planet*, (Margulis), *Biophilia*, (Wilson) *Gaia: A New Look at Life on Earth* (Lovelock) and the concept of "living matter" from Vladimir Vernadsky in his book *The Biosphere*. These views have much in common with theories of emergent complexity and self-organizing systems found in the earlier and inspiring works of Prigogine and Stengers and Jantsch.

There is also a confluence with religious thinkers who study Earth sciences, such as Pierre Teilhard de Chardin (1959, 1964), Thomas Berry, Mary Evelyn Tucker, Sigurd Bergmann, and many more. All are trying to consider ecological exigencies within a renewed conversation between religion and science, as well as with a reevaluation of "religion". As the pressure mounts to move towards an ecological imaginary, and as many cultures continue to be rooted in, and develop within religions, then *religion* or religions need to be involved. Given the social influence, albeit uneven, of religions, they could play a significant role, and provide a strategic, beneficial intervention in the articulation of an ecological imaginary (Taylor, Jurgensmeyer).

There is another group of companions who cross these paths, and that is the vast numbers of nature writers, and their hosts of magnificent insights, images and intuitions. These writers are not part of this study. Yet, their reflections and abilities to cross many epistemological boundaries and disciplines are exemplary of the desired blend of acuity, intelligence and inspiration.

My comments pertain to this particular intersection of religion, science and nature, and the need for an ecological imaginary. I am not claiming that the aforementioned colleagues agree about such a convergence. Further, there are myriad distinctions between and among these bodies of work that are essential to a different conversation.

For now I am privileging the confluences, not the divergences. For example, many of these works reside in a common terrain of reflection where the boundaries between culture and nature are fluid, and where differences are seen as complex relations rather than dichotomies. To blend religion and science in such ways requires flexible modes of thinking if they are to contribute to an adequate ecological imaginary. The first task is to understand the meaning of a social imaginary.

What is a Social Imaginary?

Human societies live according to a social imaginary – a complex and relational tapestry of intertwining ideals, beliefs, practices and influences. Many have identified the composite that Charles Taylor refers to as "the social imaginary", although some would use the term worldview (Aerts et al). Although it is impossible to describe all the threads that compose it, simply defined, our social imaginary is the way we imagine life and our lives together. It is an amalgam of the visions, ideas and practices that interweave to produce the quality of our communities, the questions we raise, and the moral principles that we choose. It is about governance and social patterns as much as it is embedded in our identities, fears, desires, and emotional matrix. Social imaginaries are created over time and are the result of intentional and unintentional decisions, events and consequences. Without consistent reflection and critique, ideological assumptions become sedimented in a society, at times inaccessible. Such concealed or unexamined aspects of a social imaginary are carried forward, and inconspicuously inform future concepts, discussions and actions (Taylor, Dalton).

Although a complex interweave and interplay of many elements, it is possible to identify key ideas and practices that develop this relational tapestry. For example, in post industrialized Euro-Western countries, notions of a capitalist economy, of democratic government and of human rights are key components of the present social imaginary. Science is elevated as a prevalent mode of knowing. Technological expertise, scientific achievements, images of progress, and a sense of entitlement to the resources and benefits of the whole world are operative in organizing and propelling social relations (Dalton). Rights to the goods, services and natural resources are enshrined in elaborate beliefs about the nature of reality, and the meaning and purpose of being human. These rights exist within a hierarchy of values that are the organizing principles of social relationships and to the world around us.

For much of the past twenty to thirty years, many people have addressed ecological issues by examining and critiquing the history, contours and limits of this Euro-western social imaginary. The work involved extensive ideological excavation by historians, deep ecologists, environmental philosophers, ecofeminists and those working on the ideals and theories embedded in the social imaginary that has led to vast ecological ruin in the name of progress (Eaton, 2005). It became clear, as illustrates Rosemary Radford Ruether, that the cultural-symbolic levels are the ideological superstructures that reflect and sanction the social, economic, political and religious orders. It was equally evident that there is a "logic of domination" endemic to the governing Euro-western social imaginary (Warren). Yet there are not straightforward connections between the theoretical and lived cultural aspects. Such work has been exceedingly important, enabling many to grapple with and critique the ideological and social constructions than have led to this difficult impasse.

However as much as it clears debris and exposes concealed influences, such uncovering does not lead to a new social imaginary. The processes of change from one social imaginary to another are not straightforward. The governing worldview needs to be seen as inadequate. Its basic presuppositions about, and orientation to *reality* or the *world* must be contentious or disputed. This gives space for marginal or alternative social imaginaries to gain ground.

Currently key aspects of the governing Euro-western social imaginary are in flux. New ecological insights and images are entering the fray. An ecological imaginary adequate to this era will require crucial insights from religion and science, among other elements. I propose three insights that are relevant for a bridge between the natural sciences and religious imagination. These insights could open up possibilities of new modes of awareness of the links between aesthetics, ethics and a viable future. These are: 1) nature as force; 2) symbolic consciousness and ecological imaginary, and; 3) religious challenges.

ONE: NATURE AS FORCE

Ecological literacy is a prerequisite for an ecological imaginary (Orr). Understanding as much as possible about the rhythms, limits and activities of specific ecosystems as well as planetary dynamics are of inestimable value. Yet we are always interpreting nature, and we can only see the natural world through a lens. Familiar lenses or "imaginaries" would be as a mechanism, an adversary, a system, or a living being. Each approach or lens results in distinct observations, value judgments, emotions and types of rapport.

The lens here is the idea of force. The image of nature as force is often related to immense and immediate power, such as earthquakes, tsunamis, volcanic eruptions or hurricanes. While these are forceful, there are other aspects of the natural world that are also types of force, yet are more subtle, ubiquitous, dynamic and persistent. These are creativity, ingenuity, inter-relatedness, and beauty. Each will be briefly discussed.

A) CREATIVITY

The natural world is fundamentally creative. At all biological levels, from bacteria to cells to ecosystems, the creative interactions and organization for life are staggering. Even non-living systems, such as the hydrologic cycle, are innovatively interwoven, from each living cell to planetary climate processes. With close attention to the meaning of "alive" as well as to the mechanisms that sustain life, the distinctions between living and non-living, or static and dynamic, blur. This realization led James Lovelock and Lynn Margulis to consider the whole Earth as a living process; the Gaia hypothesis. They observed that the processes of the natural world cannot be described as mechanical, predictable and derivative. Rather they are dynamic, creative and astoundingly interrelated. A few examples will indicate this.

The creativity of animals is astounding. Just animal habitats alone reveal immense creativity: under, on or above ground; in seas, forests, deserts, and cities; on or in other animals and plants, and alive, dying or dead. The originality and variety of mating rituals, reproduction, parental care, education of the young, leadership structures, and social codes are ingenious. Animal protection systems – diversions, noises, teeth, claws, armor, tusks, size, speed, and agility – are nothing less than innovative. The Cenozoic era has seen an expansion of life forms with the flourishing and diversity of birds, fish, flowers and mammals – not as discrete species – but within intricate webs of life systems impossible to replicate, let alone imagine. Such creativity is an underlying and persistent force of nature.

B) INGENUITY

A second force of nature could be called ingenuity. Again there are many ways to describe ingenuity in the natural world. Photosynthesis, for example, although a formidable and primordial Earth process, has had to be ingenious in transforming sunlight in various conditions: innumerable plant forms, reduced or excess oxygen, humid and arid environments, and with different and changing chemical concentrations. There are currently three distinct photosynthesis processes, with several others prior. One could label photosynthesis as adaptive, but to be adaptive requires experimentation, invention, even imagination, all of which define ingenuity.

A second and intriguing example of ingenuity is seen in how desert animals survive heat and water problems. The biological processes of all animal tissue require a relatively narrow temperature range. When this range is exceeded, the animal dies. Desert animals have evolved both behavioral and physiological mechanisms to solve the heat and water problems. In terms of heat, many birds, mammals and reptiles are active primarily at dawn and dusk. Some birds, such as the kingbird, continue activity throughout the day, but always perch in the shade. Desert mammals often have long appendages to dissipate body heat. The enormous ears of jackrabbits, with their many blood vessels, release heat in the shade. Their relatives in cooler regions have much shorter ears. A few desert animals, such as the round-tailed ground squirrel, enter a state of estivation when the days become too hot and the vegetation too dry. They sleep in the hottest part of the summer, and hibernate in winter to avoid the cold season. Desert Toads remain dormant deep in the ground until the summer rains fill ponds. Then they drink, eat, double their size, mate, and return underground. Kangaroo Rats live in underground dens that they seal off to block out heat and to recycle the moisture from their breath. They have specialized kidneys with extra microscopic tubules to extract most of the water from their urine and return it to the blood stream. Unlike others, these rats can manufacture water metabolically from the digestion of dry seeds. It is ingenious.

c) Interrelatedness

In the natural world it is impossible to find any life-form that is not bound up with others. Nothing is impermeable. Bacteria are everywhere, in the millions. Gene activity is dynamic (Margulis). Photosynthesis and water systems are involved with virtually all living organisms. The complexity and bio-interrelatedness of the hydrologic cycle is a feat of engineering paralleled by none. The interactions and exchanges among insects, flowering plants, and birds are astonishingly elaborate. The communication processes in a garden among minerals, enzymes, proteins, bacteria and photosynthesis, which is lived out in plants, insects and animals are unbelievable and impossible to describe.

Interrelatedness is seen in intricate communal relationship. Most animals exist in familial or social structures: pods, herds, packs, flocks, colonies, hives, prides, gaggles. Plants and insects also live in groups. Cellular interrelatedness is complex beyond human intelligibility. Overall, the biosphere is a vigorous network of relationships. Yet, even something "non-living" – such as a volcano – is related to seemingly extraneous phenomena. There are many types of volcanoes, and overall they function to release pressures from concentrated magma as well as plate tectonics. Also, and somewhat inexplicably, volcanic activity is involved in stabilizing Earth's atmospheric temperatures, which is a planetary process. More unusual to grasp is that some volcanoes tend to erupt when inorganic nutrients are eroded from chemical weathering. Although a trendy phrase, the image of a *web of life* is precisely the structure of the biosphere.

d) Beauty

Earth activities – the aurora borealis, rain, volcanic upheavals or earthquakes, thunder and/or lightening, rainbows, and desert, water or wind storms – all have shaped and magnified our sense of beauty. The presence and power of the oceans, of dawn and dusk, of deserts, mountains, prairies and forests are breath taking. Consciousness of space – horizons, vistas, caves, and pastures – has spawned endless representation. When trees, flowers and animals are added, the panoply of reality in which we are immersed overtakes us. The natural world inspires and is beautiful. If we pay attention, it is easy to be overwhelmed with magnificence, and marvel at the elegance, splendor and exquisite grandeur of the Earth. It evokes a composite interplay of emotions and ideation that form the notion of beauty. In a very real way, the natural world has shaped our sense of beauty and allowed us to "participate" in Earth dynamics.

As a species, we are deeply responsive to beauty. This is pertinent here due to the profound yet non-linear relationships between aesthetics and ethics. Much attention has been paid to developing ethics from reason and jurisprudence. It is more difficult to develop ethics from aesthetics, but not less potent (Bergmann). Humans are "wired" to experience beauty. Such experiences arouse emotions and evoke intuitions, more so than engaging rationality. In the language of religious experiences, we speak of wonder and awe. Often the response is reverence. A renewed attention to aesthetics and ethics, within a framework of the beauty of the natural world is timely. Some are doing so, using the term evolutionary aesthetics (Voland and Grammer).

IMPLICATIONS

These descriptions of nature, interpreted as force, are within the aforementioned blend of science and humanities. Such interpretations open up horizons of meaning and new possibilities that reductionist or mechanistic approaches fail to do. Such views are not less rational; they are simply more than rational. With such a wide lens, a shift of comprehension occurs because a large range of human responsiveness is included. This could be understood as a move from critical realism to naïve realism, and even to aesthetic realism (Siegel). To gaze upon the natural world as such transforms and enlarges what is seen, informing our ecological imaginary.

It is evident that the Earth inspires the human psyche and imagination, and has for millennia. The beauty of the Earth is a formidable force. It is also true that showing images of natural beauty is a familiar tactic of contemporary eco-spiritualities and eco tourism. But to present "nature" as picturesque scenery confines our appreciation of the Earth as alive, creative and ingenious in three ways. First, the natural world is seen as static and elsewhere, a place we visit but do not inhabit. Second, and more subtle, is that such images of the natural world, and by extension the natural world itself, become stimuli for our experiences, or a playground for leisure. This utilitarian gaze blinds us to seeing the inherent integrity of the natural world. And third, even when associated with the phrase "the Earth is our home", we miss the deeper fact that we belong to, are emergent from and a living part of the Earth, its processes and forces.

To take seriously that we are of the Earth or a living dimension of the Earth is an immense challenge to the customary social imaginary. It feels awkward and irrelevant, even if indisputable. Yet, we need to genuinely consider the images that humans are living matter (Vernadsky), walking talking minerals[2], or the Earth walking. Others have described humanity as the self-consciousness element of Earth's crust, or the Earth reflecting back on itself.[3] Then we begin to see ourselves as more than living among or succumbing to the forces of nature. We are one of the forces of nature. The point is to accentuate the depth of continuity between the Earth processes and ourselves. This does not override differentiations, or ignore the innumerable distinctions between nature and culture, the social constructions of nature, or that our lives are replete with mediated experiences. However to presume sharp demarcations between humans and "nature" is the norm. Herein lies one of the obstacles embedded within the current social imaginary and operative religious imagination that hampers the advancement of an adequate ecological imaginary.

We need to recognize that we live on a thin layer of culture over a vast expanse of nature. Increasingly it is recognized that we know very little of the deep realities of the Earth, and its 4.4 billion year geo-genesis. To persistently speak of humans and "the environment" is ridiculous in the face of planetary dynamics, evolutionary processes, and emergent complexities. But there is more. Not only is the Earth our home, it is our source. Specifically, the Earth has played a crucial role in the formation of human consciousness, and understanding this aspect is the second and necessary insight for of an ecological imaginary.

Two: Symbolic Consciousness and Ecological Imaginary

The Earth from which *homo sapiens sapiens* emerged and developed, the Cenozoic era, is nothing less than imagination gone wild. The depth of rapport between humans and the Earth would have been astonishing, and frequently overwhelming. It would have evoked, by necessity, representation (Dixon, Berry). The capacity to construct a systematic representation of the world would require a symbolic consciousness, which is the focus of this section.

Within the evolution and development of the hominid species emerged the capacity to navigate the world symbolically.[4] Anthropologist Terrence Deacon described the ways in which the human brain evolved so as to enable us to engage with each other and the natural world through symbols. This capacity for symbolic interaction is what Deacon calls a "shared virtual reality"[5] that is, a web of symbolic communications by which we indicate and experience parts of reality in indirect yet shared ways.

Little is known, and less understood, about the evolution of this symbolic consciousness. Communication, signs, representations and imagery are all foundational to symbolic consciousness and language development. The use of tools requires the capacity to imagine, and indicates a nascent form of symbolic consciousness. Although there are traces of tool use for over two million years, it is only educated guesses that connect tools with communication systems, technique capacity, brain-mind activities and evolutionary processes. Still, when a rock becomes a tool, it becomes more than it is. There is a surplus of meaning; otherwise the rock is just a rock. In symbolic processes, something becomes other than, or greater than it is. Reality becomes layered with meaning, and is then experienced within this enlarged meaning.

The formation of a consciousness that could function symbolically and sustain the capacity to manoeuver and co-ordinate images, thoughts, emotions, intuitions and insights was acquired over millennia. This symbolic, metaphoric and imaginative mode of being is the *modus operandi* of humans. A symbolic consciousness is the way humans process and navigate the world.[6] It is not through or with symbols or images that we think and comprehend. It is within symbols (Dixon).

Further, we inter-connect symbols to make a systematic representation of the world, which provides cohesion, orientation and capacity to navigate the world. Humans are incapable of existing outside of symbolic renderings of the world. However symbolic power and energy are undecipherable outside of the context, and are not readily translatable or transferable. To be meaningful, symbols must be invested with emotion and cognition, and they vary in complexity and purpose. Although the dynamics of symbolic functioning can be dissected into aspects involving external realities of culture and context, and internal realities of emotions, cognition, ideation, and identity formation, this provides a superficial, even false, understanding. These facets are inter-related in ever-moving exchanges, within a sea of influences.

Experiences are transmuted into a system of images to cope with the complexity of life and sustain a genuinely human existence.[7] Within the move from consciousness to self-consciousness, further developments of symbolic psychic structures took place. The capacity to act with conscious purpose, and to become aware of that, engenders a self-consciousness wherein the self has a purpose, and becomes other than it was. Further, these symbolically linked activities are nestled within social narratives – systematic symbolic representations or social imaginaries – of the world.

This slow emergence of human capacities is at the base of all human imagination, creativity and potential (Dixon, Deacon, Van Huesstyen). Dynamic and evolutionary potencies of consciousness were actively shaping the contours of the imagination, the symbolic structures of the self, and the primary mode of being of humans: the symbolic species. Symbolic vocabulary, techniques, imagery and depictions have changed, but the various mechanisms of symbolic consciousness, including symbols, gestures, signs, metaphors, rituals, imagination, abstractions and representations remain the navigation apparatus of *homo sapiens sapiens.*

EARTH AND SYMBOLIC CONSCIOUSNESS

Earth symbolization is considered to be the earliest systematic representations of the world. Earth activities still impress upon human consciousness, often in powerful ways, evoking intense affect – terror, joy, awe, inspiration, sadness, calm, love – which require mediation and representation. Historically, humans blended their experiences of the natural world with expressions of inner dynamics. For example, the transitions of dawn and dusk, sunrise and sunset, or seasons are frequently the chosen metaphors for personal or social transformations. Conversely, Earth symbolism reveals that humans insert a new process – the metaphoric or symbolic act – into the structural energies of the natural world (Dixon).

Some argue that potent experiences of the natural world are a blend of material, mythic, and psychic facets. Humans are not only "responding" to these realities or simply projecting emotions and images onto them. Nor are the symbolic expressions about something beyond to which the symbol refers. These are dynamics experienced within ourselves in rapport with the dynamics of the places and spaces. For example, experiences of caves or forests are described in terms of intimacy, intensity, envelopment or interiority. Again the stress is on the continuity between humans and the natural world.

The phrase "the immensity of the forest", is explored by Gaston Bachelard is his eloquent book *The Poetics of Space*.[8] Bachelard understood that the immensity felt in the forest and described as "of the forest", is an immensity experienced within our self-consciousness. It is an *intimate immensity*, as he calls it, attached to an expansion of being or a consciousness of enlargements. When encountered as such, the forest becomes immediately sacred by virtue of its otherness – which we perceive within ourselves. We describe these experiences as something mysterious or eternal, of losing oneself and going deeper into a limitless world. Bachelard used the term the *material imagination*.

What is significant here is that Bachelard sought to explain the affective, rather than intellectual/cognitive, dimension of material experience and imagination. Firstly, humans transform material by valorizing it:

It is not *knowledge* of the real which makes us passionately love it. It is rather *feeling* which is the fundamental value. One starts by loving nature without knowing it, by seeing it well, while actualizing in things a love which is grounded elsewhere. Then, one seeks in it detail because one loves it on the whole, without knowing why.[9]

The emphasis on the significance of these sentiments dovetails with aspects of the work of American pragmatist, Charles Pierce, as developed by Eugene Halton. In 1902 Peirce wrote about three developments of the mind: the rational, the progressive and the instinctual mind. The rational is the most recent in evolutionary development, hence the most immature. The conclusion is that the instinctive impulses, sentiments, dreaming, imagination, and memory – the community of passions – are the more mature. The rational mind requires this community of passions for optimal functioning.[10] Analysis is not enough. As Rabbi Heschel says, "What we cannot comprehend by analysis, we become aware of in awe."

Implications

Symbolic consciousness, the intimate immensities, and these more mature parts of human evolutionary development have been the foundation of what we now call religious imagination and sensibilities. Religions and complex social imaginaries are symbolic representations of the world. These insights are powerful and relevant to anyone trying to develop an ecological imaginary, and specifically to those in the field of religion and ecology. They are pertinent to ecological ethics, as well as to grappling with the complexities of religion. Yet, oddly, few religious scholars and even less theologians consider symbolic consciousness to be central to an understanding of, or relevant theories about, religion. Furthermore, even fewer think through the implications and layers of meaning of the basic fact that humans, as a symbolic species, are emergent from Earth processes. The hyper-rational, analytic modes of knowing inhibit both science and religion from attending to and validating the realm of intimate immensities, imagination and profound intuitions of humans, not as separate from but rather as immersed within Earth realities. Yet to understand nature as a force of creativity, ingenuity, inter-relatedness and beauty coupled with an evolutionary understanding of human emergence and symbolic consciousness could be inspirational to the field of religion and ecology, and to the realm of religious imagination. The third section addresses some of the religious challenges.

THREE: RELIGIOUS CHALLENGES

Religions are vast in myriad ways: chronologically, culturally, and ideologically. They are endlessly diverse, as well as having varied cultural impacts. Each religion is full of insights and bias, of constructive and destructive legacies, of corruption and liberation, of conserving and utopia impulses. The sheer historical influence on cultures indicates that religions can be a decisive dimension of human societies. Religions are multifaceted composites, and to understand them requires the analyses of several disciplines. From the viewpoint of social imaginaries and symbolic consciousness, religions represent the most complex of both.

The field of religion and ecology is now well established, and with extensive conversations and publications. Extraordinary efforts have created this field for over two decades. Of particular interest is *the Forum on Religion and Ecology*, now the largest international multi-religious and multidisciplinary project of its kind. With conferences, publications, and a detailed website, it is engaged in exploring religious worldviews, texts, ethics and projects in order to broaden the understanding of the complex nature of religious responses to current ecological concerns. A publication series, *Religions of the World and Ecology*, is ten volumes on specific religious traditions of the world and their ecological implications. This project involved over 800 scholars, religious leaders, and environmental specialists around the world.[11] These efforts, as well as others, have launched an intense quest to involve religions on ecological concerns.

There are countless initiatives with respect to specific traditions that retrieve relevant texts or teachings, reinterpret existing themes, and reconstruct past insights with present knowledge. Exceptional work is being done identifying symbolic, scriptural and ethical dimensions. The focus has been primarily on religions as distinct social movements and communities, with the objective of mobilizing them to play a role in ecological sustainability. In this view religions are potent yet discrete social realities with a plurality of beliefs. Individually and together they have considerable social, economic and political influence. Thus this array of work is invaluable.

However, it is not novel to suggest that Eurowestern cultures are impoverished in the face of this level of social and ecological problems. Or further, that these problems have their roots within the very religions, worldviews, or social imaginaries of these cultures. The connection between religion and the contemporary crises – while not direct – must be substantial.

There is a great need to examine the social imaginaries embedded within and out of which we consider religion. It is urgent we assess the reality maps and assumptions embedded within religious claims about reality. For example, it has been widely recognized that Euro-western worldviews are filled with dualistic thinking: matter is understood as in opposition to spirit, thought to emotion, culture to nature, humans to other animals, humans to nature, etc. These habits of mind, or social imaginary, have affected how we think about the world, but they do not represent reality. More so they blind us to seeing our interrelatedness, our dependence, or that matter and spirit are intimately interwoven. The strong anthropocentrism prevent the insights of our radical connections with the natural world.

It is also imprudent to assume that religions can adequately respond to this level of social-ecological problems in their current forms. These religions did not develop from either an overt ecological consciousness or crisis situation. The key doctrines solidified in isolation, and are ill equipped for multidisciplinary or multi-religious exchange. Some religions, and in particular Christianity, ignore or use outdated science. Therefore, if religions are part of the problem, then the religious challenges are substantial. From a larger horizon still, we must recognize that most religions that ever were are no longer. Countless specific religions have emerged, flourished and become extinct. Current traditions will also change.

The preoccupation here is about the nature of religion, rather than any particular tradition, or methods of retrieval or reinterpretation. Even the word *religion is* tricky. Although it is common to name specific world religions, it is not an accurate representation. Most religions have developed from, or are amalgamations of, other religious traditions. Religion and culture are mutually embedded to the point that distinctions are difficult.

Religions are fluid, and are often in transition. It is evident today that religions are in a large transition, both in their self-understanding, and within an epistemologically postmodern, global, multi-religious context. Rabbi Schachter states:

Many religious structures have become ossified remnants of another time. All traditional systems – Moses, Jesus, Mohammed, and Buddha – were embedded in the social and economic systems in which they arose. Their reality maps are obsolete.[12]

In this vein, the demands of a global ecological era require spirituality not religion, as suggests the Dalai Lama.[13] Some call for wisdom and ethics rather than dogma, as does theologian Hans Küng. Others, such as Ewert Cousins, claim that we are entering a second axial age – a new phase of religious consciousness – in which original insights and energies are possible.[14] In the face of the ecological crisis, Thomas Berry suggests that the era of religion, as we know it, is over. He believes that religions cannot respond to this magnitude of crisis in their current form. But also, we cannot respond without them. Thus it seems that religions, and the meaning of religion, are in transition.[15]

Of the many potential approaches to understanding religion, and religious responses to the ecological crisis, I am privileging one that integrates religion into human symbolic processes. The premise here is that while religions are important players with cultural clout, "religion" is a psychic-symbolic mode of reasoning. Religion is an archetypical, primal and evolutionary process of symbolic consciousness and reasoning. The emphasis here is on religion as a mode of symbolic engagement, emerging with the earliest forms human consciousness. What are now termed "religions" are specific yet complex symbolic processes of consciousness that have been profoundly shaped by, and even rooted in, the natural world.

From this angle, religions are seen as part of the evolutionary development of humans as a symbolic species; an emergent phenomenon within human consciousness and a later cultural formation. Such an approach affirms that religions, and what they represent in terms of consciousness, are more, rather than less, inherent to humans as a species. In addition, religions need to be seen as a very recent development in human history. Thus this view focuses more on the nature of religious consciousness and imagination and less on specific regions or even "world religions". It is about the phenomenon and nature of religion, on how the religious imagination operates, and on how to harness it. The present optic is that religions, par excellence, are symbolic and systematic representations of the world, and have the imaginative capacity to deeply shape and orient worldviews – social imaginaries. Here is a place of strategic intervention for religion.

What I am suggesting is that there is so much more to the reality of religion that could be explored in depth. The approach taken here is that religions, meaning a form of complex social imaginaries, are understood as the navigation tool of humans. When brought together with the profound work of the evolutionary Earth sciences, then the potential contributions of religions to this era are strong. In order to do this, however, we need to get real about religion, phenomenologically. Many operate with a truncated theory of religion. Religions are much more than a set of beliefs, cultural behaviours, texts and traditions. In one sense, those reflecting on or adhering to religion need to delve into the realms of religious consciousness, depth awareness and religious imagination. As Albert Einstein claimed, paraphrased here "problems cannot be solved at the level of consciousness in which they were created. We shall require a substantially new manner of thinking if human kind is to survive"[16] Religions, in a renewed form, could play a significant role here. One such way would be to draw on the deep traditions of spiritual awakening.

We need a spiritual vision that teaches us how to be present to the Earth, on Earth's terms. Spiritualities come from the realm of insights rather than data. Spiritualities are teachers of consciousness.[17] Spirituality is like breathing, as intimate and as vital as breath. It is about desire, a zest for life, and the ability to feel awe and wonder. Spirituality is the capacity to experience reverence in the face of the immensity and elegance of existence. Developing a spiritual consciousness is often described as moving from death to life, from sleep to consciousness, from illusion to enlightenment, from confinement to liberation, or from confusion to clarity. A spiritual vision adequate for our ecological era requires an awakening to the Earth. For this to occur we need the best of Earth sciences.

Authentic respect for the natural world informs a depth of vision that leads to a most profound religious response. If we contemplate the elegance of the Earth, and the fact that we emerged from and are animated by these great processes, we are inspired and energized. Such reflection informs and sustains a vision – a place from which to think and act (Eaton, 2007). Such awareness leads to a profound spiritual and ethical awakening, and insightful political actions. To see and know the Earth as such requires a new way of perceiving. The brief exploration of nature as force reveals that there are new images to be explored and nurtured. To understand, even minimally, the immense and elaborate planetary climate systems is stunning and breath-taking. To contemplate the Earth – from the microbiotic and genetic levels to the dinosaurs, the processes and life-forms – is to enter a fantasy beyond human imagination. If we attend, even briefly, to the dynamics of water, the inventiveness of birds, the ingenuity of insect communication, and the emotions of mammals, how is it possible not to be overwhelmed by the creativity, diversity, power, and beauty? Religions need to be about awakening to these deeper dimensions of reality, and they could have a crucial and constructive role to play in our era.

Furthermore, we cannot leave the public debates about religion and the ecological crisis in the hands of a right wing religious agenda, reductionist science, or impoverished cultural worldviews. And, as evidenced daily, not all religion is constructive. Superficial notions of religion or the reiteration of religious dogma will not suffice. Protectionist and triumphalist stances prevent common efforts. Religions need to return to their roots, within religious imagination, symbolic consciousness, and really into the very dynamics of Earth processes.

Conclusion

The suggestion of this chapter is that in the development of an ecological imaginary, we need a bridge between the natural sciences and religious imagination that rests upon recent insights about the evolution of symbolic consciousness. The assumption is that such a bridge may contribute to a nascent and ecological counter-imaginary; counter to the governing and unsustainable one. In this blend of insights of science and religion, one can see flexible modes of thinking coupling with new images from both disciplines. More work needs to be done. Further reflection on the relationships among Earth sciences, evolution, symbolic consciousness and religious imagination is also essential. And it is not evident how these topics can contribute to a practical agenda. Yet there are undeniable relationships between aesthetics and ethics, and between a social imaginary, an ethical imagination and practical action.

Regardless, the future requires the best of religions. Religious offer a language for a profound sense of wonder and awe in response to the "intimate immensities" of existence. Wonder is an authentic response to the elegant universe of which we are citizens, and is a decisive part of the intelligence of the human animal who recently emerged from the stunningly "numinous creativity" of Earth. Wonder is also the most intimate heart of religious experience. Wonder can galvanize human energy, imagination, wisdom, insight and the best of religions. To learn of Earth dynamics – of creativity, ingenuity, complex entanglement, beauty – educates the ethical imagination, affirms religious sensibilities and teaches the ways of Earth. That is a viable contribution to an ecological imaginary for our time.

Notes

1. The term *ecological imaginary* is borrowed and restyled from Charles Taylor's social imaginary, although others use it in comparable ways. See also Castoriadis.
2. Margulis and Sagan, 49.
3. Berry, 198
4. This understanding of symbolic consciousness comes from several sources: Deacon, Dixon, van Huyssteen, Lewis Williams, Greenspan and Shanker, and Pfeiffer.
5. Deacon, 23.
6. In depth research into the development of symbolic consciousness, the affective dimensions, and the complex inter-relations among symbol, language, emotion and thought processes is evident in Greenspan and Shanker.
7. Dixon, 49.
8. This stellar book describes in depth how humans interact with spaces via the imagination, symbolic consciousness and interiority.
9. Bachelard, 155, quoted in Kaplan, 4.
10. Halton, 45-46.
11. The astounding and exponential growth in work in religion and ecology testifies to the necessity and creativity in the field. One significant effort from Mary Evelyn Tucker and John Grim gives a good indication of the breadth and depth, conferences, publications, and activist and academic initiatives of these efforts: see The Yale Forum on Religion and Ecology, <http://www.fore.research.yale.edu>.
12. Barasch.
13. Dalai Lama.
14. Küng, (2002), (1998), Cousins, 209-219.
15. Berry, 87.
16. There are many variations of this quote.
17. For an expanded version of these ideas see Eaton (2008), 1-4.

References

Aerts, D., Apostel, L., DeMoor, B., Hellemans, S., Maex, E., vanBelle, H., et al. (2007), *World views: From fragmentation to integration*, Internet ed. Brussels: VUB Press. <http://www.vub.ac.be/CLEA/pub/books/worldviews.pdf>, 8 January 2009.

Barasch, Marc Ian (2000), "Two for the Road: Religion's Path Ahead," *State of the World Forum 2000*. <http://www.simulconference.com/clients/sowf/dispatches/dispatch23.html>, 8 May 2009.

Bekoff, Marc (2007), *The Emotional Lives of Animals: A Leading Scientist Explores Animal Joy, Sorrow, and Empathy – and Why They Matter*, Novato California: New World Library.

Benyus, Janine (2002), *Biomimicry: Innovation Inspired by Nature*, New York: Harper Perennial.

Bergmann, Sigurd (2011), "Aware of the Spirit: In the lens of a Trinitarian aesth/ethics of lived space", in: Bergmann, Sigurd and Eaton, Heather (eds.), *Ecological Awareness: Exploring Religion, Ethics and Aesthetics*, (Studies in Religion and the Environment 3), Berlin/Münster /Zürich/Wien/London: LIT, 23-40.

Berry, Thomas (1988), *Dream of The Earth*, San Francisco: Sierra Club Books.

Castoriadis, Cornelius (1998), *The Imaginary Institution of Society*, translated by Kathleen Blamey, Cambridge Mass.: MIT Press, (originally published in French in 1975).

Clark, John (2004), "A Social Ecology. 07. An Ecological Imaginary", <http://raforum.info/spip.php?article1050\&lang=fr>, 10 January 2009.

Cousins, Ewart (1999), "The Convergence of Cultures and Religions in Light of the Evolution of Consciousness," *Zygon, Journal of Religion and Science* 34, 2, 209-219.

Dalai Lama, His Holiness (1999), *Ethics for the New Millennium*, New York: Riverhead.

Dalton, Anne Marie (2009), "Communion of Subjects: Changing the Context of Questions About Transgenic Animals", *Worldviews: Global Religions, Culture and Ecology* 13, 1-11.

Deacon, Terrence (1998), *The Symbolic Species: The Co-evolution of Language and the Brain*, New York: W. W. Norton.

Dixon, John (1996), *Images of Truth: Religion and the Art of Seeing*, Atlanta: Scholars Press.

Eaton, Heather (2008), "Responding to Climate Change: Reflections on Scientific Realities, Spiritual Imperatives", *The Ecumenist: A journal of theology, culture and society* 45, 2 Spring, 1-4.

— (2007), "The Revolution of Evolution," *Worldviews: Environment, Culture, Religion* 11, 1, 6-31.

— (2005), *Introducing Ecofeminist Theologies*, London: T & T Clark.

Gelbspan, Ross (1998), *The Heat is On The Climate Crisis, The Cover-up, The Prescription*, New York: Basic Books.

Goodenough, Ursula (2000), *The Sacred Depths of Nature*, USA: Oxford University Press.

Goudzwaard, Bob et al. (2007), *Hope in Troubled Times: A New Vision for Confronting Global Crises*, Grand Rapids: Baker Academics.

Greenspan, Stanley and Shanker, Stuart (2004), *The First Idea: How Symbols, Language, and Intelligence Evolved from Our Primate Ancestors to Modern Humans*, Cambridge Mass.: Da Capo Press.

Halton, Eugene (2007), "Eden Inverted: On the Wild Self and the Contraction of Consciousness," *The Trumpeter* 23, 3, 45-77.

Harding, Stephan (2006), *Animate Earth: Science, Intuition and Gaia*, White River Junction, Vermont: Chelsea Green Publishing.

Haught, John (2003), *Deeper than Darwin: The Prospect for Religion in the Age of Evolution*, Boulder: Westview Press.

Havenaar, Johan et al. (2002), *Toxic Turmoil: Psychological and Societal Consequences of Ecological Disasters,* New York: Springer.

Hawken, Paul (2007), *Blessed Unrest: How the Largest Social Movement in History is Restoring Grace, Justice and Beauty to the World*, New York: Viking.
Jantsch, Eric (1980), *The Self-Organizing Universe*, Oxford: Pergamon Press.
Jurgensmeyer, Mark (ed.) (2005), *Religion in a Global Civic Society*, Oxford: Oxford University Press.
Kaplan, Edward (1972), "Gaston Bachelard's Philosophy of Imagination: An Introduction",*Philosophy and Phenomenological Research* 33, 1, 1-24.
Kauffman, Stuart A. (2008), *Reinventing the Sacred: A New View of Science, Reason and Religion*, New York: Perseus.
Kaufman, Gordon (2004), *In the Beginning: Creativity*, Minneapolis: Fortress.
Kolbert, Elizabeth (2006), *Field Notes from a Catastrophe: Man, Nature and Climate Change*, New York: Bloomsbury.
Küng, Hans (2002), *Tracing the Way: Spiritual Dimensions of the World Religions*, New York: Continuum.
— (1998), *A Global Ethic for Global Politics and Economics*, Oxford: Oxford University Press.
Lewis-Williams, David (2002), *The Mind in the Cave: Consciousness and the Origins of Art*, New York: Thames and Hudson.
Lovelock, James (1982), *Gaia: A New Look at Life on Earth*, Oxford: Oxford University Press.
Margulis, Lynn and Sagan, Dorion (2007), *Dazzle Gradually: Reflections on the Nature of Nature*, White River Junction, Vermont: Chelsea Green Publishing.
Margulis, Lynn (1998), *The Symbiotic Planet: A New Look at Evolution,* New York: Basic Books.
Mayr, Ernst (2001), *What Evolution Is,* New York: Basic Books.
McKibben, Bill (1989), *The End of Nature*, New York: Random.
— (2004), *Enough: Staying Human in an Engineered Age*, New York: Holt Paperback.
Monbiot, George (2008), *Bring on the Apocalypse: Six Arguments For Global Justice*, Toronto: Anchor.
Orr, David (1992), *Ecological Literacy: Education and the Transition to a Postmodern World,* Albany: SUNY Press.
Pearson, Clive (2001), "On Being Public about Ecotheology", *Ecotheology* 6, 1, 42-59.
Pfeiffer, John (1982), *The Creative Explosion: An Inquiry into the Origins of Art and Religion*, New York: Harper & Row.
Prigogine, Ilya and Stengers, Isabelle (1984), *Order Out of Chaos: Man's Dialogue with Nature*, New York: Bantam.
Radford Ruether, Rosemary (1991), "Ecofeminism: Symbolic Connections Between the Oppression of Women and the Domination of Nature", (Loy H. Witherspoon Lecture in Religious Studies), Charlotte: University of North Carolina, 1-17, (reprinted in: C.J. Adams (ed.), *Ecofeminism and the Sacred,* New York: Continuum 1993).
Sahtouris Elisabeth (2000), *Earthdance: Living Systems in Evolution,* San José, CA: iUniverse Publication.
Siegel, Eli (1981), *An Explanation of Aesthetic Realism*, New York: Definition Press.
Taylor, Charles (2004), *Modern Social Imaginaries,* Durham: Duke University Press.
Teilhard de Chardin, Pierre (1964), *The Future of Man*, London: Collins.
— (1959), *The Phenomenon of Man*, London: Collins.
Tucker, Mary Evelyn (2003), *Worldly Wonder: Religions Enter their Ecological Phase*, Chicago: Open Court.

van Huyssteen, Wentzel (2004), *Alone in the World? Science and Theology on Human Uniqueness*, Grand Rapids, MN: Eerdmans.
Vernadsky, Vladamir (1997), *The Biosphere,* edited by Mark Mc Menamin, (trans. David Langmuir), New York: Springer, (first published in 1926).
Voland, Eckart and Grammer, Karl (eds.) (2003), *Evolutionary Aesthetics*, New York: Springer.
Warren, Karen (ed.) (1994), *Ecological Feminism*, New York: Routledge.
Weisman, Alan (2008), *The World Without Us,* New York: Picador.
Wilson, E.O. (1984), *Biophilia*, Cambridge Mass.: Harvard University Press.

Waterwash and the Zen Art of Pragmatism

Lillian Ball

Working to have a positive effect as an environmental artist and activist, I have thought long and hard about potential ways to make a difference and inspire community action. How can an appreciation of place engender public involvement? What kind of visual strategies reinforce the scientific and ethical values protecting natural spaces? The need for restoration and revitalization of areas challenged by stormwater issues is widespread on Long Island's rural North Fork, in fact in waterfront areas worldwide. This area still has a farming and fishing economy now being overtaken by tourism. The WATERWASH concept occurred to me full blown after a discussion with the senior Southold town ecological planner – the transformation of a neglected area into a contemplative public outreach space could inspire community commitment to solving non-point source pollution problems.

This brainchild was not easy to bring to life, however, especially with an artist as lead agent. It was a continuing process, taking over 2 years and much soul searching to complete. After local input, a town-owned boat ramp was selected on an Inlet feeding Long Island Sound, right off a major county road. It had a serious grading problem that allowed road runoff to scour ditches beside the boat ramp, flowing directly into the Inlet and washing out the Spartina aterniflora growing there. Phragmites Australis (an invasive in our area, though native to Europe) was overtaking the disturbed shoreline, further destroying biodiversity.

Many local scientists and stormwater experts were consulted on the WATERWASH concept and my National Fish and Wildlife Foundation grant proposal was met with solid response. Previous projects in other parts of the country using the ecological restoration approach to sustainable infrastructure had proven valid. Scientists from Cornell Cooperative Extension, the Natural Resources Conservation Service, and the Department of Environmental Conservation- Restoration, Stormwater, and Shellfish departments all contributed to developing the site plan. Though initially submitted as a town project, the grant was taken over by the Group for the East End which was integral to it's success.

The permitting procedure was also one that challenged my abilities, since the skill to negotiate bureaucracy is rarely found in an artist's toolbox. Final permission needed to be obtained from the town as well as state and federal permitting agencies. They all had reservations about liability, as well as not being entirely convinced about the effectiveness of green infrastructure. A zen approach was required. Seems to me that

1 WATERWASH Mattituck, Signage uses filmstrip visual concept to attract viewers to educational information, © *Lillian Ball 2007-2009*

artists are uniquely prepared to follow through in the face of adversity. It often makes them the right personality type for such ventures as well as contributing creative thinking outside the box. Without that kind of tenacity, it is amazing anything can be accomplished in the web of bureaucracy surrounding these efforts.

The area was graded and some of the resulting clean sand was used to restore the ditch beside the boat ramp and the scoured spot behind the swale. Great care was taken to engineer adequate uptake across the site with specific pavement percolation through the sand substrate and upper layer of local pea gravel. Both Spartina patens and Spartina alterniflora were planted there amongst the jute and hay netting and secured by substantial chinked bluestones. Swale planting was rushed into action in early July for native warm weather grasses like the Panicum virgatum and Schizazachyrium scoparium. For the bottom of the swale, Hibiscus moscheutos was used for color since it thrives in our freshwater wetlands along with contrasting Chelone glabra. Community interaction was crucial, both Group for the East End and Mattituck High School volunteers helped with the plantings as well as cutting the Phragmites. A post consumer recycled glass permeable pavement filters non point source pollution from the parking area down into the groundwater. In the US, our landfills are overflowing with saved but unused glass because new glass from China is cheaper. A final piece of the ecological puzzle has not been easy to implement. Water

2   WATERWASH Mattituck, Hibiscus moscheutus blooming in bioswale absorbs nitrogen + phosphorus in stormwater, © *Lillian Ball, 2007-2009*

quality testing is integral to gauging the success of the stormwater remediation on water quality. Future projects will have the monitoring costs included in the grant.

November 9th, 2009 the Opening Press event, attended by over 70 people, was a satisfying finale to the saga. There are currently several more WATERWASH projects in the works, one on the Southern part of the Bronx River in NYC. The actual investment in time, energy, and funding means future sites must be carefully chosen, considering human, social, and scientific challenges. The ethical values of public servants, community participants, and the artist as lead agent must converge in a miracle of timing. Urgent factors of climate change will also require more coastal resilience. These processes rarely come together without considerable effort, education, and long-term coordination. Therefore the final impacts cannot be assessed without considering cultural relationships or until ecological systems are truly embraced.

How can we possibly measure a place's value to the inhabitants inspired by it? What kind of environmental experience or philosophy encourages people to be moved by and motivated to preserve nature? When we watch school classes reading the WATERWASH® signs, or see a boat returning with happy fisherfolk, or catch kayakers lunching on the benches adapted from the visionary Aldo Leopold's plans, we can see the landscape in action. There between form and function, lies an op-

3 WATERWASH Mattirtuck, Kayakers enjoy lunch and the view before they use boat ramp, © Lillian Ball 2007-2009

portunity for artist and scientist alike to inspire the community in restoring natural resources.

Until one is committed, there is hesitancy, the chance to draw back, always ineffectiveness concerning all acts of initiative (and creation).

There is one elementary truth, the ignorance of which kills countless ideas and splendid plans: that the moment one definitely commits oneself, then providence moves too. All sorts of things occur to help one that would never otherwise have occurred.

A whole stream of events issues from the decision, raising in ones favor all manner of unforeseen incidents and meetings and material assistance which no person could have dreamed would have come his way.

Whatever you can do, or dream you can, begin it. Boldness has genius, power, and magic in it. Begin it now.

(J. W. Goethe)

CALL AND RESPONSE

DEEP AESTHETICS AND THE HEART OF THE WORLD

Beth Carruthers

> Already my gaze is on the hill, that sunlit one,
> up ahead on the path I've scarcely started.
> In the same way, what we couldn't grasp grasps us:
> blazingly visible, *there* in the distance –
>
> and changes us, even if we don't reach it,
> into what we, scarcely sensing it, already are;
> a gesture signals, answering our gesture ...
> But we feel only the opposing wind.

(R. M. Rilke,
A Walk, from *Uncollected Poems*)

INTRODUCTION

I am and have been for some years working with the idea of a Deep Aesthetics. Such an aesthetics would in the first place subvert the way we commonly think of the aesthetic, which is often reductive. It would also, as I think it, present aesthetic perception, aesthetic engagement, as a way to better, more ethically sound, human-world relations. While the discipline of Environmental Aesthetics to some extent addresses this, my interest is specifically in whether aesthetic engagement might help us arrive at a deep and necessary shift in our understanding of human, culture, and world. In this sense Deep Aesthetics would resonate with Deep Ecology. Deep Ecology asks us to consider the human as environed with other beings in a matrix of inter-relations, overturning the traditional hierarchy of human at the top of an evolutionary ladder; it asks us to make decisions of how to live and act in the world as responsible co-members of an ecosystem community, rather than as masters of an external mechanised nature. I think of deep aesthetic engagement as a profound opening of perception, a way of "seeing anew", and also as a path to more caring and responsible human-world relations.

This might appear to be expecting a great deal from aesthetics, which is not the first thing that comes to mind when considering questions of how to improve troubled human-world relations. Rather, the aesthetic is commonly thought of as frivolous, expendable, indulgent, a set of rules for art appreciation, or a mere matter of personal preference; a sort of icing on the cultural cake – enjoyable, but in the face of real life, of social and environmental problems, not terribly relevant, and at times quite distracting from what really counts. For example, in commenting on cultural attitudes toward beauty in his paper *Beauty and the Contemporary Sublime*, art critic Jeremy Gilbert-Rolfe remarks that

Beauty, in being frivolous, and in that trivial and irrelevant, is always subversive because it's always a distraction from the worthwhile, which lets us know it's worthwhile by not being beautiful.[1]

In this view, while beauty may contain a generally disregarded power to subvert, it is a power that removes us from what is normally considered worthwhile. Not only is the "worthwhile" not beautiful, beauty actually undermines our awareness of the worthwhile through distraction.

Some environmental philosophers seem to share this view of the aesthetic dimension as a kind of distraction. An example can found be in Holmes Rolston III's problematising of the relationship of "beauty to duty" in his essay *From Beauty to Duty*, where he repeatedly finds difficulty in the relationship between traditional aesthetic values and environmental well-being and decision-making.

In contrast, and in support of a role for the aesthetic in environmental ethics, Emily Brady, in her book *Aesthetics of the Natural Environment* points out that

Several philosophers have suggested . . . the idea that an aesthetically sensitive relationship to nature can engender a benevolent attitude towards it.[2]

In addition to questions as to the value and role of aesthetics in environmental thought, what might comprise such an "aesthetically sensitive" relationship is also a subject of debate, with some attention focused on whether or not one must have scientific knowledge in order to arrive at genuine aesthetic appreciation of the natural world.

My interest here does not lie in locating this essay within ongoing debates in the academic field of Environmental Aesthetics, so I will not include such ongoing conversations here. Rather, my interest is in exploring other thinking vis-à-vis the potential role of aesthetic engagement in bettering the human-world relationship. Hence, for the purposes of this essay, I have for the most part chosen to exclude the usual sources for environmental aesthetics: Arnold Berleant, Alan Carlson, and Emily Brady, among others. Neither do I include discussion of an "ethics of care", as explored by ecofeminist scholars. This is not because these are unhelpful ideas, but simply because I am exploring another route. I also wish to note that while I speak of relational, or inter-relational aspects of the aesthetic, these comments do not refer to Niccolas Bourriaud's *Relational Aesthetics*.

This enquiry argues for the aesthetic as a powerful engagement providing opportunities for reconfiguring troubled human/world relations. In pursuit of such an aesthetics I began trolling among disciplines, starting with the phenomenological streams arising from Merleau-Ponty and Heidegger, as well as with my own years of experience as art practitioner and curator. I explored the writings of scholars in Environmental Aesthetics, and those of phenomenologically influenced thinkers such as ecologist Neil Evernden and anthropologist Tim Ingold. Most recently, I have been delving into the ideas of psychologist James Hillman on the aesthetic and world soul. Overall, my interest is and has been in exploring the implications of combined perspectives, and so my approach transgresses traditional disciplinary boundaries.

Finally, being more interested in this instance in process than in conclusions, this essay offers perhaps more of the former than of the latter.

Longing and Belonging

Aesthetics is a way of being, a stance toward the world; an aesthetic experience requires a relationship between a seeking subject and a responsive world. But scenery is a stockpile of usable commodities.

(Neil Evernden,
The Natural Alien)

A number of things drew me into this search for a Deep Aesthetics. The first, and most compelling, was my conviction that we have in this culture been avoiding, or dismissing something vital in the human-world relationship – more, that we have essentially blinded ourselves to experiencing essential interconnections – and that what can open us to these vital aspects of relationship is a particular kind of experience available to us by way of aesthetic engagement.

I arrived at the term "Deep Aesthetics" in part by way of a comment made by Holmes Rolston III in concluding his essay *From Beauty to Duty*. He suggested that for aesthetics to be considered "an adequate foundation for an environmental ethics", it would depend on "how deep your aesthetics goes".[3]

The etymology of the term "aesthetic" is to perceive with the senses – sensory perception. It is this root, or radical, meaning to which I turn in my search for a Deep Aesthetics – a more adequate foundation, as I see it, for an aesthetics inherently engaged with world and other, and by way of this engagement, engendering not necessarily duty, but more ethical behaviours arising from love, belonging, and a resultant responsibility of relationship. Moreover, the aesthetic may be key to sudden transformations, perceptual shifts in our apprehension of self, world and other.

For many years I have been seeking ways that we might come to *desire* change within ourselves and our world so passionately that we will do everything we must in order to achieve it – passion greater than our fear of the unknown, greater than our desire for immediate gratification. Along the way I have become intrigued by the writings of James Hillman on the aesthetic and world soul. I am attracted by his forthright use of slippery terms such as beauty, love, heart, and soul – the more slippery they are, the more they challenge our controls and definitions. And I find it particularly intriguing that he does not seek to present ethics (in a formal sense) as a response to the suffering of the world. It is my own thinking that ethics as we have them could seem too inevitably a product of the kind of thinking and worldview that has nurtured a severely dysfunctional human-world relationship, and so they are largely incapable of getting us out. I offer the example of Val Plumwood's critique of a moral extensionism wherein moral standing may be granted to non-humans through an extension of existing human values, which are themselves predicated on dualist thought. Because of it being so predicated, such extensionism can only be problematic and inherently flawed. I suspect that any ethics arising from such an ontological basis would embody and reaffirm that ontological stance.

It is to *aisthesis* in its essential meaning as sensuous perception that James Hillman turns when he considers how best to remedy the malaise of human separation from world, or the troubled split between an individual soul and the *anima mundi*, or world soul. He describes the growing disruption he sees in individual psyches as the expression of a greater, culture-wide disruption and malaise. He explains that the individual soul, or psyche, is in fact not independent, but a part of the greater world soul, the *anima mundi*, and we completely deny and disregard this. We have ontologically, if not materially, split ourselves from the greater, environing world, denying that we are in essence part of both the natural world and the *anima mundi*. The result is that as the world, and world soul, suffers, we suffer. Continued focus on an independent individual psyche will do nothing to repair the real malaise, but will only serve to reinforce it.

Hillman believes that our Western ontology of separation of human from world, which, in the words of philosopher Monika Langer "effectively *uprooted* humans and rendered them homeless"[4] has resulted also in a state of narcissism, which he also describes as being a state of *anasithesis*, the opposite of *aisthesis*; a disconnection "between what is thought, said and written and what the senses see, the heart feels, and the world suffers".[5] He explains that in this state, as we go about our lives, gaze about us, we have trained ourselves to see only ourselves, our own interests reflected, projected. Erazim Kohak would agree. In his book *The Embers and the Stars*, he remarks to the effect that we are now so embedded within this troubling ontology and its artefacts – which include the basic structures of our sciences, lifestyles, philosophies, technologies, languages and even our thoughts – that everywhere we turn our attention it is affirmed and reaffirmed, like an ever-repeating song or story. This is the world we have come to know as ours, and it is so challenging to see or think otherwise, that, in the words of Langer, "even those whole heartedly committed to eliminating the dualism of this ontology and reversing the degradation to natural systems frequently perpetuate the dominant paradigm themselves."[6]

The systems we have put in place – systems of belief, social, political, language –

tell us stories each day about our special status. They sing sweet songs of entitlement – it's all just fine, it is appropriate for humans to use the world in any way we choose. We're in charge, it is our destiny, we are superior to world and other animals ... These systems are massive, with many branches and significant inertia, all of which push back against change. They know how to carry a tune and they play "our" song all day and all night.

They give us the everyday world we know so well – the world of endless lattes, iPhones, and strawberries in mid-winter, products which seem to magically materialize as we wave paper or plastic about. Yet at the same time our lived, bodied, sensuous experience of living and being in the world whispers the background story – the story of belonging and of the origins of things. That how we have configured our world of comfort and convenience contradicts our belonging in and to the world is clear, and places us in the uncomfortable position of needing to change, which we readily perceive as an undesirable request to relinquish a world of comfort. Yet at the same time it is the hidden world of belonging that sustains us. This is truly an untenable situation, and the increasing tension of it underlies our culture like an unstable foundation constructed on a flood plain. Rather than seek deep change, which might lead to entirely new ways of being in and with the world, we seek to fortify our position with technological developments, and nurture our belief in these, although these are rooted in our existing ways understanding the world and ourselves. We approach challenges with solutions that treat the world as a mechanism that we can manage, provided we discover the right processes and formulae. One example of this approach is geo-engineering.

Psychologist Piero Ferrucci, citing classic social psychology studies of creating group consensus, notes that a group will create consensus among themselves even in the case where their agreement contradicts what they know to be true. "In other words, the group decides how we see and interpret the world."[7] It is also the case that most people will hold to the familiar, rather than risk an unknown.

As we see only human culture, and see that culture as somehow outside a world, acting upon a world external to ourselves, we become self-referencing and self-absorbed. In this way we have made ourselves profoundly (and dangerously) alone, locked within the palace of our self-reflexive ontology and its artefacts. The question is – how to escape this labyrinth?

THE SMILE OF THE WORLD AND THE OPENING OF THE HEART

To live without beauty, because we are incapable of seeing it around us, and thus to think we live in a world in which it does not exist or is not possible, will lead to desperation. And if this criterion is forgotten, we will live in a world that makes no sense ... Moral indifference reigns, and all values are reduced to zero.[8]

... below the ecological crisis lies the deeper crisis of love, that our love has left the world.

That the world is loveless results directly from the repression of beauty, its beauty and our sensitivity to beauty. For love to return to the world, beauty must first return, else we love the world only as a moral duty.[9]

It seems much easier to call for ontological change and even consider what such change might be, than it is to actually arrive at change. And arrive we must, I believe, if we are to see long-term and significant betterment of human-world relations. Yet at the same time, to paraphrase Hillman from a recorded interview: "... I [often] wonder less how to shift the paradigm than I wonder how (we) ever got so far off base."

The question remains – how to change? This is how Hillman put the question: "What can stir our depths equal to the depths of ecological need? Duty, wonder, respect, guilt, and the fear of extinction are not enough." His response is "only love" will answer, will be enough; "a desire for the world that affords the vitality, the passionate interest on which all other efforts rest ... elow the ecological crisis lies the deeper crisis of love, that our love has left the world."[10] Simply put, for James Hillman the remedy for the separation of self and world – and ultimately the suffering of the world – is to reawaken the heart, and his prescription for doing so is clear. It is beauty that stirs and opens the heart.

Without getting into what can only be a lengthy discussion of just what beauty is or might be, I briefly offer some of Hillman's discussion: "suppose we were to imagine that beauty is permanently given, inherent to the world in its data, there on display always ... an inherent radiance ... a display that evokes an aesthetic response."[11] Drawing from the Greeks, he describes beauty manifested in the world as the smile of Aphrodite, which enhances any ordinary thing, causing it to shine forth, lighting up the world. I am reminded here of Heidegger saying that when objects (or beings) in the world are not perceived by us as either tools or "standing reserve", they can then "shine forth" for us in their own being. And this shining forth is almost always a surprise, because we are caught up in viewing the world in self-referential terms of utility and resource. If beauty indeed opens the heart, then it is to world and other that we are opened. Hillman speaks of *aisthesis* as "the *appearance* of the *anima mundi*".[12] In Heideggerian terms, we might say *aisthesis* is how the world soul, the *anima mundi*, presences for us.

Psychologist Piero Ferrucci describes the "shining forth" quality of beauty in the world, in our environment, as "the *numinous*: The force that sometimes emanates from nature and certain works of art and that leaves us in awe before the *mysterium tremendum et fascinans* (the awe-inspiring mesmerizing mystery)."[13] This is Hillman's smile of Aphrodite in the world. Ferrucci goes on to comment that "I felt as though lots of superfluous pieces had fallen off me: anticipation, cultural prejudices, past experiences ... Instantly I felt purified and taken to the essence."

Our cultural beliefs almost always shape our perceptions, or the usual path of aesthetic engagement. Accounts of aesthetic experience reflect a structure meant to shape our perceptual experience and engagement; a map of how to proceed that we are told is the whole of the territory. And this territory follows the boundaries of our beliefs and ideologies, defining the perceptual lay of the land as refined to fit particular kinds of cultural interest. Much is excluded and much that does not fit is denied. It is useful to think of this process as "backgrounding" and "foregrounding", terms used in psychology, in the study of learning, and in seeking to understand autism. Val Plumwood, in *Feminism and the Mastery of Nature*, also uses the term "backgrounding" to describe relationships of hidden, or denied, dependency. I use these terms here in both the context of a necessary process of learning and being in the world.

That we choose our engagement, however "automatically", and that we interpret what and how the world presents, is reminiscent of Heidegger's description of the clearing, where we encounter Being as beings – and interpret them. Perception requires that one notice, or attend to an object, or an other. For Heidegger, there is a "clearing", or opening, about human beings which allows them to perceive, to select out an other as a discrete being which *could* then presence, or shine forth in its own being for us, were we to permit this.[14] It is most often the case that we sense the other, and then fit this other into the closest match of a familiar shape, or location, on our pre-drawn map of the world. A bear is such, a tree, so. Yet a bear is surely encountered and perceived differently by a Nunavut hunter than by a resident of Shanghai, for example. That interpretations and engagements differ, at times radically, among cultures, might cause one to think of aesthetic perception as hopelessly subjective. At the same time, this evidence of differing perception shows promise for bettering human-world relations. Because cultural maps differ, perceptions of world and other differ. Changing the maps can then change perception. That maps and perceptions do change is clear. Adopting a mechanistic worldview was a significant shift for Western culture and it is easily seen, for example, that many First Nations people in Canada have adopted the maps, the worldview, of Western culture, while others have not.

In ancient maps of the world, where the edges of information thinned and fell away, it was often written: "here be dragons". This idea of going too far, of falling off the edge of the world, might be a good analogy here. To go somewhere so unfamiliar, so different from what we admit, holds both fear and wonder. Even an uncomfortable known may be preferable to an unknown. What might cause us to let go of the map, make us risk terror and help us encounter wonder?

In Daniel Conrad's 1999 film on aesthetics, *Seducing the Guard*, Canadian writer John Gray paraphrases Freud in telling us "All visions must pass a guard at the gate to the mind before you can see them."[15] We each of us have a guard at the gate of our mind, of our conscious awareness, and if something is unacceptable to this guard, if it does not meet the criteria, then the guard rejects it. Psychologists and mediators are also familiar with this "guard", which is known to them as "reinforcement bias", the automatic allowing of only that which fits our worldview and accepted norms.

Gray goes on to say that in order for something to get past the guard, the guard must be seduced or distracted. Artists do this in part by using familiar and acceptable forms to deliver subversive content. Gray, being a writer, uses the example of the form of a sonnet. To my mind, the fact that our artefacts enforce beliefs, ontology, a map of the world, means that our artefacts can also subvert these. The form can be as familiar as a building, a painting, a photograph, or a film. If art were not powerful in its action, dictators through history would not have bothered to control, vilify and outlaw art. Media theorist and scholar Marshall McLuhan claimed a role for art "to create the means of perception by creating counterenvironments that open the door of perception to people otherwise numbed in a non-perceiveable situation."[16] The power of art is significant, as is that of beauty – and this power comes about by way of aesthetic engagement.

Another aspect of the aesthetic, or aisthesis, that Hillman brings forward is surprise. Ferrucci also mentions surprise as a quality of beauty. "We never know", he tells us, "when beauty will appear." When we experience beauty, when it appears, we are "in a state of mindfulness that does not admit distraction or escape. We are here with our whole being. This is our *kairos*, as it was called in ancient Greece: the moment of opportunity, the timeless instant when revelation comes."[17] Beauty confronts us with spontaneity.

Another way to get the past the guard at the gate is to short-circuit the program, if you will. The guard can be overwhelmed, stopped in its tracks. What might have this salutary effect are those moments when we are caught and held by beauty, so that everything stops, when "we are here", as Ferrucci says, "with our whole being". Writer James Joyce referred to this as "aesthetic arrest".[18] Hillman describes the experience as a quick intake of breath, a gasp, as reflexive as a moan of pleasure or wincing in pain. He tells us "this quick intake of breath is also the very root of *aisthesis* in Greek, meaning "sense perception", and it goes back to Homeric meanings of "I perceive" and "I gasp, struggle, for breath" as well as "I breathe in".[19] In this sense then, the moment is a taking in of the world. He goes on to say that "This aesthetic reaction which precedes intellectual wonder inspires the given beyond itself, letting each thing reveal its particular aspiration."[20] Before judgement and cognitive framing, the world floods in, the *anima mundi* holds us within it. We look upon the face of the world and the world returns our gaze. It is at this moment that we can know without doubt that we are in the world, we belong in the world, we are held in the embrace of the world.

For moments that can seem long indeed we are brought out of our self-referential dream, and revealed to us is a world of other powers, agencies and beings with which we co-habit a world. Being drawn from our frame can be a vertiginous experience and we most usually head back to the ontologically familiar as quickly as possible. Can beauty hold us in this open state long enough to truly see differently, to make different choices about who we are and want to be in the world? Along with Hillman, I believe it can.

Although many speak of the fleeting nature of that moment of aesthetic arrest, could it be that this moment can be prolonged, or that we may be so changed through a moment of spontaneous apprehension and interconnection that we discover our understanding has shifted, the ontological cage unlocked? Philosopher Michael Zimmerman, drawing from *Being and Time*, describes Heidegger's clearing, or open, as where we encounter and interpret beings – beings are revealed and Being itself is "unconcealed" in the open. Beings acquire meaning through this encounter, traditionally with this meaning rooted in usefulness, in being resource in our world.[21]

Think now of the clearing, or open, as both a primary space of contact among beings, and a moment of choice in how we each perceive the other, opening possibilities for experiencing beings and the world itself as relationship rather than as resource. No matter how brief this moment, we may be changed by it.

... our inner growth is spontaneous ... hink of the memorable episodes in your life: A chance encounter, falling in love, the birth of an idea, a sudden moment of happiness, a creative inspiration. Almost all the decisive moments of our life come unexpectedly. We may prepare the ground, but the experiences themselves are not within our control. They are surprises.[22]

To approach this another way, I now draw from Merleau-Ponty's thinking, by way of Monika Langer: "For Merleau-Ponty, self and non-self, human and non-human intertwine in a mutual enfolding, *such that comprehension itself becomes a relation of embrace with the other*."[23] Resonating with his ideas of "Flesh", such a connecting, an intertwining of Being would hold within it the intimate interrelations and presencing of beings in the world and of the world itself. And once knowledge of this embrace is foregrounded in our awareness, I believe it can be clearly seen that we have a responsibility of relationship in the world that reaches well beyond the human.

Beauty seduces, beauty terrifies, beauty smiles upon us – and beauty opens us to the world, revealing. I have made some strong claims for beauty, but none so strong as does Hillman, who tells us that beauty is "not merely a cultural accessory, a philosophic category, a province of the arts, or even a prerogative of the human spirit. It has always remained indefinable because it bears sensate witness to what is fundamentally beyond human comprehension."[24] He may be saying here that beauty is the face of the divine. It may also be the case that he is saying beauty is the face of Being itself, as the smile of Aphrodite, the manifesting *kosmos*. *Kosmos*, according to Hillman, is "an aesthetic term, best translated into English as fitting order – appropriate, right arrangement".[25] This speaks to an implicit moral order in the world, one that is inextricably intertwined with beauty, and one which we can participate with, as we open ourselves to, or are opened by, beauty, and through beauty to the *anima mundi*.

Beauty, for Hillman, is both an epistemological necessity, as that which attracts us into life, as well as an ontological necessity, grounding the sensate particularity of the world. It is the face of things themselves. "What remains when all perishes is the face of things *as they are*. When there is nowhere to turn, turn back to the face before you, face the world."[26]

NOTES

[1] Gilbert-Rolfe, 47.
[2] Brady, 258.
[3] Rolston, 140.
[4] Langer, 117.
[5] Langer, 117.
[6] Langer, 117.
[7] Ferrucci, 49.
[8] Ferrucci, 186-187.
[9] Hillman (1998), 264.
[10] Hillman (1998), 264
[11] Hillman (1998), 267.
[12] Hillman, (1992), 113.
[13] Ferrucci, 60.
[14] Heidegger, *On the Essence and Concept of Physis in Aristotle's Physics B*.
[15] Gray, in *Seducing the Guard* (film) by D. Conrad (Moving Images Distribution, 1999). Freud, 193.
[16] McLuhan and Zingrone, 342.
[17] Ferrucci, 66.
[18] Joyce (1992) *Portrait of the Artist as a Young Man*.
[19] Hillman (1998), 271.
[20] Hillman (1992), 47.
[21] Zimmerman, 77-78.
[22] Ferrucci, 67.
[23] Langer, 115.
[24] Hillman (1998), 270.
[25] Hillman (1998), 268.
[26] Hillman (1992), 48-49.

REFERENCES

Brady, Emily (2003), *Aesthetics of the Natural Environment*, Tuscaloosa: University of Alabama Press.
Evernden, Neil (1993), *The Natural Alien*, 2nd ed. Toronto: University of Toronto Press.
Ferrucci, Piero (2009), *Beauty and the Soul: The extraordinary power of everyday beauty to heal your life*, New York: Penguin.
Gilbert-Rolfe, Jeremy (1998), "Beauty and the Contemporary Sublime", in: Bill Beckley and David Shapiro (eds.), *Uncontrollable Beauty: Toward a New Aesthetics*, New York: Allworth, 39-52.

Gray, John McLaughlin (1999), in: *Seducing the Guard* (film) by D. Conrad (Moving Images Distribution).
Freud, Sigmund, "The Interpretation of Dreams", in *The Basic Writings of Sigmund Freud*, trans. A. A. Brill, New York: Modern Library, Random House.
Heidegger, Martin (1939), "On the Essence and Concept of Physis in Aristotle's Physics B, I", in: Will McNeill (ed.), *Pathmarks*, Cambridge: Cambridge University Press 1998, 183-230.
Hillman, James (1998), "The Practice of Beauty", in: Bill Beckley and David Shapiro (eds.), *Uncontrollable Beauty: Toward a New Aesthetics*, New York: Allworth, 261-274.
— (1992), *The Thought of the Heart and the Soul of the World*, Putnam, Connecticut: Spring Publications.
Joyce, James (1992), *A Portrait of the Artist as a Young Man,* New York: Penguin Books.
Langer, Monika (1990), "Merleau-Ponty and Deep Ecology", in: Galen A. Johnson and Michael B. Smith (eds.), *Ontology and Alterity in Merleau-Ponty,* Evanston: Northwestern University Press, 115-129.
McLuhan, M. and Zingrone, F. (eds.) (1995), *Essential McLuhan*, Toronto: House of Anansi.
Rilke, Rainer Maria (1997), *Uncollected Poems*, trans. Edward Snow, New York: Farrar, Straus and Giroux.
Rolston III, Holmes (2002), "From Beauty to Duty", in: Arnold Berleant (ed.)., *Environment and the Arts: Perspectives on Environmental Aesthetics,* Aldershot, Hampshire, UK, and Burlington, VT: Ashgate, 127-141.
Zimmerman, Michael (2003), "Heidegger's Phenomenology and Contemporary Environmentalism", in: Charles S. Brown and Ted Toadvine (eds.), *Eco-Phenomenology: Back to the Earth Itself,* Albany: State University of New York Press, 73-101.

Landmarks of the Sacred in Times of Climate Change

Climate Justice, Icons, and Policy

Thomas Heyd

Introduction

In this paper I argue that the disruption as a result of climate change of meaningful, identity-giving, landmarks and landscapes, especially those considered sacred, should be addressed by policy, insofar as it calls upon climate justice. I also suggest that the appeal of iconic species, landmarks and artworks, may constitute an effective tool for generating action on climate change.

I begin by drawing attention to the threat posed by climate change to culturally significant landmarks and landscapes, some of which are considered sacred. As an example, I point out that for certain populations the loss of mountain glaciers poses a particularly striking case of landmarks under threat. I proceed by clarifying what is central to the idea of the sacred, and how the disturbance of the sacred in the landscape may constitute a problem from the perspective of climate justice. After this, I point to the potential inherent in iconic images, and in artworks appealing to such images, for facilitating a fuller grasp of the implications of climate change at the personal level. I conclude that the disturbance of culturally significant sites and icons, especially those perceived as sacred, should be considered in policy, both from the point of view of climate justice and from the point of view of communication of the reality of climate change.

Culturally significant landmarks and landscapes, and climate change

The disturbance and loss of emblematic landmarks and landscapes constitutes one of the important, and so far under-discussed, consequences brought on by climate change (also see Adger et al.). For instance, the rapidly increasing thaw of ice in the Arctic means not only that a millennial landscape is threatened but that livelihoods from hunting become more difficult for Inuit. This change may also be contributing to an increased rate in the loss of local, indigenous knowledge systems and ways of living, because traditional behavioural patterns become inapplicable, as new, non-traditional patterns of exploitation of the land and the sea (oil and gas drilling, ship transport routes, military installations) rapidly intrude, under the new environmental circumstances.

Furthermore, for many coastal communities around the world, increases in sea levels mean the loss of beaches, growing risks from storm surges, and losses for recreational and tourism activities. Environmental changes, due to climate change, are not only important because of their economic and practical consequences, though, but may also have importance at the level of cultural change issuing in challenges to community self-understanding, insofar as landscape features play important roles in the symbolic mapping of the world for the people affected.[1] So, in the course climate change, places traditionally valued for fishing or for growing crops (as in Bangladesh), constitutive of individual and community identities, may be lost, and, in the case of some Pacific island states, entire homelands foreseeably will disappear (Adger et al.). While lessened flows of rivers due to the retreat of mountain glaciers, moreover, suppose difficulties for riparian populations dependent on such resources for irrigation and drinking water, deglaciation, as we will see, also has repercussions for many people's self-understanding, due to the particular cultural significance of glaciers.

The anthropologist Ben Orlove points out that glaciers play a special role in people's lives due to two factors: first, they tend to be perceptually salient, and second, they are subject to considerable cultural framing (Orlove, Orlove et al.). Concern about glacial recession is widespread among people whose culture has developed in conjunction with glaciers, such that, in certain parts of the world, human interaction with glaciers is so significant that glaciers are considered sentient in some way. Notably, some of the people living in the Alto Adige region, Italy (Jurt), some of those in the vicinity of Mt Shasta in the USA (Orlove et al.), as well as the Tlingit and the Yukon First Nations studied by Julie Cruikshank (Cruikshank 2001, 2005), seem to feel that they share responsibility for changes in the states of glaciers, since it is believed that they are responsive to human behaviour.

In the South American Andes mountain range, moreover, the peaks and their spirits (*apus*) are treated as sacred, and in many places the loss of glaciers on summits and slopes has led to consternation among local populations (Fraser, Orlove et al.). For instance, on Mount Cotacachi, Ecuador, famed for its white splendour, the loss of its permanent snows means an important disruption of people's meaningful landscape since, according to the narratives of the local population, its peak is attributed divine standing (Rhoades 2006a, 2008). Similarly, the pilgrimage up the Sinakara Valley to celebrate the Qoyllur Rit'i Festival near Ausangate Mountain used to include the extraction of chunks of glacier ice, which were taken to respective villages as part of the ritual journey (Sallnow). In view of the shrinking glacier the practice of collecting ice has had to be abandoned since 2000 (Bolin 2001, 2009).

Insofar as climate change may occasion such upsets among landmarks perceived as sacred, this invites further clarification of what is meant by the sacred, how we are to understand the concern for the disturbance of sacred landmarks through climate change, and the consequences for policy to be derived from this situation.

THE SACRED AND DISRUPTIONS OF THE LANDSCAPE: TAKING RESPONSIBILITY

Even if some institutions, such as the UNESCO, have begun to pay attention to the effects of climate change on culturally significant landmarks,[2] the significance of threats to the *sacred* in the landscape has not been much considered as such and remains much under-discussed in contemporary climate change policy. This may be an effect of the process of rationalisation of society which, according to Jürgen Habermas (following Weber), effectively eliminates religion from our purview (cp. Habermas). Nonetheless, it may be argued that, in practice, the sacred retains a kind of intrusively determining power for human actions, such that other spheres of action have to take note once something is so identified. This is evident, for example, from the fact that even in recent years significant communal strife has developed in some countries (such as in India regarding the respective locations of Hindu temples and Muslim mosques) on the grounds of religious difference.[3]

In the light of the global, all-encompassing consequences of climate change, its effect on the sacred in the landscape should be cause for reflection. In the following I seek to clarify what the sacred is, how it is disturbed in the landscape, and what taking responsibility regarding these processes implies.

THE SACRED AND THE SACRED IN THE LANDSCAPE

The sacred is a concept that is subject to a great variety of meanings, depending on the cultural tradition with which it is associated and the methodological angle from which it is approached. There are at least two overall approaches for understanding this concept, which, respectively have been labelled substantial and situational (Chidester and Linenthal). From the substantial point of view, the sacred is really a powerful manifestation of the "essential" character of reality that can be corroborated through personal experience and phenomenological observation. In contrast, from the situational perspective, the sacred is an "empty signifier" located "at the nexus of human practices and social projects",[4] often is contested, and is recognised according to its effects in the behaviour of participants of ritualised, religious action (Smith). From this latter, situational and "constructionist", perspective, nothing is inherently sacred (Chidester and Linenthal).

So, while for Émile Durkheim the sacred is a means to bring about and maintain social cohesiveness (Durkheim), Mircea Eliade focused on the role of the sacred in the experiential life of individuals (Eliade), taking as fundamental Rudolf Otto's notion of the holy as the experience of "the wholly other" (*das ganz Andere*).[5] Here I approach the sacred from this latter perspective, since there is reason to believe that his account succeeds in portraying the *phenomenological* reality of the sacred, that is, how the sacred is experienced by those who perceive reality in its terms.

For Eliade the sacred is something that "manifests itself as a reality of a wholly different order from the 'natural' realities."[6] While the profane is the realm of the everyday, the undifferentiated, the ephemeral and the largely unimportant, the sacred is the realm of the extraordinary, the permanent and the ultimately valuable. As such, the profane is associated with the chaotic and vanishing, while the sacred is considered the realm of the perfect, brimming with order and being (Eliade).

Among other things, Eliade's classic interpretation of world religions argues that, from the perspective of traditional societies steeped in a sacralised comprehension of the world, space is neither continuous nor homogeneous but fractured by special sites that connect the cosmos or world that we inhabit to the transcendent beyond. This comes about through the irruption of the ultimately real in what otherwise is relatively amorphous, meaningless space.

In this way, the sites at which the sacred "breaks through" into this world give meaning to the layout of the land. As a consequence, sacred sites offer a kind of *ultimate orientation* that is unavailable within Cartesian or geometrical space, where all points have equivalent value. Eliade points out that for many traditional societies the temple, for instance, constitutes a direct connection to a different reality, and crossing the threshold of its gate is much more than a physical change but, rather, signifies entry into a model or representation of the original design of the world (Eliade).

People who still live according to traditional systems of knowledge (even if generally also making use of, and interacting with, modern systems) identify a multitude of distinct places and spaces as sacred (see Contreras, Anderson et al., Salick). Even in today's largely post-traditional, often secularised, societies, many places are identified as sacred. Besides those sites that have obvious religious significance, such as churches, synagogues, mosques, shrines, temples or cemeteries, there are many other sites that are similarly treated as sacred, in Eliade's sense of (re)presenting "the wholly other". The reasons for such designation are diverse.

Some sites have acquired their standing as a result of an extraordinary event, often momentous and pernicious. For example, the place in Memphis, Tennessee, where Martin Luther King was shot, the concentration camps throughout Central Europe where millions of Jews were killed under guidance of the Nazis, or the A-bomb Dome, in the Peace Park in Hiroshima, that commemorates the nuclear bombing of Nagasaki and Hiroshima.[7] One reason to view such sites as sacred may be that in these places the everyday is disturbed in such a deep way that we expect "the wholly other" to manifest itself there.

Other sites are perceived as sacred in a more celebratory sense, such as the Lincoln Memorial, which US Americans remember both for Abraham Lincoln and the site of Martin Luther King's speech "I have a dream". Such sites also seem to take us in as places of "hierophany", that is, as places where the "wholly other" shows itself in some way. Still other sites, for example, great libraries, such as the British Library, or important museums, such as the Louvre or the Prado, are treated in, what, at the risk of sounding paradoxical, may be called a "secularly sacred way", for being the repositories of extraordinarily meaningful cultural goods. Such places seem to be revered because, through the cultural goods deposited in them, they can bring us closer to a deeper understanding of reality.

Still other places are approached in reverential ways because they are *themselves* considered extraordinarily meaningful cultural goods. For example, certain archaeological sites, such as the Akropolis of Athens (home of the Parthenon Temple), Machu Picchu in Peru, or Angkor Wat in Cambodia, but also architectural works such as Le Corbusier's chapel *Notre Dame du Haut* at Ronchamp, Frank Lloyd Wright's *Falling Water*, or Mies van der Rohe's *Barcelona Pavilion*. In these cases it would seem that the sites are revered because they appear as the expression of a spirit that goes beyond the everyday.

The most straightforward evidence for supporting that these various types of sites are perceived as something approximating the sacred comes from the fact that they are treated accordingly. People make pilgrimages to these places, there tend to be ritualised ways of behaving in and around them, turning them into something else is considered quasi-sacrilegious, and what one may put inside them or in their vicinity is strictly restricted. Notably, people are not supposed to behave indecorously, which may mean not to sing nor dance wildly, not to talk loudly nor otherwise behave in "profane" ways, in churches and cemeteries, at memorial sites, in libraries, museums, archaeological sites, and so on. To break these restrictions may lead to various sorts of sanctions and reprimands. All such sites are understood to stand in stark opposition to the profane everyday, even if they are located amid the everyday, and even if some everyday functions are carried out in their space or vicinity (as the British Library is open for reading, cemeteries are weeded, and archaeological sites are policed).

Places taken to be sacred do not have to be generated by human beings, of course. Many natural features of the land, such as certain mountaintops, rivers, trees, water sources, and so on, may be perceived as sacred, though they often receive additional, constructed, markers, such as shrines, gates, temples, ceremonial roads, and so on, to highlight their special status. So, while Fuji-san indeed has a shrine associated with its peak, other venerated mountains, such as Mt Kilimanjaro, sacred to the Maasai, and Machhapuchhare in Nepal, dedicated to the god Shiva and sacred to local Hindus, do not, at least to my knowledge, have any additional markers associated with them.

Moreover, while often associated with features that have use value, such as water sources, shade or isolation from society, insofar *as sacred*, natural places function rather through their symbolic role within a meaningful landscape. So, while the waters of the Colorado River are contained at the Hoover Dam for recreational, power generation and irrigation purposes, these uses of the great river are not the reason for its special cultural standing, which occasions lay pilgrimages by presently more than 4 million people a year. (The damming of the river may even be seen as detrimental to its function as an example of the "wholly other", since such ordinary uses may be taken to be in contradiction to its specialness.)

Interestingly, sacred sites in the Menri Mountains ("Medicine Mountains" in Tibetan), located in the Eastern Himalayas, in a region overlapping Yunnan and Tibet, contain a significantly greater number of useful and unique species than the non-sacred spaces surrounding them. This suggests that there is an important interaction between the traditional designation of sites as sacred and their ecological make-up (Anderson et al.), but the explanation probably is that the treatment of the sites as sacred is responsible for the greater concentration of useful and unique plants found there, and not vice versa (Salick).

Disruption of sacred landmarks

From what we have seen, the sacred in the landscape functions as a signpost. It points toward an underlying order of the world that becomes apparent through symbolic means. Such signposts may be effective even if those who recognise them as such cannot articulate with precision how they function. Disturbances of the sacred in the landscape, though, are registered quite readily by those who share the particular cultural framework, and the upset of its integrity may lead to *a loss of orientation*, in an ultimate sense.

For example, regarding Mt Cotacachi, a mountain in Ecuador that recently lost its glacier, the anthropologist Robert Rhoades tells us that "Mama Cotacachi, the local name of the sacred mountain, is a feminine power requiring reverence and special dedication."[8] Accordingly, "the loss of the glacier and decline of water resources is thought by some to be God's punishment for unacceptable actions by the communities (e.g., deforestation, grazing, infighting and moral decline)."[9] Apparently, the loss of the glacier on Cotacachi constitutes significant problems for local populations, not just on the practical level of everyday needs, such as for water.

The concern of these communities for the loss of the glacier needs to be understood, furthermore, within the larger context of traditional Andean conceptions of "Pachamama" or the natural world, according to which the latter deserves respect *as such* and is not simply regarded as a resource for the services that it may supply human populations (see Bhagwat).[10] Incidentally, it is precisely on the basis of such considerations that Ecuador, which is a country with a largely indigenous population, has become the first sovereign nation to enshrine the rights of nature in its national constitution (*Constitución de Ecuador* 2008), where it has dedicated a whole chapter (Chapter 7) to these rights.[11]

Taking responsibility

People in the Andes face a diversity of risks from glacial retreat, ranging from catastrophic landslides to eventual water scarcity in the dry seasons. To address the resulting vulnerability careful monitoring is required, but also active dialogue across institutions and communities, since short and long term goals and risk projections may receive different weightings depending on degrees of information, capacitation to respond, the priorisation of basic needs; political, economic and engineering determinants; as well as individual risk-taking patterns (see Bury et al., Carey 2008).[12]

Importantly, as we have seen, diverse communities also have to contend with the disruption of sacred landmarks.

For the people who live in traditional communities that only marginally participate in the fossil-driven economies of our times, the disruption of sacred places, in conjunction with the increased risks arising for their day-to-day working and living environments, brought about by climate change, constitutes a problem that has been created elsewhere, and for which they, objectively, have little if any responsibility. Interestingly, Rhoades reports that younger members of the communities around Cotacachi diverge from their elders in *not* attributing *to themselves* the blame for the deglaciation of the peak, alleging, rather, "that the changes are due to global warming caused by industrial nations like the United States." Rhoades points out that this is the result of a cultural change, since "They glean this information from the press and local NGOs."[13]

The fact that many communities living according to traditional cultural frameworks perceive their universe as disrupted as a result of the actions of peoples from societies where fossil fuels are burnt in great quantities raises important ethical concerns that should be understood in terms of climate justice (also see Orlove et al.). From the perspective of the people affected, the issue is not only that individuals and communities are harmed through the physical changes of the land, but that for them the loss of marks of the sacred in the landscape means that the order of the world is being upset in a fundamental way.

This is an issue that climate change policy has largely neglected, but ought to consider. So far, progress on the incorporation of the perspectives on the sacred of populations who perceive that their traditionally significant landmarks are threatened by climate change has been rather slow and extremely limited (see Salick 2009). If "climate justice" is to become more than a convenient catchphrase, efforts to give voice about these matters to indigenous people at climate change policy venues must certainly increase.

Significantly, threats to the iconic sites in the landscape that may in some way be considered "sacred" do not only pose a challenge to climate change policy in terms of climate justice, but also may generate opportunities for attaining personal insight and comprehension regarding the reality of global warming. We consider this point next.

ICONIC SITES IN THE LANDSCAPE: OPPORTUNITIES FOR INSIGHT

We are witnessing that, despite the great advances in climate science, as summed up in the Assessment Reports of the IPCC (Inter-governmental Panel on Climate Change), large sections of populations in the Western World, especially in North America, remain complacent about the need to address climate change, and some are even unconvinced about its reality. This situation can be partially explained by the fact that climate change is a process that is difficult to register, as such, through one's personal, observational experience. While we think that we should be able to trust our own observations regarding weather and climate, recent research suggests that our unaided assessments of climate, in any case, tend to be inaccurate (Strauss and Orlove). Consequently, our grasp likely is even *more* unreliable regarding *changes* in climate.

So, engaging the public about global climate change is difficult, among other things, because this phenomenon is perceived as spatially and temporally distant and hard to capture in personal experience. The notion of "climate" already supposes a level of abstraction beyond weather. Insofar as climate is an average over weather events spread out in time, change in this factor is hard to give a reliable interpretation to from a non-expert perspective that relies on personal experience. The perception of threats to iconic landmarks, however, may provide significant leverage in creating a personally meaningful grasp of the reality of climate change.

Iconic images

In a recent study, Saffron O'Neill and Mike Hulme define icons as "a tangible entity considered worthy of respect; something to which the viewer can relate and for which they feel empathy".[14] Reference to icons under threat is common,[15] and may be an effective way to overcome information overload in the communication of complex issues about which there may be a perception of uncertainty.

Climate change has been brought home to the Canadian public, for example, by pointing to the threat to survival that the decrease in Arctic ice means for polar bears, who need to be able to access pack ice to hunt but cannot swim for indefinite periods of time to return to land.[16] Similar appeals are made with reference to the possible extinction of king penguins in Antarctica, due to decreasing quantities of fish in their rapidly warming waters (Le Bohec et al.). One may add the case of the Edelweiss plant in the Alps, which has long been an icon for Alpine landscapes and may become an icon for climate change, in the light of the need for the flora in this region to migrate upward along this mountain ranges' slopes as temperatures rise in the area (Grabherr).

As such, these species seem to have "signal value" for the threat of climate change. Notably, the meaning of the potential disappearance of these emblematic species seems to go beyond the concern for the decrease in biodiversity to which their extinction would contribute, but rather points toward the disruption of something even greater: insofar as the extinction of such species stands for the disturbance of the integrity of our world, it signifies something akin to the disruption of sacred landmarks.[17]

Even physical science seems to make use of iconic images in order to illustrate consequences of climate change. Accordingly, "abrupt climate change", consequent to crossing certain "tipping points" or thresholds, generally is represented by certain key events, such as the loss of the Greenland ice sheet, the shutdown of the North Atlantic thermohaline ocean conveyor, or the break-up of the West Antarctica Ice Sheet. Such visually effective images signal a radical break with a relatively comprehensible and comfortable climate trajectory, as known throughout the Holocene, and the entry into a realm of mostly inscrutable climate chaos (cp. Burroughs).

AESTHETIC SALIENCE OF ICONIC IMAGES AND LANDMARKS

Interestingly, iconic images as well as landmarks considered sacred, be they natural or humanly-made, generally are perceptually and aesthetically salient. In Europe, the Middle East and the Maghreb, for example, churches and mosques stand out among other buildings through their usually sightly steeples and minarets, while in Japan Shinto shrines and Buddhist temples announce themselves through visually attractive, winged *torii* gates, amid varied urban and natural spaces. Churches, synagogues, mosques, shrines and temples normally present themselves with architectural designs and interior furniture intended to generate aesthetic appreciation among the faithful.[18] Natural sites treated as sacred also tend to stand out in some aesthetically appreciable way, and confirm this supposition.

For example, mountain peaks, such as Fuji-san or Mt Kilimanjaro, revered by Japanese and Maasai, respectively, stand high above everything else like beacons, and have a beauty that has attracted the attention of poets and writers like Matsuo Bashō and Ernest Hemingway. In Australia, pristinely clear pools of water as well as striking rock outcrops that contrast in exquisite ways with the surrounding wide open, mostly dry, "bush" land, represent Ancestors from Dreamtime to the Aborigines. Intriguingly shaped rock formations, located on the Northern edge of Seoul, revered for their resemblance to a praying buddha, make the wandering traveller wonder if they were not sculpted as art by human hands. A spring in a lush green space dedicated to the god Asklepios in ancient Greek times, at Lissos on the island of Crete, visited for the allegedly divine curative power exercised there, still delights for its tranquility and unusual green splendour, which must have been a constant as long as the source produced water.

Since the confrontation with aesthetically salient things draws our attention in an extraordinary way, this suggests the potential instrumental value of artworks, intentionally made to address climate change. Such works have been produced as of late. For example, Alfio Bonanno, an Italian Arte Povera artist representing Denmark, participated in the climate change art show *Melting Ice, a Hot Topic* in Oslo with a site-specific sculpture called *Ark* (2007). It consists of the wooden frame of a boat balanced on top of trees outside the Nobel Peace Centre museum building, dramatising the impact of sea level rise due climate change in places such as Bangla Desh.

Katie Paterson, a Scottish artist, created a rather more subtle work called *Vatnajökull (the sound of)* (Paterson 2007, 2008), which consists of a live phone-line to an underwater microphone placed in Jökulsárlón lagoon, Iceland, which is an outlet glacial lagoon of the Vatnajökull icecap. The melting of the glacier could be followed aurally by phoning a telephone number in the UK from anywhere in the world, which allowed audience members to hear the crashing sound of icebergs falling into the lake, as well as sounds of gurgling and of the scraping of ice against ice.

1   Tea Mäkipää and Halldór Úlfarsson, *Atlantis*, 2007-2009, part of the exhibition "WANÅS 2009 – Footprints", Wanås Foundation, Sweden; © photo: Anders Norrsell

This piece attempts to tap into deep-seated human needs of security and comfort by illustrating a drastic end to those need satisfiers. It also represents our cultural "turning a blind eye" to the issue of climate change; an audio track of people talking calmly about everyday concerns plays on a continuous loop inside the sinking house. (Comments by a visitor to the piece, Charlotte Barrow)

Similarly, the work with the richly allusive title *Atlantis* (2007-2009) by Tea Mäkiää and Halldór Úlfarsson, shown at Wanås Foundation, Sweden, offers to our view a life-size, one-family house that is in the process of sinking under the waters of a lake (see illustration 1). It addresses the shelter that makes possible our lives and the deep-seated fears about losing it. As such, the one-family house represents the hopes of the average citizen in many countries, at least in the Northern latitudes, and its imminent demise underwater seems intended to unsettle our everyday complacency by pointing toward the disastrous consequences of floods and storms, whose increase in intensity is an already present and, foreseeably, increasingly common consequence of climate change.

In all of these cases, the art object *bundles* a diversity of conditions and processes constitutive of "abrupt climate change" into a picture representing harm to particular things that represent the integrity of the world *as a whole*. In short, the use of iconic images or sites to illustrate the current threat of climate change may be a way to visualise how careless human activity may bring about the erosion of the order of the world.

Conclusion

Previous to the present, relatively calm, Holocene, the global climate was much more variable and prone to repeated, rapid changes (Burroughs). This means that human beings have undergone many severe changes in weather patterns throughout the 200,000 years of existence of modern *Homo sapiens*. We do not know with certainty how previous generations of human beings perceived the periods of rapid temperature increases and decreases during of the chaotic climates of the Pleistocene, but confronting them would have required relatively frequent, drastic adjustments in locations of habitation, modes of living, and livelihoods, often within single lifetimes.[19]

In many ways, conditions this time around are significantly different from previous occasions of climate change, due to the rapid development of technology, accumulated and accelerating environmental degradation, rapid loss of biodiversity, an overwhelmingly large and still growing world population, increasingly unequal entitlements, the militarisation of nations, and a quilt of cultures representing human groups that are pressed by the market system to compete rather than to cooperate in the face of resource scarcities. Nonetheless, we have reason to be hopeful for the future as we realise that *we are here today* because human beings already have *repeatedly* managed to weather through previous periods of climate change somehow (Burroughs).

This being said, it is sobering to think that it is not some geological or cosmological process, but human beings, who have unwittingly provoked the present process of accelerating global environmental change, with uncountable life-changing consequences for human and non-human life. The fact, however, that we can *still* importantly modify this process (through thoroughgoing mitigation and adaptation actions) should be perceived *both* as a tremendous challenge *and* as a grand opportunity for action. As such, it calls for deep reflection on responsibilities and on possibilities for action.

One of the most fundamental characteristics of human beings is our need to organise life as meaningful. For this, people require orientation. Such orientation is often provided by symbolically laden places, landscapes and landmarks that may be considered as sacred. When those places, landscapes and landmarks are in crisis, as it increasingly is the case due to anthropogenic climate change, this calls for urgent reconsideration of our perspectives on life. Things cannot stay the same: *either* we transform the contemporary structures and processes of producing livelihoods and everyday life, *or* the fundamental conditions of life will change even more drastically than already is to be expected, due to the lagtime of effects from the greenhouse gases accumulated in the atmosphere over the last century.

From the discussion offered here I conclude that, for at least two distinct reasons, culturally significant landmarks should constitute focal points for climate change-oriented policy. First, the threat to iconic landmarks considered sacred should be an issue from the perspective of climate justice and responsibility. Second, insofar as cultural landmarks and artworks that bring into play iconic images can generate understanding and focus attention on the reality of climate change, they may serve to motivate individuals and communities to address this all-encompassing phenomenon with demands for action on mitigation and adaptation. In sum, we ought to develop policy that recognises responsibilities for climate change-based disturbances in culturally significant sites, and should consider greater use of iconic, culturally significant, markers, including artworks, to engender action on climate change across wide sectors of society.

NOTES

1. Also see the special issue of *Global Environmental Change* (2009) on "Traditional peoples and climate change", and Jan Salick and Nanci Ross' introduction to the issue.
2. The UNESCO has developed additional protection guidelines for particularly threatened sites listed under the World Heritage Convention (World Heritage Convention 2007).
3. Notably, moreover, even in highly secularised countries, such as Iceland and Japan, road building and urban development has to approach with caution places considered sacred. According to local understanding in these countries, spirit beings ("little people" and *kami*, respectively) are present in various features of the landscape, including rocks and mountains (regarding Iceland, see Lyall).
4. Chidester and Linenthal, 5.
5. Certainly the details of how the sacred is understood vary greatly across human groups, even if Eliade proposes that there are reasons to believe that the concept, as developed through his research in the history of religions, is applicable in most cultures. I propose that Eliade's concept is useful enough for our purposes, insofar as it is applicable across religious systems and is realised by determinable differentiations in the conceptual and physical construction of spaces and places in the landscape.
6. Eliade, 10.
7. Other sites might be equally sacred to some, but are neglected because of intentional or accidental historical amnesia, such as the site where Manitoba's champion of the *métis*, Louis Riel, was hung, or the places, near the Tiergarten Park in Berlin, only marked by small letter-sculptures spelling out their names, where the intellectual revolutionaries Rosa Luxemburg and Karl Liebknecht were murdered.
8. Rhoades (2008), 44.
9. Rhoades (2008), 44.
10. Also see Carey (2007), on the narrative of glaciers as endangered.
11. Bolivia also expressed its concern for the integrity of the natural environment in the face of climate change by organising the "World People's Conference on Climate Change and the Rights of Mother Earth" in 2010, intended as a response to the largely unsuccessful 2009 Copenhagen UNFCC Conference. Since then, Bolivia has called for an international court of climate justice.

12 Also see Mark's argument for a transdisciplinary perspective with regard to the management of vulnerability arising in connection with the retreat of Andean glaciers.
13 Rhoades (2008), 44.
14 O'Neill and Hulme, 403.
15 See e.g. "Ten Climate Change 'Icons' Announced" (2009).
16 The WWF has an active Polar Bear Conservation campaign in which polar bears function as iconic images for climate change (WWF no date). The question whether polar bears are endangered, and their role as "icons", became the subject of controversy in 2008. While various groups, including Greenpeace, asked and obtained May 14, 2008, the listing of polar bears as threatened under USA legislation, the Inuit Circumpolar Council (2008) argued against it on the grounds that using polar bears as an "icon within a global environmental struggle" does not take into account the impact that this will have on Inuit communities that earn important revenues resulting from trophy or sport hunting this animal by Southern tourists.
17 Slocum agues that local icons are to be preferred, for their effectiveness, over national or global ones. Saffron O'Neill and Mike Hulme address Slocum's point through an empirical study that compared the value of "global" and "expert-led" icons with "local" and "non-expert" icons in Britain. They found that reference to locally meaningful, non-expert, icons under threat work best to generate engagement among the general population. Their conclusions should have important implications for the use of icons in communications with the general public. It does not invalidate reference to the more "global" icons, such as polar bears, mentioned here though, since there seem to be particular constituencies for diverse icons. To judge by popular responses to media reports, the threats to polar bears due to loss of ice in the Arctic certainly seem to be of concern to Canadians, for example.
18 It is relatively rare to find cases such as a synagogue tucked away among ordinary houses, or a Daoist temple hidden on a third level floor of an apartment building, as we find in Córdoba, Spain, and in Victoria, Canada, respectively. It is, similarly uncommon to find the places of worship of any religion bare of features with intentionally created, aesthetically interesting, characteristics. The most recent theory about prehistoric cave art claims that this manifestation was associated to shamanism (Clottes and Lewis-Williams), which suggests that a perception of the sacred would have been present even then. This suggests that there is a very long-lasting (*longue durée*) conjunction between the presentation of the sacred and aesthetically relevant features.
19 We can gather some hints about the changes that they lived through from the material culture remaining in the archaeological record, for example, in prehistoric art. On a very rough time scale, Delluc and Delluc link specific motifs in cave art representations to climatic development, suggesting that future research of the changes in prehistoric rock and mobile art may provide us with some understanding of how people perceived those periods of change.

References

Adger, W. Neil, Barnett, Jon, Chapin III, F. S. and Ellemor, Heidi (2011), "This must be the place: Under representation of identity and meaning in climate change decision-making", *Global Environmental Politics* 11, 2, 1-25.

Anderson, Danika M., Salick, Jan, Moseley, Robert K. and Xiaokun, Ou (2005), "Conserving the sacred medicine mountains: a vegetation analysis of Tibetan sacred sites in Northwest Yunnan", *Biodiversity and Conservation* 14, 3065-3091.

Bhagwat, Shonil A. (2009), "Ecosystem Services and Sacred Natural Sites: Reconciling Material and Non-material Values in Nature Conservation", *Environmental Values* 18, 417-427.

Bolin, Inge (2001), "When Apus Are Losing Their White Ponchos: Environmental Dilemmas and Restoration Efforts in Peru", *Development and Cooperation* 6, 25-26.

— (2009), "The Glaciers of the Andes are Melting", in: Crate and Nuttall, 228-239.

Bonanno, Alfio (2007), *Ark*, at the exhibition *Melting Ice, a Hot Topic*, Oslo: Nobel Peace Centre.

Burroughs, William J. (2007), *Climate Change in Prehistory: The End of the Age of Chaos*, Cambridge: Cambridge University Press.

Bury, J.T., Mark, B.G., McKenzie, J., French, A., Baraer, M., Huh, K.I., Zapata M. and Gomez, J. (2011), "Glacier recession and human vulnerability in the Yanamarey watershed of the Cordillera Blanca, Peru", *Climatic Change* 105, 1-2, 179-206.

Carey, Mark (2007), "The History of Ice: How Glaciers Became an Endangered Species", *Environmental History* 12, 3, 497-527.

— (2008), "The politics of place: inhabiting and defending glacier hazard zones in Peru's Cordillera Blanca", in: Ben S Orlove, K. Wiegandt and B. Luckman (eds.), *Darkening Peaks: Glacier Retreat, Science and Society*, Berkeley and Los Angeles: University of California Press, 229-240.

Chidester, D. and Linenthal, E.T. (eds.) (1995), *American Sacred Space*, Bloomington and Indianapolis: Indiana University Press.

Clottes, Jean and J. David Lewis-Williams (1998), *The Shamans of Prehistory: Trance and magic in the painted caves*, New York: Harry N. Abrams.

Constitución de Ecuador 2008 (*Ecuador Constitution*; Ecuador: Asamblea Constituyente); for an English translation of chapters 1 and 7, see <http://hettingern.people.cofc.edu/Environmental_Ethics_SP_10/Equador\%20Constitution\%20Rights\%20of\%20Nature\%202008.htm>, 23 July 2011.

Contreras, Daniel A. (2010), "Landscape and Environment: Insights from the Prehispanic Central Andes", *Journal of Archaeological Research* 18, 241-288.

Crate, Susan A. and Nuttall, Mark (2009), *Anthropology and Climate Change: From Encounters to Actions*, Walnut Creek, Cal.: Leftcoast Press.

Cruikshank, Julie (2001), "Glaciers and climate change: Perspectives from oral tradition", *Arctic* 54, 4, 377-393.

— (2005), *Do Glaciers Listen? Local Knowledge, Colonial Encounters, and Social Imagination*, Vancouver and Toronto: UBC Press.

Delluc, Brigitte and Delluc, Gilles (2006), "Art paléolithique, saisons et climats", *Comptes Rendus Palevol* 5, 203-211.

Durkheim, Émile (1965), *The Elementary Forms of Religious Life*, trans. Joseph Ward Swain, New York: The Free Press, (French original: *Les formes élémentaires de la vie religieuse*, 1912).

Fraser, Barbara (2009), "Climate Change Equals Culture Change in the Andes", *Scientific American*, October 5, <http://www.scientificamerican.com/article.cfm?id=andes-climate-change-glacieramaru-agriculture>, 23 July 2011.

Grabherr, Georg (2009), "Biodiversity in the high ranges of the Alps: Ethnobotanical and climate change perspectives", *Global Environmental Change* 19, 167-172.

Habermas, Jürgen (1984), *The Theory of Communicative Action*, trans. Thomas McCarthy, Boston: Beacon Press, (German original: *Theorie des kommunikativen Handelns*, Frankfurt am Main: Suhrkamp 1981).

Inuit Circumpolar Council – Canada Office (2008), *ICC Canada Backgrounder On USA Environmental Groups' Polar Bear Lawsuit*, 14 January, <http://www.inuitcircumpolar.com/files/uploads/icc-files/PR-2008-01-14-BackgrounderPolarBearsJan142008.pdf>, 27 July 2011.

Jurt, Christine (2009), "Perceptions of Natural Hazards in the Context of Social, Cultural, Economic and Political Risks: A Case Study in South Tyrol", Ph.D. dissertation, Department of Anthropology, University of Bern.

Le Bohec, Céline, Durant, Jo'el M., Gauthier-Clerc, Michel, Stenseth, Nils Chr., Park, Young-Hyang, Pradel, Roger, Grémillet, David, Gendner, Jean-Paul and Le Maho, Yvon (2008), "King penguin population threatened by Southern Ocean Warming", *Proc Natl Acad Sci* (*PNAS*) Vol. 105, 11 February.

Lyall, Sarah (2005), "Building in Iceland? Better Clear it with the Elves First", *New York Times*, <http://www.nytimes.com/2005/07/13/international/europe/13elves.html>, 24 July 2011.

Mark, Bryan G. (2008), "Tracing tropical Andean glaciers over space and time: Some lessons and transdisciplinary implications", *Global and Planetary Change* 60, 101-114.

O'Neill, S.J. and Hulme, Mike (2009), "An iconic approach for representing climate change", *Global Environmental Change* 19, 402-410, <http://pubs.giss.nasa.gov/abstracts/2007/Hansen_etal_2.html>.

Orlove, Ben S. (2009), "Glacier Retreat: Reviewing the Limits of Human Adaptation to Climate Change", *Environment: Science and Policy for Sustainable Development*, May-June, <http://www.environmentmagazine.org/Archives/Back\%20Issues/May-June\%202009/Orlove-full.html>, 15 July 2012.

Orlove, Ben S., K. Wiegandt and B. Luckman (2008), "The place of glaciers in natural and cultural landscapes", in: Orlove, Ben S., Wiegandt, K. and Luckman, B. (eds.), *Darkening Peaks: Glacier Retreat, Science and Society*, Berkeley and Los Angeles: University of California Press, 3-19.

Otto, Rudolf (1926), *The Idea of the Holy: An Inquiry Into the Non Rational Factor in the Idea of the Divine*, trans. John Wilfred Harvey, Oxford: Oxford University Press, (German original: *Das Heilige: Über das Irrationale in der Idee des Göttlichen und sein Verhältnis zum Rationalen*, 1917).

Paterson, Katie (2007), *Vatnajokull (the sound of)*, London: Slade School of Fine Art.

— (2008), *Vatnajokull (the sound of)*, at the exhibition: *Encounters Katie Paterson*, Oxford: Modern Art Oxford.

Rhoades, Robert, Zapata Ríos, Xavier and Aragundy, Jenny (2006), "Climate Change in Cotacachi", in: Rhoades (2006), 64-74.

Rhoades, Robert (2006), *Development with Identity*, Oxon UK: CABI Publishing.

— (2008), "Disappearance of the Glacier on Mama Cotachachi: Ethnoecological Research and Climate Change in the Ecuadorian Andes", *Pirineos* 163, 37-50.

Salick, Jan, Amend, A., Anderson, D., Hoffmeister, K., Gunn, B. and Fang, Z. D. (2007), "Tibetan Sacred Sites Conserve Old Growth Trees in the Eastern Himalayas", *Biodiversity and Conservation* 16, 3, 693-706.

Salick, Jan and Ross, Nancy (2009), "Introduction: Traditional peoples and climate change", *Global Environmental Change* 19, 137-139.

Sallnow, Michael J. (1987), *Pilgrims of the Andes: Regional Cults in Cusco* Washington, D.C.: Smithsonian Institution Press.

Slocum, Rachel (2004), "Polar bears and energy-efficient lightbulbs: strategies to bring climate change home", *Environment and Planning D: Society and Space* 22, <http://www.rslocum.com/Polar\%20bears\%20and\%20energy\%20efficient\%20lightbulbs\%20strategies\%20to\%20br.pdf>, 27 July 2011.

Smith, J. Z. (1978), *To Take Place: Toward Theory in Ritual*, Chicago: University of Chicago Press.

Strauss, Sarah and Orlove, Ben (2003), *Weather, Climate, Culture*, Oxford/New York: Berg.

"Ten Climate Change 'Icons' Announced" (2009), *National Geographic Daily News*, December 14, <http://news.nationalgeographic.com/news/2009/12/photogalleries/091214-climate-change-red-list-species-animals/>, 22 July 2011.

Wolf, Barbara and Orlove Ben (2008), "Environment, history, and culture as influences on perceptions of glacier dynamics: The case of Mt. Shasta", in Orlove, Ben S., Wiegandt, K. and Luckman, B. (eds.), *Darkening Peaks: Glacier Retreat, Science and Society*, Berkeley and Los Angeles: University of California Press, 49-67.

World Heritage Convention (2007), "Climate change threatens UNESCO World Heritage sites", April 10, <http://whc.unesco.org/en/news/319>, 24 July 2011.

World Wildlife Fund (no date), *Polar Bear Conservation – WWF: A Leader in Polar Bear Conservation*, <http://www.worldwildlife.org/species/finder/polarbear/polarbear.html>, 27 July 2011.

Representations of Reality, Constructions of Meaning

Netherlandish Winter Landscapes during the Little Ice Age and Olafur Eliasson's Glacier Series

Philipp Meurer

Climate Change and Artistic Innovation

"Little Ice Age" is the common term for a global phase of colder climatic conditions between the warmth optima of the Middle Ages and modern times. On the basis of climatologic surveys using ice and mud coring or the analyses of tree-rings, an average reduction in temperature of 1.5° C between the early 14th and the mid-19th centuries could be traced.[1] The lower temperature did not only affect the severity of the winter-months but also general weather conditions and everything that was dependant on them. Numerous historical weather records are preserved which correspond to the scientific data. Written sources, such as chronicles, diaries, journals and illustrations on flyers, illustrate long frost periods, frozen rivers, storms, floods, crop failures, and famines.[2]

In spite of the strong annual variability, there are temperature minima traceable in the second half of the 16th and the last quarter of the 17th centuries. One of the severest winters of the 16th century was recorded in 1564/65.[3] During 1565 Pieter Bruegel the Elder (1525/30-1569) painted his famous winter scene *The Hunters in the Snow* for the Antwerp merchant Nicolaes Jonghelinck (fig. 1).[4] This panel is not only one of Bruegel's most popular paintings, but it has also been used as artistic evidence for the Little Ice Age.[5] The coincidence is of course striking. It is the first winter landscape on panel with an impressive scale of 117 x 162 cm. Furthermore, it marks the beginning of an increasing popularity of the genre, which continued during the 17th century in the Northern provinces of the Netherlands, the new state *Republiek der Zeven Verenigde Nederlanden*.[6]

In this paper, I will question the assumed relationship between climatic processes and visual art. If its reference to reality is not only documentary, what other aspects have to be considered? Which layers of meaning played a role for artists, buyers, and viewers? Regarding art as an elementary human reaction to the world, the problem is obviously silhouetted against a larger framework of questions. How did early modern humans aesthetically cope with environmental change? Did they really cope with a change as such or rather with a hard time in the recurrent perils of life?

Bearing these questions in mind, I first take a closer look at Bruegel the Elder's winter landscape and its relationship to the pictorial tradition of seasons. In a second step, I extend the scope to the development of the genre in the Northern Netherlands asking how pictorial inventions contribute to the construction of identity. Finally, I dare to take a short outlook on contemporary art, which deals with environmental issues taking the *Glacier Series* (1999) by the Danish-Icelandic artist Olafur Eliasson (born 1967) as an example. Although a diachronic comparison always bears the risk of fallacies, I want to question whether knowledge of contemporary art does not only distort our perception or if it also helps us to discover new aspects of historical paintings.[7] Accordingly, it is my general interest whether some characteristics of aesthetic behaviour towards the environment persist over time.

LOCAL ART, GLOBAL CLIMATE

For many scholars, a direct or even causal relationship between the Little Ice Age and the winter landscapes is evident. The positions range from radical opinions, which regard climate change as a catalyst for artistic change (here the invention of winter scenes), to moderate ideas, which consider these paintings as reflections of the weather within a general development towards naturalism.[8]

It is helpful to consider the basic propositions necessary for the assumed relationship of art and climate.[9] The fundamental proposition maintains that the main purpose of any image is (and has ever been) to mirror the visible world in an objective, photographical way. Thus, art buyers would expect paintings whose objects had been viewed and exactly reproduced by the artists. Accordingly, any change of the displayed objects would therefore indicate changes of the real world, which had been observed by the artists. The more these changed attributes are portrayed in these paintings, the more evident the respective changes appear. In compliance with this perspective, the popularity of winter scenes after Bruegel's cornerstone is a prime example of this case.

Unfortunately, there is no written evidence that Bruegel did not make his inventive winter-paintings as a direct reaction to the deteriorating climate, or that he was not inspired by a hard winter, at least to some extent. We only have the paintings themselves and the artistic tradition in which they emerged. These, however, engender arguments that the snow scenes are not mere documents of the climate or certain weather events, but must be seen in a wider and more sophisticated context.

The first critical argument against a direct relation is very simple. The Little Ice Age was, of course, a global phenomenon that did not only concern Flanders. The emergence of the winter landscape was, by contrast, quite a local development, firstly unique to the artistic environment of Bruegel and other Flemish artists. The winter of 1565, however, was as hard in Flanders as in Holland. Accordingly, we must therefore ask why there was no such phenomenon, for example, in Amsterdam only 200 km north of Brussels. After the winter landscapes became popular in the Northern provinces as well, we could again ask why there was no artistic response in the rest of Europe.[10] Other countries also excelled with achievements in landscape painting, but followed divergent thematic priorities. Pastoral concepts with a new subtlety in colour and atmosphere were made by Italian masters like Titian. Winter landscapes, however, are almost unique for the Netherlands. Apparently, there were also other requirements necessary for the development of the winter genre, for instance a particular artistic climate or a tradition of particular interests and skills. This argument is again strengthened by the fact that the popularity of winter scenes abated during the last quarter of the 17th century although some of the winters in these decades were also extremely cold.[11]

CALENDARS AND SEASON-PAINTINGS

Returning to the *Hunters in the Snow*, it first has to be stated that it is no single work but part of a series of six panels which showed the seasons of the year. The series, of which only five paintings are preserved, was commissioned by the merchant and humanist Nicolaes Jongelinck to decorate a room in his country house outside Antwerp.[12] The *Hunters in the Snow*, now commonly associated with December and January, conclude the course of the year.[13] Being the only snow scene on an equal footing with paintings of the other seasons, the uniqueness of this winter scene has to be put into perspective. It is still an echo of an iconographic tradition that can be traced back to the calendars of medieval manuscripts. Lavishly executed calendars emerged especially during the Late Middle Ages as parts of Books of Hours that are devotional texts for laypersons. The respective parts contained not only pages with dates and holidays, but also characteristic depictions of the months. Each month is usually defined by the particular human activity corresponding to the course of the year. One of the most famous Books of Hours is the *Très Riches Heures du Duc de Berry*, which was made by the Limbourg brothers between 1411 and 1416 (fig. 2). As one of the earliest snow landscapes in art, the February page shows typical occupations like wood chopping. More emphasis is placed, however, on the intimate view into the farmhouse where a noble woman and a peasant couple are warming themselves by a fire. Instead of simple stereotypical activities, the Limbourg brothers already tried to visualize the universal grip of winter in a more sophisticated way. On the one hand, there is a distinction between the couple which shows its private parts quite unashamed and the woman who bashfully turns away. On the other hand, both share the existential experience of cold like everyone else.

Of course, the tradition of illuminated calendars was transformed and further developed in Pieter Bruegels series of the seasons 150 years later. Instead of twelve book illustrations, we have six large panels with independent landscapes. Nevertheless, basic characteristics remained unchanged. Despite its innovative qualities, Pieter

Bruegel's series is also distinguished by an ambition to construct a fundamental human experience. However, this experience was only possible in its entirety taking nature and the course of the year into account. An image of winter needed the image (or at least the imagination) of summer as a complement. The complementary piece within Bruegel's series is accordingly a summer scene. Its title, *The Corn Harvest*, names the depicted activity typical for the season.[14] Analogously, the image of spring had to be completed by an image of autumn. This "holistic" way of thinking was not only essential for Bruegel but also for the later development of the winter genre in the Northern provinces. Many winter scenes, for example that of Jan van Goyen, were made with a pendant summer scene and it is likely that they were often placed on opposite walls. Even winter scenes without pendants demonstrated that they were only parts of all the seasons by displaying the typical activities for the respective months. In spite of their growing naturalistic appearance, they are not spontaneous responses to the climate but rather paradigmatic constructions of winter.

Winter as an Aesthetic Experience

The iconographic tradition of the seasons is not the only topic which has to be mentioned. Just as important for the emergence of the winter genre is the general development of landscape painting in the Netherlands. It is important to highlight a few characteristics of Bruegel's winter scene to explain its crucial position in this development. As a comparison, I want to draw on the February page of the *Tres Riches Heures* again. Although this book is far ahead of its time, there are remarkable differences in the rendering of landscape.

The scene by the Limbourg brothers is divided into different areas regarding space and function. The main emphasis has been put on the farmstead in the foreground. The vantage point seems to fit to the ascending ground behind the farmstead, but a certain inconsistency of proportions and perspectives is discernable. A donkey driver and a woodcutter seem to be too large for their distance within the pictorial space. The spatial situation of the hills and the distant village is unclear. Although the landscape defines and also intensifies the characterization of winter, it is a subordinate background to the scenery in the foreground.

In comparison, the *Hunters in the Snow* features a more consistent pictorial space, although it also has different zones. A cuneiform hilltop at the left side of the panel marks the foreground. The group of hunters with their dogs strive away from the viewer down to a wide valley with a village. The beholder's gaze follows the hunter's direction and sweeps over houses, frozen ponds, skaters, and a river that meanders towards the sea at the horizon; it only stops at a cliffy mountain range that encloses the valley on the right.

As indicated by the path of the hunters and the respective direction of the viewer's gaze, the main emphasis is directed towards the landscape. The objects and figures are important, but subordinate to the landscape as a whole. Despite several attempts to localize the scenery, it has to be noted that it is purely imaginary.[15] Single elements may have been taken from sketches Bruegel made during his voyages through Flanders or the Alps, which were then integrated in the fictitious composition.

The single elements or zones are ably connected to create a harmonious impression of space. Compositional breaks like the steep slope in front of the hunters are wellbalanced by the sequence of hills, trees, and houses. The result is a plausible illusion of geographic coherence.

The impression of coherence is not only created by means of composition, but also by the colouring. A central element is the white snow covering every object and leveling the differences in distance and height. A structuring effect, however, is obtained by the darkness of the bare trees and branches. Equally important is also the cold greenish blue of the sky that is mirrored by the sheets of ice. Together, a subtle atmosphere is evoked that contributes to the suggestive power of the winter image.

Finally, the integration of the figures has to be mentioned. In contrast to the February page of the *Tres Riches Heures*, the figures are not placed in a stage-like setting but embedded in the landscape as its natural protagonists. The different work or leisure activities fit to the structure of the landscape. The stocky appearance of the warmly wrapped figures blends perfectly with an impression of coldness. A sense for laconic humour is revealed by details like the dog turning tiredly to the spectator or the hunters, who only caught a fox but pass a tavern whose name "The Deer" ("dit is in't hert") is written on a crooked sign above the door. This ironic view on the futility of human striving goes hand in hand with the timeless regularity of winter.[16]

The visualization of experience is a crucial aspect for the understanding of the painting in a double sense: The togetherness of humans and their basic natural conditions is not only pictured, but also transmitted to the beholder by the vehemence of experience in front of the canvas. If the terms "realistic" or "naturalistic" can be applied to this painting, then in the latter sense rather than in a simply descriptive one. Bruegel's skilful construction of winter is clearly an aesthetic one. Of course, there are elements of closeness like the hunters which seem to take beholders by the hand and lead them into the image. The panoramic view through the valley, however, creates the degree of distance which is necessary for aesthetic contemplation.

A VARIETY OF WINTERS

Bruegel's art was extremely popular not only in Flanders, but also in the Northern provinces. Some compositions like the famous *Winter Landscape with Skaters and a Bird Trap* were often copied, mostly by his son Pieter the Younger.[17] Prints of Bruegel's design were widely distributed and affordable for many people. Of course, other Flemish masters painted winter scenes as well. Artists like Lucas van Valckenborch (1530-1597) or Joos de Momper (1564-1634/35) adopted features such as the high vantage point with a panoramic view on a crowded ice sheet, but they placed a little more emphasis on anecdotic elements like defecating peasants or stumbling lovers. Perhaps his successors did not convey the experience of winter as intensively as Bruegel, but they nevertheless came up with a similar repertoire of elements and similarly strived to create a particular wintery atmosphere. Funny scenes or the joys of winter were always accompanied by indications of its bitter aspects.[18] The typical tasks of the winter season also implied an admonition: Only those who secure enough food, firewood, and other necessities can amuse themselves on the ice. Moreover, depicted dangers like fires, stumbling skaters, or figures who sink through thin ice always remind the beholders of their fragile human existence. Vanitas symbols were typical for all artistic genres of this epoch. However, winter landscapes offered new possibilities and shades of meaning. Skaters, for example, could be indications of the slipperiness of human life or just symbolize that practice is necessary to master a matter.[19]

Some other winter motifs were commonly used but not necessarily connected with landscapes. The personification of the seasons, for example, was a popular subject that dated back to antiquity.[20] The seasons were often represented by human figures of different ages with characteristic attributes. Spring was commonly associated with a young person, winter accordingly with an old man or woman warming up next to a fire or carrying a brazier as in Philips Galle's print based on the design of Maerten van Heemskerck (fig. 3).

The equation of the human age groups with the course of the year is particularly interesting. It exemplifies how deeply early modern humans imagined themselves as integral parts of natural or cosmologic cycles. Old age referred to the "winter of life" and winter was a natural part of the divine order.

The personifications could also be combined with more figures in an allegorical scene. Sometimes the seasons were represented by mythological divinities. Aelous, ruler of the wind, Boreas, the north wind, or the two-faced Janus symbolized "winter" in this tradition. The connection with the cosmological model was illustrated for example by the signs of the zodiac or by Janus. His face looking backward was often an old man's face, while the face looking ahead and expecting the future belonged to a young man.[21] Like all other subjects and iconographic models, the allegoric scenes were widely spread by prints and emblem books.[22] It is likely that the popularity of the depictions of winter and their use as a decoration, memento, or admonition also implicated a certain magical conception. Having a picture of winter within its seasonal context effectively meant getting hold of it. The contemplation of such a depiction helped to reassure beholders of the predictable character of the seasons. Weather and nature in general were imponderable enough, but one could be sure of the divinely ordered cosmologic cycle and that each hard winter is followed by spring.

The iconography of the seasons is a broad field of study that can only be touched briefly here. Yet, it was necessary to demonstrate the rich variety of traditions and notions interrelated with the seasons. It can be mentioned again that these images of winter were constructions of meaning within a cyclic view of nature rather than

EFFŒTI MENTIRE SENIS SPECIEM ALGIDA BRVMA. CORPVS ABOLLA DVPLEX OPERIT, PLANTAS QVE CALONES.
HISPIDA BARBA RIGET PELLITVS TEMPORA VDO. EXANGVES QVE MANVS FOCVLVS FOVET IGNE CORVSCVS.

3   Philips Galle after Maerten van Heemskerck, Winter, 1563, Engraving, 21,7 x 25 cm, Rijksprentenkabinet, Rijksmuseum, Amsterdam, The Netherlands, photo: © Rijksmuseum, Amsterdam

descriptive echoes of certain weather events. In this respect, they differ fundamentally from journals, flysheets, and similar sources.

Coping with the Cold

Pieter Bruegel the Elder, who died 1569 in Brussels, still lived long enough to see the beginning of the 80 Years' War that was going to determine the development of the Netherlands.[23] The revolt against Spanish governance triggered by centralistic politics, high taxes, and rigorous ordinances against Protestants in particular began in the years 1566-68. The new governor, the Duke of Alba, was sent by the Spanish king, Philipp II, to regain control. In doing so, brutal persecutions and punishments forced thousands of people to flee. As a result of the following acts of war, an enormous demographic increase occurred in the more liberal provinces of the north, which declared their independence in 1579. The number of refugees even increased after the fall of Antwerp in 1585. The population of the former economic and cultural capital decreased dramatically.

Among the immigrants were also many artists who settled in the towns of Holland like Amsterdam, Haarlem, or Leiden. Despite the war, they contributed to growing prosperity and profoundly influenced the local art scene. The first Dutch winter landscapes painted by artists like Hendrick Avercamp (1585-1634) in the first decade of the 17th century continued to show many Flemish elements. Avercamp, who specialised in winter landscapes, only eventually lowered the horizon line and reduced the anecdotic character of the staffage. Thus, he contributed to the development of the "realistic" Dutch landscape style which remained popular until 1670, encompassing artists such as Salomon van Ruysdael, Art van der Neer, or Jan van Goyen (1596-1656).[24]

Van Goyen's *Ice Scene with the "Huys te Merwede"* of 1638 may be considered typical for the new realistic style (fig. 4).[25] At the beginning of his career, van Goyen also portrayed winter scenes with a Flemish influence including "summer" pendants often painted with round formats. At first sight however, the mentioned painting appears to be a spontaneous and unsophisticated view of an ice sheet with skaters. The actions of the staffage are not particularly selective or narrative. On the contrary, movement appears frozen during its natural activity on the ice. Peasants in horse-drawn sleighs, skaters, and colf-players[26] turn their backs to the beholders and seem to be randomly distributed. The enormous sky with its sunlit clouds, the pallid light on the foreground, and the hazy distance evoke a delicate wintery atmosphere. In short, the landscape is presented as a direct record of a winter day in Holland.

Just the same, a closer examination reveals a carefully composed structure. The vertical elements on the left side of the canvas, the tree, and the mast of the ship correlate with the refreshment tent on the right that has a Dutch ensign on its top. Together they form a second framing within the composition. The two skaters in the foreground to the left of the push-sledge and the tent are the only figures which move directly in the direction of the beholder. Being additionally emphasized by one of the few colour stains of the painting, i.e. the red jacket of the front skater, they establish a link to the viewers and incorporate them in the activities on the ice. Moreover, the group helps to counterbalance the weight of the cuneiform bank on the left with the groups of figures in front of it.

The pictorial elements, however, are not only harmoniously distributed but carefully arranged to induce the illusion of pictorial depth. Imaginary diagonals run roughly from the inn on the left bank and from the top of the tent at the right to the distant ruin.[27] Corresponding diagonals begin at the feet of the left and right figures in the foreground and culminate again in the ruin, which serves as a vanishing point. The spatial effect is even intensified by the lighting. At first, the beholder's gaze sojourns on the activities in the shadowed foreground, but then, it is drawn into the sunlit distance.

The compositional features exemplify that van Goyen's painting is no pictorial document in the sense of a naïve reproduction of nature. It is also no "veduta", meaning that it is no exact portrayal of an existing landscape. Van Goyen was a prolific draughtsman and made hundreds of sketches on his excursions throughout the Dutch countryside. The actual paintings, however, were produced in the studio as was common among 17th century artists. During the work process, the drawings were not simply transferred to the paintings. Their purpose as mnemonic devices or pictorial components always complied with a compositional intention; parts were selected, changed, or left out. This also applies for those paintings which can be topographically identified. Important buildings, for example church-towers, were enlarged, and rows of houses were moved together or pulled apart.[28]

Although the master narrative of "Dutch realism", regarded as a faithful adoption of nature, is still influential, it has been put into perspective by some important studies.[29] They show that even the direct and unsophisticated appearance of the Dutch landscapes was bound to new representational conventions and to a high appreciation of artistic virtuosity. These skills, however, were no longer displayed with ostentation like in Flemish winter landscapes with their variety of different anecdotic scenes. On the contrary, just the straightforward, naturalistic appearance of Dutch landscapes required a particular but unobtrusive virtuosity.[30] This type of disguised artistry was much concerned with the developing cultural identity of the Northern Netherlands that was open for innovations. According to the new self-consciousness, artists could adopt, vary, or even ignore classical landscape conventions inherited by the Flemish mannerist tradition. The use of inventiveness and imagination, synonymous with the Dutch concept "uyt den geest", resulted paradoxically in the emergence of plausible fictions of the Dutch countryside.[31]

This also applies for van Goyen's *Ice scene with the "Huys te Merwede"*. Its constructed verisimilitude, however, is not an end in itself but is linked to the Dutch self-image and an idealized conception of life in winter. It is remarkable that some of the depicted elements are clearly accentuated. First and foremost, the sunlit appearance of the ruin on the horizon line, the Huys te Merwede, has to be mentioned. Although it is not placed on the vertical centre line of the canvas, it has an emphasized position between the mast of the boat and the tent. Van Goyen, however, did not only select a particular landscape section. The two main groups of figures in the foreground leave an empty space and allow an open view on the distant building as if the figures were flanking the lines of sight.

The castle Huys te Merwede appears frequently in works of Dutch landscape artists. Situated near the town of Dordrecht, it was built in the 14th century for the lords of Merwede.[32] Although it fell into disrepair long before the 80 Years' War, it was an important landmark that commemorated Dutch history. It is not meant that the Dutch wished themselves back to feudal times, but the ruin demonstrated that the young republic already had a rich historical past coequal with Rome and its monuments.[33] A second layer of meaning is accordingly the allusion to the Golden Age of antique mythology. On an equal footing with the realistic style, there was a broad interest for pastoral subjects in 17th century Holland, traceable in literature but also in painting and graphic art. Ruins were integral parts of this context. Against this backdrop, the depiction of the sunlit ruin in the Dutch winter landscape by Jan van Goyen can be regarded as a self-confident evocation of the Dutch Arcadia.[34]

The identity-forming aspect is amplified by details such as Dutch flags on the tent and the masthead on the left. More important than tracing single iconographic elements, however, is their integration in the interplay of the winter atmosphere and human activities. A remarkable characteristic of Dutch winter landscapes is the absence of negative aspects of the cold, which is noticeable in van Goyen's painting as well.[35] The people on the ice display everyday life, in which the seasonal activities are integrated as natural, self-evident elements. Winter is taken as an inevitable natural fact. Moreover, labour and leisure are as typically bound to Dutch identity as is the flat, watery land with the enormous sky above. In short, the depicted citizens on the ice are ostentatiously and blithely braving the cold rather than only coping with it. Again it can be stated that the Dutch winter landscapes of the 17th century were no mere reactions to climate fluctuations, but sophisticated constructions of meaning which combined early modern concepts of nature, a new aesthetic notion of the native landscape, and the formation of identity. This applies in a similar way to the many different winter subjects in addition to ice scenes, be it sleigh rides, hunting scenes, or peasants outside an inn.

FILM-STILLS FROM A BIRD'S EYE PERSPECTIVE

The documentary character of Olafur Eliasson's *Glacier Series* of 1999 seems to be obvious at first sight (fig. 5). Forty-two aerial photographs of glaciers are arranged in a rectangular grid.[36] The spectator is able to recall similar vistas from newspapers, magazines, or television documentaries. However, the various faces of the icy phenomenon are impressive. Some glaciers cower on a mountain peak like a zoomorphic life-form, some roll down to the sea like a white stream of lava. Attempts to describe the scenes fail to capture the forcefulness of the sequence, which immediately evokes our knowledge of present global warming: deglaciation, sea-level rise, floods, and storms. Paradoxically, the distant vantage point intensifies these threatening associations because only a certain distance allows us to experience the actual fragility of the huge ice sheets. The photographs captured parts of nature which we know are in danger of disappearance.[37]

Beholders could stop here and turn to the next work of art, at best being inspired to contemplate on the global situation and their own behaviour. The topical, documentary and perhaps admonitory aspects, however, are only a primary layer of understanding. A reason to continue reflecting on the *Glacier Series* could be its conceptual appearance: the presentation of the picture series as an art work, the further thematic context and, first and foremost, the way it is composed. As in his other landscape series, Eliasson chose a moderate calendar format for the single prints. Thus, he avoided the illusionistic effect that would have been induced by a large-sized art work. In the latter case, the beholder would have not only tended to empathize with a large image of nature but would also have been distracted by reminiscences on Romanticism and the aesthetics of the sublime. The small format, however, reveals the photographic character of the images.[38]

The series exposes its representational function. This is amplified by the systematic and apparently objective character of the work.[39] "Distance" turns out to be a key concept, not only as defined above, but in a wider context as the general distance between image and beholder. It is not only the loneliness and vulnerability of the pictured objects, which come to the fore, but also the isolation of the beholder, who is separated from nature by different layers of artistic strategy. The only possible approach is reconsidering the images as such. Their bird's eye perspective, for human observers only possible by airplane or helicopter, demonstrates again the gap between the icy wilderness and the technical human realm. Glaciers are hostile regions which make ordinary walk-in access difficult and dangerous. Accordingly, no human traces can be found in the images. The beholder is repelled to the mediated field of experience in the exhibition. The small photographs exemplify that distance is also a matter of proportion. A commensurable view on the huge glaciers is only achieved by the sequence of representational layers: the window of the aircraft, the view-finder of the camera, the selection and composition of the artist, and the public display. The beholder is not only inspired to reflect on epistemic possibilities, but also on human smallness and the conditionality of life.[40]

A second key concept is "time". Every photograph only captures a short moment of an ever changing reality. From a human perspective, however, glaciers have a slow pace of change. Although being sensitive to the slightest climate fluctuations, they take hundreds or thousands of years to grow. Moreover, their actual movement downwards is almost imperceptible. It can only be deduced by secondary phenomena like ice calving or melting water. In addition, the traces of the flow are engraved in the glacial surface. The overall structure with its crevasses and faults not only reveals enormous forces but also the temporal aspect. It is the only indication for movement conserved by the photographs. By exhibiting moments within long natural processes the series can transmit allegorical character. The images emblematise the general flow of time as well as the relation between geological periods and the life spans of the spectators. Contemplating the *Glacier Series*, they do not only view film-stills of a climatologic drama but also of the perpetual drama of life and nature.

THE CHALLENGE OF CONTEXT

Herewith we return to the opening questions. As in the early modern winter landscapes, the relationship of art and reality in the contemporary photo series is bound to a sophisticated texture of meaning rather than to documentary purposes. Moreover, Eliasson's mimetic approach is scrutinised by the particular strategies of the art work. With our present knowledge, this aesthetic reaction to the world includes environmental change but refers to the human condition. Of course, the understanding of every work of art is bound to a particular context, whether it is topical, historical, or anthropological. For an interpretation of the *Glacier Series* as a critical response to global warming, it is necessary to know basic propositions of the related scientific debates. The implications in regard to representation and perception, however, can only be understood by knowing facts about photography, about the particular production of the photos, and, first and foremost, about the history of media.

These are, of course, only a few factors indispensable for the respective understanding. Various contexts have different ties to society and culture and different intersections among themselves. The Little Ice Age context related to climate change in general is a contemporary context imposed retrospectively on Netherlandish winter landscapes. This is not necessarily wrong, but, in fact, it can be an interesting inquiry into the documentary potential of these images. Yet, it is a relatively young and, in a manner of speaking, "thin" context; it only scratches the pictorial content that is deducible by the present-day beholder. However, the iconographical context of the winter landscapes – including their texture of meaning within Netherlandish culture – has to be reconstructed by historical research. It can be perceived as a "thick" context with numerous links to occidental history.[41] In addition, this context corresponds largely with the anthropologic dimension as defined above. It is likely that this general understanding would not be equally accessible in every cultural or historical environment. Nevertheless, the approach is relatively easy for beholders familiar with modernism and contemporary visual culture, because their common visual knowledge widely depends on early modern achievements.

Accordingly, the extended context of the *Glacier Series* can be traced by a self-reflected beholder who is – perhaps unknowingly – influenced by the respective semantic traditions and deciphers flowing structures of glaciers as metaphors for time. Finally, it can be stated again that the aesthetic reactions to the environment of both areas of investigation go far beyond topical or documentary purposes. The fundamental difference between contemporary positions and early modern art, however, is again that the latter was characterised by the faith in an immutable and divinely ordered nature with coldness, ice, and snow being integral parts. This is, to a large extent, lost today. What we have gained, however, is an awareness of the fragile balance of nature and humankind. With this awareness and a particular aesthesia, it is possible to challenge the considerations on climate change with the millennia-old quest for the human condition and vice versa.

Representations of Reality, Constructions of Meaning

1 Pieter Bruegel the Elder, The Hunters in the Snow, 1565, oil on wood, 117 x 162 cm, Kunsthistorisches Museum, Vienna, photo: © Kunsthistorisches Museum, Vienna

2 Paul, Jan and Herman van Limburg, February page of the Tres Riches Heures du Duc de Berry, 1413-1416, miniature, 29 x 21 cm, photo: © bpk, Berlin, RMN, René-Gabriel Ojéda

4 Jan van Goyen, Ice Scene with the "Huys te Merwede", 1638, Panel, 37,5 x 61 cm, Stedelijk Museum De Lakenhal, Leiden, The Netherlands, photo: © Stedelijk Museum De Lakenhal, Leiden

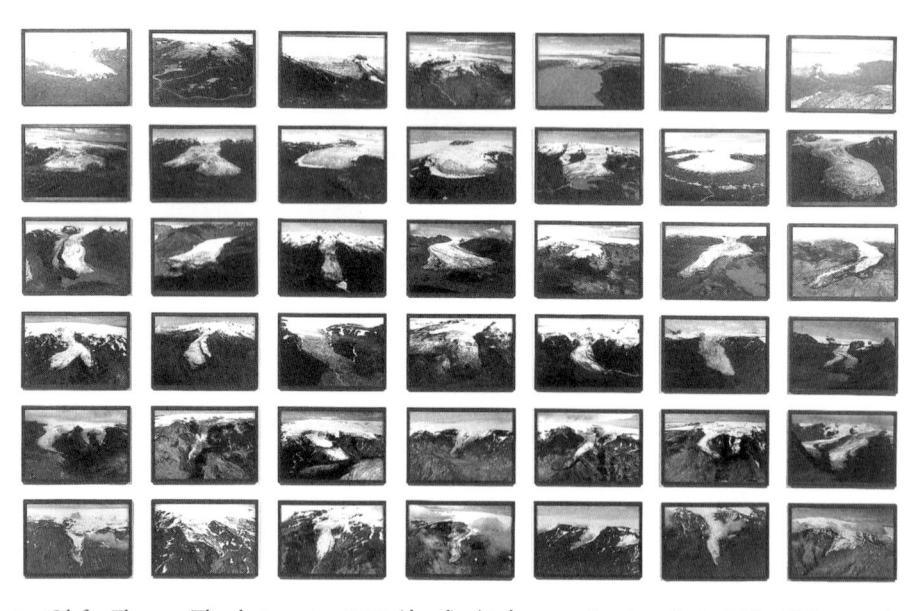

5 Olafur Eliasson, The glacier series, 1999 (detail), 42 chromogenic prints, Series 244 x 404 cm, each 34 x 50 cm, Photo: Jens Ziehe, Courtesy of the Solomon R. Guggenheim Museum, New York, © 1999 Olafur Eliasson

Notes

1 Negendank, Brüchmann, Kienel, 55-62. Other scholars use different time frames, e.g. Ariane van Suchtelen. For her, the Little Ice Age began with the first temperature minimum in the middle of the 16th century. See van Suchtelen, 12. For more bibliographical references see also Behringer (2005), 415-508.
2 A seminal work is the climate history of Jan Buisman, *Duizend jaar weer, wind en water in de Lage Landen*, see Vol. 3. For an overview see Glaser, 195f.
3 Glaser, 118. A significant Brabant chronicle of 1665 is quoted in van Straaten, 75, (abridged also in van Suchtelen, 12).
4 On the life and work of the artist see Sellink, 201-211.
5 The particular preference to use Bruegel's *Hunters in the Snow* as an image of historical reality has been recently demonstrated by the cover of Wolfgang Behringer's book (2009). On the Little Ice Age see 117-195.
6 For a comprehensive historical overview see North, 23-65.
7 Contemporary art does not only depend on old masters but changes our notion of them as well. An intriguing study has been carried out by Mieke Bal, 1-25. For the general hermeneutical problem see also Krüger, 55-74.
8 As an example for a strong position see Lamb, 233f. Lamb stated for instance, that Bruegel's *Adoration of the Magi in the Snow* in the Oscar-Reinhart-Collection in Winterthur was directly inspired by the hard winter of 1565. This hypothesis can be refuted due to a new restoration, which revealed that the correct year of production is 1563, not 1567. See Sellink, 126. A more modest position is presented by Negendank, Brüchmann, Kienel, 56.
9 A critical discussion of propositions is found in Lawrence O. Goedde's essay. Goedde (2005), 311-321, argues for a qualified response to the unusually cold winters but also stresses the selective and constructive character of the renderings of nature.
10 Goedde (2005), 314.
11 Ibid. 320.
12 More information in Sellink, 138-140.
13 Good surveys of the discussion about order, attribution to the months and interpretation are presented by Sellink (see above) and Herold, 89-110.
14 Pieter Bruegel the Elder, *The Corn Harvest (August-September)*, 1565, Oil on wood, 118 x 161 cm, Metropolitan Museum of Art, New York.
15 For references to scholars attempting to localize the place see Herold, 82.
16 In Bertram Kaschek's most recent monograph on Bruegel's season paintings, the author, 261-301, traces an eschatological background as the key to understanding the series. According to Kaschek, details like the flying magpie or the tiny bird-trap on the slope in the center of the painting are intended to remind viewers of the Last Judgment. Numerous literary sources are presented to support this iconographical content, e.g. Augustine's *Confessions* or Sebastian Franck's *Chronica* of 1536 (282, 285f.). Hardly any of these significant texts, however, are directly linked to Bruegel's paintings. Admittedly, it is important to emphasize the context of salvation history, which was highly relevant for early modern culture. The season series, however, allows different approaches – as Kaschek, 263, himself concedes. Hence it is emphasized here that the eschatological content is not the master key that fits to every question. It should be noted that eschatological and cyclic

aspects of nature and creation are not necessarily contradictory but work together within the ambivalent structure of meaning.

17 Pieter Bruegel the Elder: Winter Landscape with Skaters and a Bird-Trap, 1565, Panel, 37 x 55,5 cm, Koninklijke Musea voor Schone Kunsten, Brussels. According to Sellink, there are no fewer than 127 copies. See 212-213.

18 The iconographical subjects are summed up in van Suchtelen, 16-35 (with more references).

19 Van Suchtelen, 16-20. Here again, Bruegel the Elder created an early and influential example with his print *Skaters by the St. George's Gate in Antwerp,* 1560.

20 An important reference is the *Metamorphoses* of Ovid. See van Suchtelen, 28-35.

21 See also van Suchtelen, 33-35, for examples and references.

22 Van Straaten provides a brief survey and pictures of prints and emblems.

23 For the following paragraph see Blockmans, 111-140.

24 These are of course only three artists among many others who created winter scenes. For a survey see van Suchtelen, 50-70.

25 See van Suchtelen, 102-103 and 162.

26 "Colf", a forerunner of "Golf", was a typical Dutch game that had its origins in the Middle Ages but became extremely popular in the 17th century. Although it could be played all year round, it is a frequent element of Dutch ice scenes. See van Suchtelen, 26.

27 See van Suchtelen, 102, and Vogelaar, 104.

28 See Buijsen, 33, and Sluijter, 45f.

29 See Goedde (1997), 132f. and 140f., for a critical account. Echoes from the paradigm of realism can still be found in van Suchtelen, 54.

30 Goedde (1997), 143.

31 Goedde (1997), 133, 136f. and 143, here also more references for literature on the important concepts "naer't leven" and "uyt den geest".

32 <http://cms.dordrecht.nl/dordt?waxtrapp=rhqboDsHaKnPxBaBRLH>, 14 February 2012.

33 See Levesque, 73-113, for a deliberate analysis of this subject on the basis of Jan van de Velde's print series. On the comparison with Rome see pages 102-106.

34 See Levesque, 109-113.

35 On the selective character of Dutch landscapes see Goedde (2005), 320f., and Goedde (1997), 134-136.

36 The order of the series varies in different reproductions; the original arrangement seems to have 6 lines and 7 columns, as pictured in Engberg-Pedersen, 459, Blessing, 38f., and <http://www.deutsche-guggenheim.de/e/ausstellungen-truenorth01.php>. Other reproductions show only 40 photographs with 5 lines and 8 columns. See e.g. <http://pastexhibitions.guggenheim.org/moving_pictures/highlights_12a.html>, 14 February 2012.

37 On the aspects related to global warming see e.g. Lerup, 62-63, and Blessing, 37.

38 See Eliasson (2001), 18-20, Eliasson (2008), 254-255, and Blessing, 37.

39 See Eliasson (2001), 20. Eliasson emphasizes that all his photographic series also work as studies or sketches for his installations. Generally, he only exhibits them separately. It is just this quality, however, that confirms their status as independent art works because it opens a separate space for reflection.

40 Although Eliasson rejects a naíve romantic approach, he draws on theoretical paradigms

of Romanticism. The reflected adoption of nature and the possibilities of representation were key aspects for authors like Friedrich Schlegel, but also for artists like Caspar David Friedrich. These questions are again crucial for postmodernist discourses and also for contemporary approaches to nature. See Meurer, 17-26, 50.

41 The antagonistic use of "thin" and "thick" contexts is owed to Clifford Geertz's methodological concept of "thick description". In contrast to Geertz, it is used here to characterise the range of a semantic structure within visual traditions. Due to the time-dependency of the observer, however, it is important to emphasise a self-reflected perspective here as well. See Geertz, 7-24.

REFERENCES

Bal, Mieke (1999), *Quoting Caravaggio: Contemporary Art, Preposterous History*, Chicago and London: University of Chicago Press.
Behringer, Wolfgang (2005), "'Kleine Eiszeit' und Frühe Neuzeit", in: Behringer, Lehmann and Pfister, 415-508.
Behringer, Wolfgang (2009), *Kulturgeschichte des Klimas: Von der Eiszeit zur globalen Erwärmung*, München: Beck.
Behringer, Wolfgang, Lehmann, Hartmut und Pfister, Christian (eds.) (2005), *Kulturelle Konsequenzen der kleinen Eiszeit*, Göttingen: Vandenhoeck & Ruprecht.
Blessing, Jennifer (2008), *True North*, New York and Berlin: Guggenheim Museum Publications and Ostfildern: Hatje Cantz Verlag.
Blockmans, W. P. (1999), "The Formation of a Political Union: 1300-1600", in: J. C. H. Blom and E. Lamberts (eds.), *History of the Low Countries*, New York and Oxford: Berghahn Books, 111-140.
Buijsen, Edwin (1996), "De schetsboeken van Jan van Goyen", in: Vogelaar, 22-37.
Buisman, Jan (1996-2006), *Duizend jaar weer, wind en water in de Lage Landen*, 6 volumes, Franeker: Van Wijnen.
Eliasson, Olafur (2001), Interview with Jessica Morgan, in: Morgan, 16-23.
Eliasson, Olafur (2008), *Landscape*, Interview with Anna Enberg-Pedersen and Philip Ursprung, in: Engberg-Pedersen, 252-267.
Engberg-Pedersen, Anna (ed.) (2008), *Studio Olafur Eliasson: An Encyclopedia*, Köln: Taschen.
Geertz, Clifford (1983), "Dichte Beschreibung: Bemerkungen zu einer deutenden Theorie von Kultur", in: *Dichte Beschreibung: Beiträge zum Verstehen kultureller Systeme* (1. ed. 1973), übersetzt von Brigitte Luchesi, Frankfurt am Main: Suhrkamp, 7-43.
Glaser, Rüdiger (2008), *Klimageschichte Mitteleuropas: 1200 Jahre Wetter, Klima, Katastrophen,* Darmstadt: Wissenschaftliche Buchgesellschaft.
Goedde, Lawrence O. (1997), "Naturalism as Convention: Subject, Style, and Artistic Self-Consciousness in Dutch Landscape", in: Wayne E. Franits (ed.), *Looking at Seventeenth-Century Dutch Art: Realism Reconsidered*, Cambridge: University Press, 129-143.
— (2005), "Bethlehem in the Snow and Holland on the Ice: Climatic Change and the Invention of the Winter Landscape, 1560-1620", in: Behringer, Lehmann and Pfister, 311-321.
Herold, Inge (2002), *Pieter Bruegel: Die Jahreszeiten*, München: Prestel.
Kaschek, Bertram (2012), *Weltzeit und Endzeit: Die "Monatsbilder" Pieter Breugels d. Ä.*, München: Wilhelm Fink.

Krüger, Klaus (1997), "Geschichtlichkeit und Autonomie: Die Ästhetik des Bildes als Gegenstand historischer Erfahrung", in: Otto Gerhard Oexle (ed.), *Der Blick auf die Bilder: Kunstgeschichte und Geschichte im Gespräch*, Göttingen: Wallstein, 55-85.

Lamb, Hubert Horace (1995), *Climate, History and the Modern World*, 2. ed. London and New York: Routledge.

Lerup, Lars (2001), "(Art) Objects are Conservative and Processes are Radical: On the Disappearance of the North Pole and the Liquidation of Art", in: Morgan, 62-67.

Levesque, Catherine (1994), *Journey through Landscape in Seventeenth-Century Holland: The Haarlem Print Series and Dutch Identity*, Pennsylvania: The Pennsylvania University Press.

Meurer, J.-G. Philipp (2012), *Natur im Bewusstsein der Differenz: Franz Gertsch und Caspar David Friedrich*, Münster: LIT.

Morgan, Jessica (ed.) (2001), *Olafur Eliasson: Your only real thing is time*, Boston: Institute of Contemporary Art and Ostfildern: Hatje Cantz.

Negendank, Jörg F. W., Brüchmann, Cathrin und Kienel, Ulrike (2001), "Die kleine Eiszeit und ihre Abbildung im Klimaarchiv Binnensee", in: *Die "Kleine Eiszeit": Holländische Landschaftsmalerei im 17. Jahrhundert*, Berlin: Gemäldegalerie, Staatliche Museen Preußischer Kulturbesitz, 55-63.

Sellink, Manfred (2007), *Bruegel: The complete paintings, drawings and prints*, Ghent: Ludion.

Sluijter, Eric Jan (1996), "Jan van Goyen als marktleider, virtuoos en vernieuwer", in: Vogelaar, 38-59.

Van Straaten, Evert (1977), *Koud tot op het bot: De verbeelding van de winter in de zestiende en zeventiende eeuw in de Nederlanden*, The Hague, Staatsuitgeverij.

Van Suchtelen, Ariane and van der Ploeg, Peter (2001), "Holland Frozen in Time: An Introduction", in: Peter van der Ploeg et al. (eds.), *Holland Frozen in Time: The Dutch Winter Landscape in the Golden Age*, The Hague: Royal Cabinet of Painting Mauritshuis Foundation and Zwolle: Waanders Publishers, 11-70.

Vogelaar, Christiaan (ed.) (1996), *Jan van Goyen*, Leiden: Stedelijk Museum De Lakenhal and Zwolle: Waanders Publishers.

BEING ON THE BEACH

EXPLORING SENSOMOTORIC AWARENESS IN A LANDSCAPE

Grete Refsum and Ingunn Rimestad

INTRODUCTION

This essay is a retrospective reflection on what may be defined as an artistically directed event of experiencing nature on a beach. It describes a collaborative, site-specific art experiment that was realized during the *Aesth/Ethics in Environmental Change* workshop on Hiddensee in May 2010. Initiated by the authors, a visual artist and a dancer/choreographer, this particular event is part of a broader, on-going artistic research project on presence and sensomotoric awareness related to nature and the environment.

Traditionally, visual artists have interpreted the world as they perceived it through form – primarily in paintings and sculptures – while dancers and choreographers have produced pleasurable entertainment, delivering gracious movements within performances. Today, in a world overflowing with goods and wastes and with an ecological crisis revealing itself through climatic change, artistic expressions may take new directions.

The project *Being on the Beach* is an artistic response to the current situation. It builds on the idea that there is a need for a culturally enhanced respect for nature and a change of lifestyle. Two premises underlie the project: a) there is a connection between sensitivity towards the environment and the respect granted it; and b) bodily awareness and a stable grounding are central to the individual's ability to adapt and change. The presupposition of the project is that increased sensomotoric awareness and improved grounding will help the individual respond more respectfully and adequately to environmental challenges.

How can we become more grounded and bodily aware of what we feel, see, hear, smell, or even taste? Choosing the beach as the site, the project applies artistic methods for exploring how we can perceive a landscape more intensely. It seeks to foster and deepen the individual's self-understanding as a part of the environment.

A beach represents a border area. Physically, the beach is situated between fluid water and firm land. Its area is unstable, oscillating in size according to the water levels. On the beach, slow geological processes are made visible: the perpetual building up and breaking down of land unfolds comprehensibly. A beach receives and gives back – sediments and objects – from two sides: from the land to the water, and from the water onto the shore. Culturally, the beach is a space where many activities take place, spanning from the laborious to the leisurely. The beach can be a metaphor of life and a place for existential reflection. *Being on the Beach,* therefore, has several layers of meaning. In this particular context, the beach serves as a concrete landscape to experience and as a point of departure for the conference theme of existential reflection on the environmental crisis.

The text, first, presents the background of the project, its artistic context and the collaboration of the artists. Second, it describes the preparatory work of the event, particularly in analysing a beach. Third, it provides an account of the planning and realization of the Hiddensee event and the responses to it. The essay concludes by rounding off the beach activity as an art category and by suggesting possible further developments.

Project Background

Artistic Context

In contemporary visual art and modern dance, various artistic expressions reflect the time in which they were created. From the 1960s onward, many visual artists literally left their gallery spaces and began looking for new sites and frameworks in ordinary and everyday spaces, including nature, in which to explore contemporary problems. Concurrently, they began to dematerialize and deaestheticize artworks as products. By doing this, art moved from being a noun and an object to becoming a process and an activity.[1] Some artists started to experiment with their bodies.[2] Furthermore, audiences sometimes were invited into the art projects as participants.[3] Thus, personal body positions and various activities – so-called performances – became included in the concept of art.

The same development occurred within the field of modern dance. Dancers and choreographers began to work in new arenas and spaces. Here also, onlookers were invited into the actual performance, thereby blurring the borders between an artwork made by professionals and the contribution of the audience.[4] In these kinds of performances, the focus is on sharing, rather than on showing off something to be admired. The American dancer and body therapist Anna Halprin (1920-) invites participants to interpret for themselves, saying: "I don't want spectators, I want witnesses who realize that we are dancing for a purpose to accomplish something in ourselves and in the world."[5]

Building upon and extending these artistic traditions of visual art and dance, the *Being on the Beach* project is a practice and process that aims to elicit new insights concerning who we are within ourselves, in our given world, and together with other people.

COLLABORATION

Being on the Beach is an interdisciplinary, collaborative project between visual artist Grete Refsum and dancer and choreographer Ingunn Rimestad.[6] In her later work, the pioneer Swedish dancer and choreographer Birgit Åkesson (1908-2001) emphasized seeing as foundational to the work of a dancer. Dance should arise from seeing reality as it reveals itself.[7] Bengt Molander, a Swedish-Norwegian philosopher, expresses the same idea in more general terms. According to him, attention or awareness in the moment of action constitutes the basis of how professionals work.[8] Similarly, we recognized that our methodical way of working rested on the same basic factors of looking, being present in the moment and responding to the situation at hand. Our responses differ according to our training: Refsum reacts primarily with her hands, starting to construct something in space, while Rimestad starts moving, involving her whole body in a spatial structure. Together, we decided to join forces and experiment with objects and body awareness (fig. 1).[9] The invitation to the conference on Hiddensee acted as a trigger for us to continue, extending this collaboration into a beach project that would involve the conference participants.

1 *Workshop on body awareness using stones, Granavollen, Norway, 2009, photo: © Anna Widén*

Beaches are rich with artistic references given that many artists have worked on beaches and with beach motifs. Both of us live close to the sea and have been acquainted with beach areas since childhood. Individually, we have worked site specifically in nature and in relation to the beach[10] or water.[11] Starting this joint project, we asked: what is a beach? What is there to see and to find? How does a beach affect us? We decided to go and look at a beach together in order to be there and to see what happened, trusting our different artistic methods and competences.

PREPARATORY WORK

EASTERN QUAY

We went to *Østre brygge*[12] on Brønnøya[13] in Oslofjorden, Norway. The reason for choosing this particular beach was one of convenience: it is a communal beach near Refsum's cabin. Our foundational and repetitive question was this: what catches our attention? We sought both outward experiences and inward responses, movements, associations, images and thoughts.[14]

Eastern Quay is a small beach edging the shallow fjord water and land. Arriving on a grey, somewhat misty weekday in April with almost no wind and approximately 10 degrees Celsius, we had the beach to ourselves (fig. 2).[15]

2 *Eastern Quay, entrance towards the South, Oslofjorden, Asker in Norway*

On our visit, Eastern Quay offered a pleasant calmness, with the intense light of spring. To begin with, we stood for a while, taking in the view of the sea and the bright daylight (fig. 3).

3 a and b   Eastern Quay towards West, shallow water towards East

We closed our eyes and became aware of the air as moist and slightly cold against our faces. Subtle sounds became audible. Gradually, the focus shifted to our standing and how our feet met the ground. We stood on small stones, wearing hiking boots on a slanting ground. The uneven ground represented an unpredictable foundation that our bodies had to counterbalance for stability.

4 a and b   Directions along the coastline and perpendicular to the water

When we opened our eyes the landscape looked different. We actually started to *see* the beach and its environment, registering the strong light and the directions of the beach, its width and breadth. At this stage, we began to document by taking photos (fig. 4).

5 a and b   Zones of materials

We noted the tidal line and recognized different zones of materials: close to the sea there were small stones, further away from the water were sand, pebbles, shells, pieces of wood and vegetation transitioning into the woodland (fig. 5).

5 c and d   Shell sediments defining the upper tide level, detail

Next, we started to pick up objects of interest. Geologically, Eastern Quay consists of eroded Ordovician limestone rocks over 400 million years old, the pebbles of which often take peculiar, longitudinal shapes (fig. 6).[16]

6 Ordovician limestone pebbles

Knowing the geology added a conceptual dimension to the experience of being where we were. Our minds tuned into geological time and evolution, which from the human perspective opens into eternity and awe.[17] At this stage, we felt that we had gained the information we needed. This is the way artists work: they use, trust, and follow their senses concerning what to do and how to act until they feel satisfied.

Summing up

In general, a concrete experience on a chosen spot results from the interplay between the person present and the environmental factors. A person encounters an environment bodily and mentally, clothed more or less for the conditions and with the baggage of her/his life, such as previous experiences, thoughts, emotions, sensitivity, and moods. The environmental factors are characterized by its natural conditions combined with the season, time of day, weather, wildlife, vegetation and cultural aspects.

Our beach visit was in spring and out of the bathing season. We were clothed for the weather and just followed our impulses, simply standing upright, closing and opening our eyes. From this modest activity, we experienced how the process of becoming bodily grounded, while shutting out vision, made us more receptive to the reality around us. When we opened our eyes, we were able to relate more deeply to the place.

This is the methodological framework we brought with us to Hiddensee.

Hiddensee

The Beach

Hiddensee Island lies as a narrow shield, protecting the German mainland from the Baltic Sea. The environment is in visible flux; the island diminishes and grows on different sides as sand perpetually washes away in one place and becomes sediment in another. Its northern coastline is protected from being washed into the sea by a barrier of huge, black stone blocks (fig. 7).

7 Protecting stone blocks

Our proposed task was to organize an art event on a local beach that involved conference participants. We chose to work on an area of the beach next to the biological station where the conference was being held. Convenience and accessibility were again decisive for the choice. Small pathways led down to the sea through narrow openings in the vegetation (fig. 8).

8 *Entrance to the beach, Northern Hiddensee, 25 May 2010*

Obviously, there is a risk of exposing oneself to the seeming endlessness of the ocean and the void of the sky. Working on sensomotoric awareness in such an environment may reveal strong emotions, ranging from fragility to robustness. On our first day of arrival, the natural forces were dramatic with hard wind and showers of rain, orchestrated by the thundering sound of waves breaking onto the shore. It was challenging to encounter these surroundings and photographic documentation was impossible. Our immediate response to this environment was that we needed time to adapt.

The task of a dancer is to balance and keep contact with several spaces: the inner personal space, the space of the scenic character to be performed, the performance's space, and the space of the outer surroundings. The challenge is continuously to coordinate these spatial layers, articulating them through body work. An essential element of this is the dialogue with the air, its temperature and humidity, how it is breathed, transpired into the lungs and expired. The dancer has to meet and balance that which is given with what is made out of it by choice, either spontaneously or controlled.[18]

We had two days to prepare the art event and, fortunately, the weather improved on the second day. Even so, we had to wear all the clothes we had to keep warm: double layers with a rain costume on top. Dressing like this does something to the bodily experience – it would have been a different experience wearing a bikini on a hot day (fig. 9).

9   *On the beach, well dressed*

We now were able to ask: what catches our attention? The sensation of the air was predominant. The wind and the waves sent powerful impulses that were perceived as different aspects of energy, expressed in sound, pressure, and visual images. We could tactilely feel the air in the wind, hear it as sound, and watch the effect of its force on the waving sea surface, on the flat grass and creeping bushes on land.

Our first impulse was to stand up against the wind, facing the sea; then, we spontaneously let the body respond. To sum up, we:
- stood against the wind
- leaned into the wind's forces
- let the wind move our bodies
- moved efficiently in dialogue with the wind
- found our way through the wind's resistance

Various body directions in space were addressed:
- facing the sea
- turning the back on the sea
- standing sideways, in two directions
- facing the ground

- facing the sky

These responses were intertwined with different body positions, with eyes open and with eyes closed:
- walking
- standing
- shifting from side to side
- rotating
- bending down
- sitting
- rolling over
- lying down

We noticed that when we turned our backs to the sea, the sound became more striking, even when our eyes were open. In this position, the movements of the swaying grass caught our attention: its degree of toughness and resilience, its mobility and availability. The question arose: can our bodies tune into similar qualities?[19] Standing, thus, became essential and our attention shifted to our feet on the ground and to our dangling arms. The effect of the gravity and the wind became something to be explored. To balance wind pressure and stability on the ground was a challenge. Wet sand is hard and one can easily stand supported. Dry sand, however, presents an unpredictable ground.

Having grounded ourselves, we were able to distinguish different materials on the sloping beach, such as sand, stones, shells, grass and wastes. In the dry sand, the marks of footprints left an ornamental structure that arrested the eyes (10).

We now recognized stones, pebbles and flints and began collecting interesting pieces, making patterns and building structures (fig. 11).

Next, the beach in itself came into focus. We found openings in the breakwater and small bays (fig. 12).

Three zones and their transition areas became clearly distinguishable: vegetation/sand, sand/shells or stones, shells or stones/sea. Each offered different microlocations of ground, stones or shells and wastes of various kinds, both natural and artificial (fig. 13).

In the bays, zones of concentrated materials created clear structures (fig. 14).

Looking more closely, we found waste materials and remnants of fish and birds (fig. 15).

Plan of the Event

After having exposed ourselves to the beach, we entered into a reflective conversation with the situation about how to structure a possible event.[20] We decided on the following structure and agreed that Rimestad would lead and instruct the group:

1. Walk together in silence down to the beach, approximately 200 meters.
2. First stop: the transition area between grassland and sand.

10 Sand marked with footprints

3. Choose a partner: walk in couples to the nearby bay, one leading, the other with eyes closed.
4. Arriving in the bay area: find a spatial position and face the sea with eyes closed.
5. Stand, balance and listen outwardly with closed eyes.

11 Pattern making

6. Open your eyes: what catches your attention?
7. Turn towards the landscape with your back to the sea. Position your body and stand for a while with eyes closed.
8. Open your eyes: what catches your attention in this direction?

12 Opening in the stone breakwater, small bays

9. Go and collect eleven objects.
10. Return with your findings.
11. New task: walk somewhere and decide on a place to stop, stand still and leave one object. Repeat this pattern until all objects are given back to the beach, then return.
12. Find a place to stand along the bay, face the ocean with your eyes closed.
13. Open your eyes, find your partner, change roles, and walk back to start.
14. At the transition area between grassland and sand, everyone opens their eyes and the event ends.

The Event

The event took place in the evening of the second day of the conference with a group of approximately 30 people.
1. The group needed time to adapt to the first instruction of walking in silence.
2. Arriving at the beach, we saw that the bay we had planned to use was occupied by a playing family. We instantly shifted to another bay further away, which made the walk a little longer.
3. People walked at different speeds, most of them quicker than anticipated, with Rimestad at the front of the group and Refsum at the rear (fig. 16).

13 a   Zones and transition area, vegetation/sand

4. Surprisingly, people placed themselves further away from the water than planned, on a contour line close to the grassland.
5. Each person reacted differently to the challenge of standing still with eyes closed. Some seemed comfortable in the situation, while others were uneasy.

13 b and c   The meeting between water and land in a bay

6. Once all eyes opened and awareness was established, the group had to be moved closer to the sea. People were invited to the contour line defining the bay.

14 a and b   Longitudinal and perpendicular directions with zones

7. Standing with their backs to the sea, eyes closed, the participants appeared more at ease.

15 a and b   Details: Shells, pebbles, seaweed, waste, with the tide border

8. At this point the group seemed comfortable with the event structure.
9. When the new task of picking objects was given, people eagerly set off (fig. 17). Some just found their objects right where they stood (18).

16 *Entering the beach and walking in couples, one seeing, one with closed eyes (video stills, Sigurd Bergmann)*

17 *People going off to pick objects on the beach (video still)*

10. Returning, the group gradually and spontaneously formed a circle. While the early returners waited for the others to arrive, they were asked to share their catches with each other. Holding the objects in their hands, the exchange was lively. The collection contained a wide variety of items to be found on the beach, ranging from objects of beauty to remains of fish and rubbish. People talked quietly, exchanging delights, ideas and findings.

18   Picking objects at the shore (video still, Sigurd Bergmann)

11. The instruction to return the objects to the beach, however, was carried out very differently (fig. 19).

19   Example of findings returned (video still)

Some walked further off and spent much more time than others. At this stage, the participants seemed to have established personal spaces in which they acted.
12. The process of gathering the group became time consuming because the participants were now operating within individual time. Upon return, the participants positioned themselves at a clear distance from one another, randomly shaping themselves into a curve parallel to the bay.[21] The wind hampered communication in such a large group, and thus, instructions had to be communicated individually:

"face the sea, eyes closed". Those who returned early had to stand for quite a long time (fig. 20).

20 The group facing the sea, eyes closed (video still)

A few left after some time.
13. When the group was gathered, standing with eyes closed, the final instruction was given. Partners quickly found each other and walked back to the starting point. The quality of the return displayed focus and calm. Participants seemed more grounded and present in the situation than in the beginning.
14. The event ended in the transition area between grassland and sand with a short "Thank you!" Surprisingly, half the group remained. Small clusters of people formed, some in silence, some talking quietly, everyone just *being* there.

PARTICIPANTS' RESPONSES

We received several oral and three written responses to the event.[22] One respondent commented (no. 1): "As we walked in silence a certain tension that builds up by talking, was released. Pleasant the silence. And yet we were still sharing something together with this special group, but now in silence and perhaps we were sharing something deeper that we cannot reach in talk mode".

Concerning the returning of the collected objects (no. 11), some were quite reluctant to do so, but for different reasons. One had sought the most beautiful objects and they had become a personal treasure. Another had selected rubbish in order to clean the beach and refused to return them.

Of those who withdrew early (no. 12), one experienced increasing fatigue during the protracted final sequence. Another could not bear to look at the black, stone breakwater: it came to represent a scary metaphor for the formerly walled – in Eastern Europe (figure 7).

One written response was highly detailed in describing the experience of the event as a whole. The instruction to walk slowly calmed the respondent down and made this person more sensitive to the environment. Likewise, closing the eyes made the respondent more aware of the grounding of the feet and the sounds of the sea. This respondent also noticed that, while walking, the sounds changed along the beach. The experience of standing with closed eyes revealed a new experience of the sea: an awareness of the grounding in the sand, the smell of the sea and the light of the sun. The respondent noticed that, when opening the eyes, the waves and the light made a new and different bodily impact. The practice of finding and replacing objects was enjoyable and was something this person was accustomed to when out in nature. The experience of being led and then leading one's partner was also appreciated. This response ended by noting, "it was a beautiful experience that sensitized me to this beach and to my body and awareness on that beach".

Another respondent wrote, "The exercise slowed me down, it made me present and open. I felt more life streaming through and out of me."

ROUNDING OFF

Art projects rarely reach conclusions. *Being on the Beach* exemplifies a contemporary artwork that is interdisciplinary, collaborative and participatory, aiming to improve and contribute to community and individual life. The work blends elements from performance, land art, ritual, environmental study and a simple walk on the beach. It represents an example of relational art, in which art may be a social experiment and a moment of encounter.[23] The main purpose of *Being on the Beach* was to organize an opportunity to explore personal sensation in nature.[24] From beginning to the end, the work was experimental. Structuring the process of the event through this retrospective analysis clarified our understanding of what actually happened and contributed to our personal theories of practice and knowledge.[25] We suggest that, theorized and set in context, as this text does, such work can be defined within the scope of artistic research.[26]

Being on the Beach is a work that operates on a scale ranging from simplicity to complexity. Within the set framework of the beach, we hoped to find a way to concretize the individual's encounter with nature on two levels: the personal and the shared. The beach is a restricted place in the world just as our body is a restricted volume in space. These outer restrictions make it possible to focus attention on separate elements: tactility through air and wind, sound through water and waves, light from heaven and sun, and our foundation related to recognizable qualities – sand, pebbles, stones, shells, grass, and wastes. In order for the event to occur, it is essential for the participants to be creative. Each individual is outstanding in her/his own way, as well as together. We wish to stress that the participants are key, they make the difference.

Such an idea brings the event nearer to ritual and liturgy, which was mentioned in the oral responses.[27] On future occasions, it would be interesting to collaborate with theologians and explore the possibilities of such communal actions.

By effecting personal experiential knowledge of the body in relation to a landscape, *Being on the Beach* seeks to create meaning by fostering continuity and connections between inner and outer life. Standing firmly on the ground and being fully present, we may be better equipped to move into the uncertain future.

NOTES

[1] Kwon.
[2] One example is the American visual artist Bruce Naumann (born 1941). In the late 1960s, he started to experiment with his body, documenting the projects in video and photo, see: <http://www.vdb.org/smackn.acgi\$artistdetail?NAUMANB>. Complete works see: <http://www.pkmgallery.com/artists/bruce-nauman/biography/>.
[3] The American Japanese visual artist Yoko Ono's (born 1933) *Cut Piece* from 1965 has become iconic, see: <http://www.youtube.com/watch?v=F2IgqYiaywU> and <http://www.youtube.com/watch?v=Zfe2qhI5Ix4>.
[4] In the American artist Mierle Laderman Ukele's *Maintenance Art* from 1973 on, she washed the stairs outside a gallery. Some people watching her at work actually started to help, giving her a hand, see: <http://www.youtube.com/watch?v=aJ9GWlFZz1g>.
[5] Halprin, 249. Cf. <http://www.annahalprin.org/>.
[6] Dance performances are by their very nature interdisciplinary. Choreographers work not only with dancers, but also with composers, musicians, costume and lightening designers, scenographers, technicians and others. In this case, however, interdisciplinarity is on the conceptual level and not merely on the performative level.
[7] Åkesson, 54. This attitude seems quite similar to the ideas of the American painter Agnes Martin (1912-2004).
[8] Molander, 119.
[9] The workshop *Body Awareness and Objects* was part of *Verksted på Vollen* (English: Workshop in the Fields), 26-29 March 2009 at Granavollen, Norway, see: <http://www.verkstedpavollen.no/>. This work was continued in Iceland at the conference *Religion and Politics of the Body*, The Nordic Society for Philosophy of Religion (NSPR), Reykjavik, 26-28 June 2009. <http://www.verkstedpavollen.no/pdf/2009\%20Reykjavik_Refsum_Rimestad.pdf>.
[10] See Refsum's contribution to the World Beach Project: <http://www.vam.ac.uk/collections/textiles/lawty/world_beach/map_gallery/index.php?section=2\&postIndex=530>.
[11] See Rimestad as Water Queen in the performance *Juv* by Dansdesign, Norway 2006: <http://dansdesign.com/blog/Gallery/index.html>.
[12] "Østre brygge" means Eastern Quay in English.
[13] "Brønnøya" means Well Island in English.
[14] This approach is inspired by traditions of body movement and sensory awareness established in Europe and the in US during the latter half of the 20th century (Adler, Brooks).

15 Unless otherwise noted, the photos are taken by the authors.
16 Additionally, Eastern Quay is rich in a variety of rhombic porphyry pebbles that stem from later, local volcanic activity, some 250 million years ago. On the geology of the Oslo Graben, see online: <http://www.mantleplumes.org/Norway.html>.
17 The cultural history was not considered.
18 Eriksen, 77.
19 This is one of the principles taught in Chinese *Tai Chi* practices, with which both Refsum and Rimestad are acquainted.
20 Schön, 93.
21 This is a natural grouping, a position of non-contact, or, in a term coined by the American anthropologist Edward T. Hall, at *personal distance* (Hall, plate 4).
22 The event was documented by video. To some this was disturbing and we promised not to publish any material that would identify the participants without explicitly receiving personal permission.
23 Bourriaud, 18.
24 Although the artistic expression of the event may seem foreign, the preparation of the event builds on traditional qualities of art, as expressed by the American pragmatist philosopher John Dewey (1859-1952): "For art is a selection of what is significant." (Dewey, 216)
25 Jarvis, 145.
26 Refsum, 17-19.
27 Macmurray.

REFERENCES

Adler, Janet (2002), *Offering from the Conscious Body: The Discipline of Authentic Movement*, Rochester, Vermont: Inner Traditions.
Bourriaud, Nicolas (2002), *Relational Aesthetics*, Dijon: Les presses du reel, (original edition 1998).
Brooks, Charles V. W. (1986), *Sensory Awareness: The Rediscovery of Experiencing through Workshops with Charlotte Selver*, New York: Felix Morrow/Publisher/Great Neck, (original edition 1974).
Dewey, John (2005), *Art as Experience*, New York: Penguin Books, (original edition 1934).
Eriksen, Anne Grete (2009), "Dialogen med rommet", in: Anne Grete Eriksen (ed.), *Koreografi ute*, Oslo: Dansdesign, 72-79.
Halprin, Anna (1995), *Moving Toward Life: Five Decades of Transformational Dance*, ed. by R. Kaplan, Hanover and London: Wesleyan University Press and University Press of New England.
Hall, Edward T. (1982), *The Hidden Dimension*, New York: Anchor Books, Doubleday & Company, (original edition 1966).
Jarvis, Peter (1999), *The Practitioner-Researcher: Developing Theory from Practice*, San Francisco: Jossey-Bass Publishers.
Kwon, Miwon (2004), *One Place after Another: Site-specific Art and Locational Identity*, Cambridge Mass. and London: The MIT Press.
Martin, Agnes (1992), *Writings/Schriften*, ed. by Dieter Schwarz, Winterthur: Kunstmuseum Winterthur: Hatje Cantz.

Macmurray, John (1961), *Religion, Art, and Science: A Study of the Reflective Activities in Man, The Forwood Lectures 1960*, Liverpool: Liverpool University Press.

Molander, Bengt (1993), "The Practical Intellect – Design and Use of Knowledge", *Nordisk arkitekturforskning* 2, 117-130.

Refsum, Grete (2008), "Artistic Research: Contribution to Clarifying the Concept", in: *State of the Arts: KHiO Annual Review 2008*, ed. by Grete Refsum, Oslo: Oslo National Academy of the Arts.

Schön, Donald A. (1983), *The Reflective Practitioner: How Professionals Think in Action*, New York: Basic Books.

Åkeson, Birgit (ed.) (1998), *– att ge spår i luften –: föreläsningar, samtal, möten;* Malmö: Propexus.

Contributors

Lillian Ball is a multimedia artist and environmental activist working in New York. Fluid imagery has been a constant in the work for over 30 years, developing into a specific focus on water quality issues. Recent work uses a variety of methods, such as sculptural game installations or video projections to address environmental concerns ranging from climate change to wetland conservation. In addition, Ball was appointed to the Southold, NY Land Preservation Committee in 2006, where she serves on an ongoing basis. A multidisciplinary background in anthropology, ethnographic film, and sculpture inform her work. She has exhibited and lectured internationally, most recently at the Queens Museum, the Seville Biennial and Reina Sofia Museum in Spain. Her numerous art awards include: two New York State Foundation for the Arts Fellowships, a John-Simon Guggenheim Foundation Fellowship, and a National Endowment for the Arts Grant. Her most recent works are the permanent WATERWASH® public projects combining stormwater remediation, wetland restoration, and educational outreach. The original prototype was installed at a boat ramp park in Mattituck, NY and was funded by the Long Island Sound Futures Fund as a concept that can be adapted to coastal situations worldwide. The newly completed (Oct. 2011) WATERWASH ABC is an innovative collaborative green infrastructure solution to stormwater runoff pollution in the Bronx River. Ball and the project partners were awarded special citations from the NY State Assembly for cooperation between local business and the community. Job skills apprentices from Rocking the Boat, a non-profit that teaches local youth to build wooden boats and do environmental work, planted over 8000 native wetland and grassland plants. WATERWASH ABC cleans commercial parking lot runoff before it enters the river, opens private property to public use, and was funded by the NY State Attorney General's Office.

Sigurd Bergmann holds a doctorate in systematic theology from Lund University and works as Professor in Religious Studies at the Department of Archaeology and Religious Studies at the Norwegian University of Science and Technology in Trondheim. His previous studies have investigated the relationship between the image of God and the view of nature in late antiquity, the methodology of contextual theology, visual arts in the indigenous Arctic and Australia, as well as visual arts, architecture and religion. He has initiated and chaired the "European Forum on the Study of Religion and Environment", and ongoing projects investigate the relation of space/place and religion and "religion in climatic change". His main publications are *Geist, der Natur befreit* (Mainz 1995, Russian ed. Arkhangelsk

1999, rev. ed. *Creation Set Free*, Grand Rapids 2005), *Geist, der lebendig macht* (Frankfurt/M. 1997), *God in Context* (Aldershot 2003), *Architecture, Aesth/Ethics and Religion* (ed.) (Frankfurt/M., London 2005), *Theology in Built Environments* (ed.) (New Brunswick/London 2009), *In the Beginning is the Icon* (London 2009), *Så främmande det lika* ("So Strange, so Similar", on Sámi visual arts, globalisation and religion, Trondheim 2009) and *Raum und Geist: Zur Erdung und Beheimatung der Religion* (Göttingen 2010). Bergmann was a co-project leader of the interdisciplinary programme "Technical Spaces of Mobility" (2003-07) and co-edited *The Ethics of Mobilities* (Aldershot 2008), *Spaces of Mobility* (London 2008), *Nature, Space & the Sacred* (Farnham 2009), *Religion, Ecology & Gender* (Berlin 2009), *Religion and Dangerous Environmental Change* (Berlin 2010), *Religion in Environmental and Climate Chnage* (London/New York 2011). Last winter he was a visiting fellow at the Rachel Carson Center for Environment and Society in München. He is editor of this series, board member of several international journals, and leader of the section for philosophy, history of ideas and theology/religious studies in the Royal Norwegian Society of Sciences and Letters.

Irmgard Blindow finished her Ph.D. in 1991 at the Department of Limnology/Ecology, University of Lund, Sweden. She worked as research assistant in the department until 2000, when she accepted a position as leader of the Biological Station on Hiddensee, University of Greifswald, Germany. Her research focuses on charophyte ecology, charophyte taxonomy and trophic interactions in shallow lakes, and includes furthermore landscape development and habitat management on the island of Hiddensee, especially in dry grasslands and coastal heathlands. She has published more than 30 journal papers.

Beth Carruthers is an environmental humanities scholar and multidisciplinary artist whose work for more than two decades has focused on community, culture and the nature of sustainable dwelling. With a particular interest in the role of perception and aesthetic engagement in human-world interactions, she has for some years been developing a transdisciplinary theory of "deep aesthetics". Related areas of work and research include post-humanist ontology and applied ethics. A curatorial and programming advisor to arts centres and groups in Canada and abroad, she is also an internationally exhibited and collected visual artist. She is widely published and cited, and lectures internationally on Arts, Culture and Sustainability. Beth is a Founding Member of the *International Environmental Communications Association*, and a longtime member of the *International Ecoart Network*. She holds degrees in the Fine Arts and Environmental Humanities, and teaches in Critical and Cultural Studies at *Emily Carr University of Art and Design* at Vancouver, Canada.

Forrest Clingerman is Associate Professor of Philosophy and Religion at Ohio Northern University in Ada, Ohio, USA. He received his Ph.D. in Modern Religious Thought from the University of Iowa. He is co-editor of *Placing Nature* *on the Borders of Religion, Philosophy and Ethics* (Aldershot, 2011) and *Interpreting Nature: The Emerging Field of Environmental Hermeneutics* (New York, forthcoming). In addition he is author of several articles and essays that have appeared in religion, philosophy and environmental studies publications. He is on the steering committee of the European Forum for the Study of Religion and the Environment and serves as co-editor (with Brian Treanor) of *Groundworks*, a new book series that is devoted to fostering a deeper conversation between theology and philosophy on ecological issues. His research investigates how place serves as an orienting hermeneutical concept in environmental thought. He is involved in working on hermeneutics can work as a method for interrogating the ideas of place found in natural landscapes, as well as human cultural works.

Celia Deane-Drummond is Professor of Theology at the University of Notre Dame. She holds a concurrent appointment between the Department of Theology in the College of Arts and Letters and the College of Science. She was elected Fellow of the Eck Institute for Global Health at the University of Notre Dame in September 2011. From 2000 to 2011 she held a professorial chair in theology and the biological sciences at the University of Chester, and was Director of the Centre for Religion and the Biosciences launched in 2002. In May 2011 she was elected Chair of the European Forum for the Study of Religion and Environment. She was editor of the international journal *Ecotheology* from 2000 to 2006. From July 2009 to July 2010 she was seconded to the spirituality team at the Catholic Fund for Overseas Development (CAFOD), working explicitly in the area of environmental justice and climate change. Since 1992 she has published as a single author or as an editor twenty-two books, thirty-three contributions to books, and forty-three articles in areas relating to theology or ethics. Her more recent books include *Creation through Wisdom* (2000), *Brave New World* (2003), *ReOrdering Nature* (2003), *The Ethics of Nature* (2004), *Wonder and Wisdom: Conversations in Science, Spirituality and Theology* (2006), *Genetics and Christian Ethics* (2006), *Future Perfect: God, Medicine and Human Identity*, edited with Peter Scott (2006, 2n edn., 2010), *Ecotheology* (2008), *Christ and Evolution: Wonder and Wisdom* (Minneapolis: Fortress/London: SCM Press, 2009), *Creaturely Theology: On God, Humans and Other Animals*, edited with David Clough (2009), *Seeds of Hope: Facing the Challenge of Climate Justice* (2010), and *Religion and Ecology in the Public Sphere*, edited with Heinrich Bedford-Strohm (2011).

Heather Eaton is Professor at Saint Paul University in Ottawa, Ontario, Canada. She holds an interdisciplinary PhD in Ecology, Feminism and Theology from the University of St. Michael's College, Toronto School of Theology. She is engaged in religious responses to the ecological crisis, particularly the relationship between ecological, feminist and liberation theologies, and connections between religion and science, and committed to inter-religious responses to ecological issues. Her books include *Introducing Ecofeminist Theologies* (London/New York 2005) and *Ecofeminism and Globalization: Exploring Religion, Culture, Context* (ed. with L.A. Lorentzen, Lanham 2003). Eaton is on the board of the journal *Worldviews: Global Religions, Environment and Culture*, the steering committee of the Religion and Ecology session of the American Academy of Religion, and she is past president of the Canadian Theological Society, and founder of the Canadian Forum of Religion and Ecology. She has taught courses in these areas at St Michael's College, University of Toronto; Faculty of Environmental Studies, York University; Faculty of Environmental Education at Royal Roads University, and at Saint Paul University. She is involved in numerous conferences, workshops, teaching and publishing in these areas. Recent work focuses on the intersection of religion, science and ecology and specifically among evolution, Earth dynamics and religious imagination.

Thomas Heyd teaches in the Department of Philosophy and in the School of Environmental Studies at the University of Victoria, British Columbia, Canada. His Ph.D. is in history of philosophy. Most of his research and publications concern ethics and aesthetics in relation to environmental issues, and in relation to cultural markers (in particular on stationary rock), often considered sacred by traditional societies. Presently much of his research interest focusses on the development of appropriate environmental policy in the light of the cultural dimensions of climate change. Publications on this topic include a special issue of the *Human Ecology Review* (December 2010). He also organised an international workshop on the cultural dimensions of climate change (University La Laguna, Spain, 2010), as well as symposia at the Climate Change Science Congress (Copenhagen, 2009), the Global Environmental Change and Human Security Synthesis Conference (GECHS, Oslo, 2009), the World Congress of Philosophy (Seoul, 2008), and the Society for Human Ecology (Washington State, 2008). His publications concerning environmental ethics and aesthetics include *Encountering Nature: Toward an Environmental Culture* (Aldershot 2007), *Recognizing the Autonomy of Nature* (New York 2005). His publications on cultural markers of traditional societies on stationary rock include *Aesthetics and Rock Art* (Aldershot 2005), *Aesthetics and Rock Art IV Symposium* (Fundham 2010), and *Aesthetics and Rock Art III Symposium* (2008). He is a member of the Rock Art Research Task Group (2010-), and has organised a series of symposia on the ethics and aesthetics of rock art manifestations at four congresses of the International Federation of Rock Art Organizations.

Philipp Meurer is a doctoral research student in the graduate school of Human Development in Landscapes at Kiel University, Germany, and holds a scholarship from the German Science Foundation. He holds a M.A. in Art History, German Literature and Philosophy from Kiel University. Meurer is engaged in the artistic perception of landscape and environmental change from early modern times to the present. His book *Natur im Bewusstsein der Differenz: Franz Gertsch und Caspar David Friedrich* (Berlin 2012) analyses similar tendencies in Romanticism and Postmodernism. His PhD project deals with the perception and imagination of foreign landscapes in early modern Netherlands with a particular focus on the formation of identity.

Konrad Ott has been fighting entropy since 1959. He is married and the father of four children. In the 1980s, he studied philosophy and history at the University of Frankfurt. In 1989, he did his Ph.D. under the supervision of Jürgen Habermas. In the 1990s, he worked as researcher and lecturer at the universities of Tübingen and Zürich. Since 1997, Ott has been a full professor of environmental ethics at the Ernst Moritz Arndt University of Greifswald. For 15 years he has worked in close cooperation with ecologists, environmental economists, and experts in international relations. His ongoing fields of research are discourse ethics, theories of justice, environmental ethics, concepts of sustainability, water resources, and ethical aspects of climate change. He publishes mainly in these fields. From 2000 to 2008, Ott was a member of the German Environmental Advisory Council (Rat von Sachverständigen für Umweltfragen) which counsels the German Government in environmental affairs. He is a member of the Board for Sustainable Development of the Protestant Church of Germany and a member of the "Deutscher Rat für Landespflege". Beginning in the winter term of 2012, Konrad Ott will take the chair for philosophy and ethics of the environment at the Christian Albrecht University in Kiel.

Grete Refsum is a visual artist and Senior Adviser at the Oslo National Academy of the Arts. She holds a degree ("hovedfag") from the Norwegian University of Life Sciences (1977), a diploma (1985) and a degree ("hovedfag") from the National College of Art and Design (1992), and a doctorate from the Oslo School of Architecture and Design (2000) In her artwork she focuses on religion and spirituality and explores how to bridge Christian traditions and contemporary culture. A broad range of projects and exhibitions – in art institutions, churches and outdoor environments – has investigated interreligious and intercultural encounters with methods of spatial design, craft, sculpture, glass, textile and painting. Recently, she has experimented with interactive projects, inviting the audience to participate in collaborative art production. She has in may ways contributed to the development of research in art and design. In 2004 and 2008 she was the editor of the Annual Review at the Oslo National Academy of the Arts, and she has contributed chapters to S. Bergmann's edited books *Architecture, Aesth/Ethics and Religion* (Frankfurt am Main and London 2005) and *Theology in Built Environments, Exploring Religion, Architecture & Design* (New Brunswick NJ/London 2009).

Ingunn Rimestad is a dance artist and pedagogue within the fields of contemporary dance, improvisation and somatic practice. Her interest lies in the relationship between anatomic functionality (the inner culture and ecology of the body), dance technique and movement expression. She has developed her personal method based on the fundamental question: what is movement expression? By continuously addressing this question, she challenges the individual to explore her/his personal body potential and possibilities, allowing movements or body expressions to happen. Since 1980, she has been employed at The National School of Dance, now Academy of Dance/Oslo National Academy of the Arts. She started her teaching career in 1973 at The Ballet School of The Norwegian Opera, and continued this work alongside her work in The National School of Dance until 2004. From 1984 to 2003, she was engaged by a group of elderly women, *The Grandmothers*; this work is documented in a film by Kjersti Martinsen, entitled *Wednesday*. Her first employment as a dancer was at The National Theater in Oslo (1972-73). In 1985, she established the company HeXakin, together with dancer and choreographer Lise Ferner, that was active for three years. Rimestad has danced in several performances choreographed by prominent Norwegian choreographers such as Anne Grete Eriksen and Leif Hernes (DansDesign), Amanda Steggell and Homan Sharifi (Impure Company). She is currently involved in a project on improvisation with the prestigious Norwegian artistic research programme.

George Steinmann is a visual artist, musician and researcher based in Bern, Switzerland. He studied painting at the University of Applied Arts in Basel, as well as painting, sound and Afro-American culture at the San Francisco Art Institute. His work focuses on the relationship between contemporary art and science and the interconnectedness of art, culture and sustainability. He has completed transdisciplinary projects and conceived multimedia based exhibitions at the Helmhaus Zürich, Salo Art Museum, Kunsthaus Interlaken, Kunstverein Kassel, Villa Elisabeth Berlin, Museum of Contemporary Art Helsinki, Kunsthalle Bern, Art Gallery of Ontario Toronto, The Contemporary Arts Centre Cincinnati, Winnipeg Art Gallery, Centre Pasquart Biel, Lokaal 01 Breda, Centre for Contemporary Art and Architecture Stockholm, Gallery Heike Strelow Frankfurt/M., Pori Art Museum, Centre for Contemporary Art Nairs, and the ERES Foundation München. George Steinmann also works as a musician, and his concerts include solo performances and tours (including many jazz festivals) with his own band and African-American artists such as Grammy Award winner Johnny Clyde Copeland. In recognition of his multidisciplinary work and lectures, George Steinmann was awarded a honorary doctorate by the philosophical-historical Faculty of the University of Bern. His books include *Blue Notes* (Nürnberg/Zürich 2007), *Komi – A Growing Sculpture* (Bern 2007) and *Art without an Object but with Impact* (Basel 2012).